JOSEPH AND NOAH

JOSEPH
AND NOAH

What ancient wisdom can teach us
about thriving in today's world

DANIEL GOZO

Quickfox

Published by Quickfox Publishing
Cape Town, South Africa
www.quickfox.co.za | info@quickfox.co.za

Joseph and Noah
ISBN paperback: 978-1-0370-2811-3
ISBN ePub: 978-1-0370-2812-0
ISBN Kindle: 978-1-0370-2813-7

First edition 2025

Edited by Louise Rapley
Cover wave art by Yuichiro

CONTENTS

INTRODUCTION

A deep recession gripped the country many years ago as a young man, fresh out of college with a four-year technical diploma, set out to find employment.

His goal was to become an electrical engineer, and he hoped to find an employer with strong training programmes and good career prospects. But after eight months of searching, he had not found a single opening or promise of work.

Desperation set in, and he began walking the streets, making cold calls on factories and industries. Some employers, tired of unsolicited jobseekers, had mounted signs at their entrances: '*Geen werk*/*Awukho Umsebenzi*' ('No jobs'). In most places, doors were slammed shut in his face. Others, more polite, urged him to try elsewhere: 'Wishing you all the best,' they would say.

Then, one day, a middle-aged guard at the gate of a large tobacco factory called after him.

'I've seen you walking down the street several times. The boss will be hiring for the grading season if you're interested … come back next week.'

Grading tobacco was not what he had studied for, but he needed to start somewhere.

The following week, he returned to find a long queue of jobseekers. The same portly guard, on duty again, explained the procedure. Thirteen positions were available, and the minimum qualification was a matric certificate.

The guard needed someone to organise the group and prepare a list of those eligible. Scanning the anxious faces, he spotted the keen young man from the previous week and called him forward.

'I'll check everyone's qualifications and send those who qualify to you. You will list only thirteen. I know you're smart, the most qualified of this group. Please count to thirteen, no more. Here's pen and paper.'

The process was quick, and soon the list was complete. The guard disappeared into the office complex, closing the large gate behind him. When he returned, it was to call in the shortlisted candidates for their formal interviews. The candidates passed through the gate one by one – thirteen in total. The process, which was performed seasonally, had stood the test of time: the guard trusted that this final step was a mere formality.

But the keen young man who had compiled the list was not among the thirteen. As the guard began to close the gate, the young man pushed forward to protest.

'I explained myself clearly, son. The boss will only take thirteen today,' the guard said. 'You didn't count yourself in. The next recruitment will be next season.'

The guard's expression transformed into the firm, unyielding look of a security official whose word was final.

In his zeal, the young man had overlooked himself. As the large gate slammed shut, he slumped to the ground, weeping uncontrollably.

* * *

Reading comprehension and literature studies in high school are favoured teaching and learning methods, much like case studies in business schools. What better way to explore success than by examining the real-life journeys of those who have walked difficult paths and emerged victorious? When they reach a fork in the road, what gives them the confidence to choose the right path? Is the answer hidden in the details of their stories, like the fine print in an insurance contract?

In writing this book, I set out to investigate the lives of ordinary people who have achieved extraordinary success, fame or wealth – people who did things differently. From ancient biblical figures of millennia past to modern-day individuals in the twenty-first century, the pursuit of the secrets of success spans generations.

I found balance in the power of three, like a tripod, a bar stool, a potjie pot resting on its three cast-iron legs, and the Holy Trinity. The eight chapters in this book are therefore divided into three parts.

The first part, with two chapters, explores patterns, cycles and catastrophes. Beneath the surface of seemingly random events, there is hidden order. Large-scale catastrophes can trigger cycles that last long enough to demand our attention and provide frameworks for making informed decisions. Ancient biblical stories, such as those of Joseph and Noah, offer guidance when examined closely. For instance, how did a youthful Joseph succeed in interpreting Pharaoh's dreams so accurately? And how did Noah have the foresight and resilience to build an ark and prepare for a flood while those around him remained indifferent?

The second part of the book spans three chapters, featuring tales of people – young and old, famous and unknown – who walked unique paths. Their lives provide not only entertainment but also valuable lessons. For example, how did a thirty-year-old woman navigate the global financial crisis of 2008 and emerge unscathed?

I believe that reading these stories is akin to experiencing the essence of someone's life through a single chapter. The devil is in the details – self-awareness and the secrets of investing, particularly in managing human emotions around money. When markets crash and panic sets in, the Joseph and Noah models offer calm guidance through the storm.

The final section of the book comprises three chapters. Some of the individuals featured became famous, leaving legacies of improving humanity, building generational wealth, establishing global brands or creating landmark tourist destinations. Others are unique in their pursuit of happiness, redefining the very concept of success along the way. Many challenge stereotypes – whether related to ageing, perceived limitations from chronic illnesses or genetic conditions, or the barriers imposed by naysayers. All of them triumphed.

* * *

The tale with which I began this Introduction was passed down from my grandpa, who had an endless reservoir of stories. Although fearing it might upset some of my classmates, I shared it during a life orientation lesson in high school. Instead, it quickly became known as the 'count-yourself-in' tale, spreading through the playground – proof that it resonated as a learning moment. It is one of the few stories that has stuck with me, replaying itself at various points in my life.

Throughout this book, as I have written about the lives of fascinating individuals who have found success, in whatever way they define it, I have remembered to count myself in too, drawing from my personal library of memories and experiences to supplement the stories.

I think my grandpa would be proud.

PART I

PATTERNS, CATASTROPHES AND FINANCIAL MARKETS

CHAPTER 1

THE JOSEPH EFFECT:
Harnessing patterns and cycles for greater success

'He shared with the men of the Old Testament and with the Oracle of Delphi the heavy burden of instant vision.'
– **Gian-Carlo Rota**

1

In a world where the constant flux of markets mirrors the unpredictable ebb and flow of life itself, we find ourselves at a crossroads of decision-making and interpretation. Financial markets often reflect each other, echoing the global trends and uncertainties that shape our economic landscape. Just as life is filled with unexpected turns and challenges, so too are the markets influenced by a myriad factors – geopolitical events, technological advancements and economic policies – that steer them in different directions.

Imagine standing at the edge of a vast ocean, watching the waves rise and fall. Each wave is unique, yet part of a larger, interconnected system influenced by the wind, tides and gravitational pull of the moon. Similarly, financial markets are part of a global system where actions and events in one part of the world can create ripples felt across continents. A policy change in the United States can impact on stock prices in Asia, for example, just as a technological breakthrough in Europe can influence market movements in Africa.

This interconnectedness means that markets often move in tandem, reflecting a shared search for direction amid a sea of information and events. Investors, much like sailors navigating the open ocean, must interpret these movements and make decisions based on their understanding of the patterns and trends. They seek to find meaning in the chaos, to predict the next wave and to position themselves advantageously for the future.

In this dynamic environment, where the only constant is change, we must remain vigilant and adaptable. By observing global trends and understanding the factors that drive market movements, we can better navigate the uncertainties of the financial world, making informed decisions that align with our goals and aspirations.

And as we stand on the brink of unprecedented technological advancements, one question looms large: what unique capabilities will AI bring to the table that traditional computers cannot? Investors and markets alike are always on edge, keenly awaiting new data, such as US wage reports, while geopolitical tensions and rising oil prices add further complexity to the financial landscape.

In South Africa, we keep a close eye on the South African Reserve Bank's decisions as well as inflation trends and market movements. The latest inflation figures occasionally surprise economists by coming in slightly lower than expected. The Reserve Bank Governor's policy stance is scrutinised for its hawkish or dovish tendencies, shaping expectations about inflation, economic health and interest rates.

The world of cryptocurrency also presents intriguing dynamics, particularly with the periodic halving of Bitcoin rewards, which affects its price by reducing the rate at which new coins are minted. These events are keenly anticipated by investors and analysts, with each halving being followed by intense speculation and market adjustments.

In our information-saturated age, news comes at us from every direction, around the clock, via television, radio, social media and countless apps. The sheer volume of data, often laced with subjective opinions, poses a significant challenge: how do we sift through it all to find reliable insights? Should we mute notifications, unsubscribe from feeds or follow influencers who seem to have a knack for spotting trends?

Reflecting on these modern dilemmas, we can draw inspiration from ancient wisdom. Take a story that has withstood the test of time, for instance: the story of Joseph from the Bible. The tale is a narrative not just of dreams and interpretations, but of a young man's journey from the depths of despair to the heights of power.

In the twenty-first century, many of us seek advice from consultants or experts. In Joseph's time, millennia ago, there were wise men and magicians but no laptops or internet. Joseph was sold into slavery by his jealous brothers, only to rise to prominence in Egypt by interpreting Pharaoh's dreams when no one else could. His tale is one of vision, courage, faith and a willingness to defy the consensus – qualities that are as essential today as they were thousands of years ago.

2

Joseph lived with his family in the land of Canaan, a large, prosperous country located in the Levant region of present-day Lebanon, Syria, Jordan and Israel. According to the book of Genesis, the land of Canaan was designated as the ideal inheritance for the descendants of Jacob, who was also known as 'Israel'. This promise was part of a divine covenant, marking Canaan as the destined homeland for Jacob's family and future generations. This inheritance symbolised the fulfilment of God's promise to Jacob and his ancestors, representing prosperity, stability and a lasting legacy for his descendents, the Israelites. In the context of Joseph's story, this inheritance underscored the significance of his journey and the trials he and his family endured to ultimately secure their place in this promised land.

Joseph had eleven brothers. His father, Jacob, whose life was marked by trials and triumphs, was a significant figure in biblical history. Jacob's story is intertwined with many pivotal moments that shaped the destiny of his descendants.

Jacob was a man who wrestled with both human and divine beings. This is why God renamed him 'Israel', which means 'he who struggles with God' (*New King James Bible*, 2004, Genesis 32:28). This struggle was emblematic of Jacob's perseverance and faith, qualities that he passed down to his children.

The name change from Jacob to Israel symbolised a profound transformation and a new beginning, marking Jacob as the patriarch of a great nation. Understanding Jacob's story and his transformation into Israel helps us grasp the deeper themes of perseverance, faith and redemption that run through Joseph's life.

Joseph was the last son in the family; having been born in Jacob's old age, he soon became his father's favourite. It did not take long for Joseph's brothers to realise that of all his children, their father loved Joseph the most. To make matters worse, as younger boys often do, Joseph regularly told on his brothers when they misbehaved, so relations between him and the brothers were strained. When Jacob had a special robe with many colours made for Joseph, the die was cast and the battle lines were drawn.

Thirteen chapters (Genesis 37–50) and 214 verses of Genesis, the Hebrews' biblical book of creation, are devoted to the story of Joseph. It is also told in the Quran: Surat Yusuf in Sura 12 covers the story in 111 verses. In both accounts, the texts reflect the main events in a similar fashion and the consequences of the events are the same.

In a research journal article about Joseph, Abdel Haleem (2007) offers perspectives regarding the story as told in the Quran versus the Old Testament. The differences lie in the emphasis and tone with which each version is recounted, the time spans involved, and the characterisation, artistic forms and colour given in each of the two texts. This difference is reminiscent of the device used in Pete Travis's 2008 action thriller film, *Vantage Point*, in which different witnesses offer differing points of view to unravel an assassination attempt made on a US president in the fictitious storyline.

The underlying themes of Joseph's story are jealousy, deceit, callousness, fateful lust, courage and faith. All events in the story contrive towards the bigger purpose of divine intervention by a distant God to save the family of Israel. Stripped of religious zeal and opportunism, the story exposes human failings, hidden agendas and survival instincts familiar to humans living on earth today.

The story of Joseph in the book of Genesis was written by Moses, who lived many years after Joseph (circa 1400 BC). Even though the story was written millennia ago, it still has great significance for current generations of people, whether they are of Jewish or Gentile origin.

3

One day, seventeen-year-old Joseph had a dream, which he related excitedly to his brothers: 'Please hear this dream which I have dreamed: There we were, binding sheaves in the field. Then behold, my sheaf arose and also stood upright; and indeed, your sheaves stood all around and bowed down to my sheaf' (*New King James Bible*, 2004, Genesis 37:6–7).

His eleven brothers reacted with shock and resentment: 'Shall you indeed reign over us? Or shall you indeed have dominion over us?' (*New King James Bible*, 2004, Genesis 37:8). The favouritism shown to Joseph by their father, Jacob, was already a source of tension, but Joseph's vivid retelling of his dream only exacerbated the existing divide. The implications of the dream for the family's inheritance could not be overlooked. Consequently, the brothers' animosity towards Joseph escalated dramatically.

Joseph had another dream, which he again shared with his brothers: 'Look, I have dreamed another dream. And this time, the sun, the moon, and the eleven stars bowed down to me' (*New King James Bible*, 2004, Genesis 37:9). This may have been the straw that broke the camel's back of Joseph's relations with his brothers.

Joseph then related this latest dream to his father, who became very worried about its meaning and the potential consequences for his son. Jacob admonished Joseph, saying: 'What is this dream that you have dreamed? Shall your mother and I and your brothers indeed come to bow down to the earth before you?' (*New King James Bible*, 2004, Genesis 37:10).

In Sura 12, vv. 4–6 (Haleem, 2007), Jacob replied to his son as follows: 'My son, relate nothing of this dream to your brothers lest they plot evil against you: Satan is the sworn enemy of man. So will your Lord choose you, teach you to interpret dreams, and perfect His blessing upon you and on the House of Jacob as He perfected it formerly on your fathers Abraham and Isaac; surely your Lord is all-knowing and wise.' Jacob, the wise old-timer, had no intention of forgetting about this dream, and brooded quietly over it. As we shall see later, there is a connection between Joseph's two dreams, which both project an outcome that has Joseph in a position of strategic status.

4

In the context of the texts, Joseph's dreams are considered to be a supernatural gift from a distant, divine God depicting a future reality. Is this view of a supernatural gift the only viable explanation for predictions? Or is there an alternative that derives from the observation of patterns in the natural environment? These questions are the subject of Judith Corey's research article for the *Journal for the Study of the Old Testament*, aptly titled 'Dreaming of Droughts …'. Dreaming of a future reality is a phenomenon located within the area of futures forecasting.

An historian at the University of California in Los Angeles, Corey examines the history of futures forecasting from Babylonian civilisation through Hermetic philosophers to modern meteorology, and from Greek philosophy to contemporary sciences (Corey, 2014).

Corey notes that a subtle introduction in the first verse of Genesis 37 – 'Now Jacob lived in the land of journeys of his father in the land of Canaan' – is a reminder of the instability of nomadic life for a sojourner or temporary dweller at the time during which Joseph's dreams were recorded. Corey believes that this instability would have had an influence on Joseph, resulting in his dreams of landing in a position of status at a time of drought. As Corey points out, the dreaming mind is fed by emotional relationships that cultivate the psychic conscious.

Babylonian civilisation is credited with excellent record-keeping. Centuries of observations were recorded by scribes employed by kings and priests in a guild fashion, from father to son, and with this discipline, the Babylonians produced the first almanacs, predicting the times of events such as sunrises and sunsets, eclipses, solstices, equinoxes, high tides, rising river levels, frost, plentiful harvests and devastating droughts. The Babylonians came up with the concept of correspondence, a model where what occurs in the macrostructure influences the microstructure (in other words, creates a ripple effect). The natural environment produces information that in turn is received via the senses, with the mind receiving a copy of the image – these are referred to as 'emanations' in this model. Dreams are experienced in the quiet of the night during sleep. The Greek philosopher Aristotle surmised that the stillness of the night acts as a catalyst that enhances the emanations.

David Brown, who has made an extensive study of Mesopotamian planetary astronomy, concluded that Babylonian astrology spread to other cultures in neighbouring regions in a process that introduced a paradigm shift and a new science (Brown & Brown, 2000). It was during this period that Babylonian astronomical science found its way into Jewish culture, creating an impact that lasted for centuries, including at the time of the writing of the book of Genesis. These are the times in which the youthful Joseph grew up, and the prevailing beliefs and culture of these times shaped him as a human being. The instability of his life as a sojourner or temporary dweller and having to deal with the vagaries of the natural environment had a significant impact on him. The events in the natural environment, past and present, intersected with his belief in the divine and influenced his resultant dreams.

5

The plot quickened when Jacob sent his beloved Joseph out to the pastures at Shechem to check in with his brothers and report back to confirm that all was well with the flocks. The brothers hated Joseph, and the two dreams in which Joseph had predicted that they would be subservient to him were fresh in their minds. They hastily plotted to kill Joseph when they saw him approaching from a distance. However, overcome by a sense of guilt, they decided instead to sell him as a slave to a caravan of Midianites travelling to sell their wares in Egypt. The brothers washed Joseph's robe in goat blood in order to create the impression that he had been attacked and killed by a wild animal, and presented it to Jacob. Jacob went into mourning, beside himself with sorrow. Not only had Joseph been his son, but he had been Jacob's favourite son.

Once in Egypt, Joseph was sold to Potiphar, captain of the guard. However, Joseph's ordeal was not over. His new owners and employers found him to be a likeable young man; his curse was his good looks – he was described in Genesis as a handsome boy – which brought him trouble. Potiphar's wife soon made lustful advances on Joseph, but he committed the cardinal error (in her eyes, at any rate) of remaining loyal to Potiphar, his master, and rejecting her advances. According to Genesis 39:12–18 (*New King James Bible*, 2004), 'she caught him by his garment, saying, "lie with me": he left his garment in her hand and fled'.

Using the robe as evidence, Potiphar's wife turned the tables on Joseph; she reported him to her husband, accusing Joseph of having attempted a sexual attack on her.

The event is painted with much more colour when told from a different vantage point. In the version of the story that is related in the Quran, some women in the city mocked Potiphar's wife, accusing her of soliciting her slave boy. This prompted the nobleman's wife to invite the women for a meal during which she presented Joseph to them. The women were charmed and hypnotised; they were so enraptured by Joseph's beauty that they found themselves cutting their fingers with their knives during the meal.

Joseph may have brought the ladies under his spell like Richard Gere in the 1980 film *American Gigolo*, but he was no gigolo. He found himself on the horns of a classic dilemma: condemned if he gave in to temptation, and equally condemned if he rejected the advances of Potiphar's wife.

According to Sura 12 (Haleem, 2007), Joseph prayed, 'Lord, prison is dearer to me than what they call me to. Shield me from their cunning or I shall yield to them and lapse into folly.'

Joseph was indeed thrown into prison, where he found himself in the company of other prisoners, including Pharaoh's previously ranked and trusted (but now errant) officers: his cupbearer (butler) and his baker (Haleem, 2007; Aling, 2003). These two officials are of immense importance in Joseph's story; this is the first time that Genesis records Joseph's gift for interpreting the dreams of others.

Joseph's faith was too strong for him to take the credit for this gift and he attributed this power to God, saying in Sura 12 that his Lord had taught him to do so (Haleem, 2007). In Genesis 40:8, Joseph says, 'Do not interpretations belong to God? Tell me them.' And so the baker and the cupbearer told him their dreams, which Joseph interpreted accurately: the cupbearer was recalled to Pharaoh's service and promoted, but the baker was killed, impaled on a pole, just as Joseph predicted. As the cupbearer had promised and when the opportunity arose, he remembered his prison mate when his fortunes took a turn for the better.

6

As Joseph had predicted, the cupbearer was duly released from prison and reappointed in Pharaoh's palace, this time in the higher role of chief cupbearer. Two years later, Pharaoh had two dreams on the same night. He found these dreams so disturbing and worrying that he woke up between them, and later could not shake them off.

The degree of importance that Pharaoh attached to his dreams was typical during ancient times. As noted earlier, Jacob had brooded over the meaning of Joseph's dreams, and Joseph had himself been so excited by them that he had felt compelled to share them with his family members, even though it was obvious that they would receive the dreams negatively. Respected Old Testament scholar Gerhard von Rad points out in his book that for the ancients, visions were so vital and imperative that the notion of keeping them private was inconceivable. In addition, dreams were taken so seriously that those who could interpret them were accorded high status in royal courts (Von Rad, 1973).

It should come as no surprise that early the following morning, Pharaoh summoned his magicians and wise men in order to consult with them. He wanted these capable men to interpret his dreams and needed this to be done quickly. It was a simple brief. But none of Pharaoh's wise men could explain their meaning.

The chief cupbearer was in attendance. Witnessing the fiasco, he suddenly recalled the young Hebrew man he had met during his time in prison. To find favour with Pharaoh, the chief cupbearer explained that Joseph had interpreted both the baker's dream and his own, and that everything had happened exactly as predicted. Pharaoh was excited to hear this, and without further ado, he ordered that Joseph be brought immediately to his chambers.

Joseph shaved before presenting himself to Pharaoh. Historians have debated the significance of this decision to shave off his beard. It appears that Joseph was a smart fellow. The Egyptians shaved routinely; in ancient

21

paintings, they are always clean-shaven. This detail had not escaped Joseph, who decided not to present himself with a full beard, as was the practice of the Hebrews. This was Pharaoh, the most powerful man in Egypt, and first impressions mattered. There would not be many more opportunities for Joseph to negotiate his way out of the dungeon and into Pharaoh's court, where he could begin to build a career for himself.

Joseph walked into the royal court and found Pharaoh ready for him. Pharaoh started by complaining that none of the wise men of Egypt had been able to interpret his dreams, and then recounted his dreams to Joseph:

> In my dream, I was standing on the bank of the Nile River, and I saw seven fat, healthy cows come up out of the river and begin grazing in the marsh grass. But then I saw seven sick-looking cows, scrawny and thin, come up after them. I've never seen such sorry-looking animals in all the land of Egypt. These thin, scrawny cows ate the seven fat cows. But afterward you wouldn't have known it, for they were still as thin and scrawny as before! Then I woke up.
>
> In my dream I also saw seven heads of grain, full and beautiful, growing on a single stalk. Then seven more heads of grain appeared, but these were blighted, shrivelled, and withered by the east wind. And the shrivelled heads swallowed the seven healthy heads. I told these dreams to the magicians, but no one could tell me what they mean. (*New King James Bible*, 2004, Genesis 41:17–24)

Joseph responded as he had to the chief cupbearer and baker: the business of interpreting dreams, he told Pharaoh, belonged to God, and he was only the messenger. This is a testament to Joseph's strong faith in the divine. But I also have a sense of the smart use of what we would now call a 'disclaimer', in case his interpretation and predictions proved inaccurate or misleading. Joseph knew that Pharaoh was a cruel man – he had only recently seen the baker being executed by being impaled on a pole – and he knew that he would be wise to use a caveat when called on to provide advice.

To understand the effect of witnessing another person being impaled, we should go back in history to Vlad III Drachul. During the fifteenth century, Vlad III rose to power while still in his twenties, ruling Transylvania and Walachia in the mountainous region of present-day Romania. He was a feared leader and warlord who had the singular aim of staying in power at all costs. His belief was that in order to be a great leader, he had to mete out morbid, sadistic and cruel punishment whenever a subject displayed even the slightest measure of dissent.

Vlad III, who inspired Bram Stoker's horror novel *Dracula*, used several ways to punish 'errant' people, including decapitation and mutilation of their noses, but his favourite was impalement. For this reason, he earned the frightening nickname *Tepes*, which in English means 'The Impaler' (CE Noticias Financieras, 2020, 2021).

Impalement was a public spectacle, carried out in full view of the citizens. The unfortunate victim would have oil and grease poured into their rectum or vagina while warriors held them down. A sharpened pole was then driven through their body, lubricated by the oil and grease, causing severe internal damage as it progressed. The pole would eventually emerge near the person's neck, shoulders or mouth.

This gruesome method ensured a prolonged and agonising death, sometimes lasting hours or even days. For added cruelty, a blunt pole might be used instead of a sharp one, prolonging the agony by preventing rapid internal damage.

Impalement was often meted out capriciously. For instance, a Franciscan friar who had reprimanded Vlad III for murdering a family of boyars was impaled by having a pole driven through his brain as punishment for his perceived insolence. In another instance, a man who had challenged Vlad about the smell of the bodies of those who had been impaled was himself impaled high enough to be able to breathe fresh air while he suffered and died – a grim mockery of his complaint.

Vlad III's unpredictable and brutal behaviour contrasts sharply with the predictability typically expected of leaders, even in medieval times. His actions provide a stark context within which to understand Pharaoh's decision to impale the baker and the peril Joseph faced when he stood before Pharaoh.

Joseph was a man of faith who displayed an incredible amount of courage on that day. First he made it clear to Pharaoh that he was only the messenger; the interpretation of dreams came from Joseph's God. And then, in what is now seen as one of the most famous forecasts in the Old Testament, which had far-reaching consequences for everyone concerned, Joseph used divine guidance to outline the meaning of the dreams.

According to him, the seven healthy cows and the seven healthy heads of grain represented seven years of prosperity. The seven scrawny cows and the seven thin heads of grain 'withered by the east wind' represented seven years of famine. In Joseph's words, this was a revelation from God – a warning – about what he was about to do. The famine was going to be so severe that any memories of past prosperity would be erased. The similarity of the two dreams was deliberate, intended to emphasise the fact that these events would happen fairly soon. Pharaoh had to take quick action; this was an emergency.

Joseph went on to advise Pharaoh that the predicted events required him to identify a wise person who would, with the support of competent supervisors, take charge of operations in the entire country. During the good years, the appointed governor and his officers should be tasked with collecting one-fifth (20%) of all grain produced in Egypt, which would be stored in Pharaoh's warehouses and guarded. The advice was precise and persuasive; such was Joseph's wisdom that the proposal was issued together with details, specifics and numbers. He assured Pharaoh that if he followed this process, he would succeed in feeding all his people through the difficult years of the famine.

Pharaoh believed everything Joseph said and was impressed by his God. Joseph's interpretation of Pharaoh's dreams showcased his wisdom, making him the perfect candidate to lead Egypt. Pharaoh made Joseph the second-most powerful man in Egypt, giving him a signet ring, fine linen clothes, a gold chain, a chariot and a new Egyptian name. Pharaoh declared that no one in Egypt could do anything without Joseph's approval.

The dreams that Joseph had had at the age of seventeen came true when he was thirty. As he had predicted, Egypt experienced seven years of abundant harvests, during which time vast amounts of grain were stored in Pharaoh's warehouses. This time of abundance was followed by seven years of severe famine. When the famine hit, the Egyptians cried out for help, and Joseph distributed the stored grain. He proved to be a capable and shrewd administrator, first selling food for money, then for livestock and eventually for land, until all the land in Egypt except that of the priests belonged to Pharaoh. Desperate, the people offered themselves as slaves in exchange for food, and Pharaoh accepted, making them his slaves.

Meanwhile, Joseph's family in Canaan was facing starvation. When Jacob heard that there was grain in Egypt, he sent his sons to buy food. When they arrived, they did not recognise Joseph, who had transformed from a spoiled favourite child into a powerful, wise leader. Joseph's mature appearance and regal attire disguised him from his brothers. Eventually Joseph revealed his identity and saved his entire family, bringing them to Egypt with Pharaoh's blessing. He told his brothers, 'You meant to harm me, but God used it for good, to save many people' (*New King James Bible*, 2004, Genesis 50:20).

The interconnection of Joseph's two dreams – his brothers' bundles of grain bowing down to his bundle, and the sun, moon and eleven stars bowing low before him – and his new status of influence in a foreign land was now complete. According to the Old Testament, it was the conclusion of what had been God's divine plan to save the family of Israel during a devastating drought. I wonder, though, how Joseph managed to achieve this with such success. The Old Testament and Sura 12 are both quite clear that this was a result of divine intervention made possible by the courage and faith of Joseph. It was a plan made by a distant God.

7

Human beings have an unquenchable desire for certainty. People make forecasts, assumptions and predictions on a daily basis in pursuit of certainty. We rely on hundreds of these assumptions every day. For instance, you probably wake up in the morning assuming you will feel well, your car will start, the roads will be clear and your office will still be there when you arrive.

In a discussion of futuristics and futures forecasting, Roland Meinert stated that while we possess empirical data about the past, we lack such data about the future; however, although we cannot change the past, we can shape the future (Meinert, 1973).

Meinert identifies four systematic techniques for forecasting the future (1973):

- Extrapolation: Analysing past data to identify patterns and build future models.
- Delphi: Polling experts for their insights.
- Simulation: Creating models to test scenarios, such as in space programmes.
- Scenario speculation: Imagining future lifestyles or consumer behaviours.

These techniques are useful in various fields, including social planning.

The study of dreams and their potential to predict the future is part of the larger field of complex adaptive systems. John Henry Holland, a scientist at the University of Michigan, pioneered research in this area. He believed that predicting the future is essential for survival, and that complex systems, which may appear chaotic, generate order and patterns over time (Holland, 1995). Living beings, including humans, create internal models based on vast amounts of data and experiences in order to anticipate future events.

In today's world, predictions about future natural events are made using data collected over centuries. The power of modern computers allows us to run complex mathematical models quickly. For example, scientists David Hodell, Mark Brenner, Jason Curtis and Thomas Guilderson (2001) studied lake sediment cores from the Yucatan Peninsula in Mexico to reconstruct the region's history over the past 2 600 years. They found a recurring drought cycle every 208 years, most likely linked to solar activity and the gravitational influence of celestial bodies. While the exact causes of drought are not fully understood, a lack of magnetic sunspot activity seems to correlate with drought occurrences. Movements of the moon and the planets as well as the occurrence of solar storms are also connected to events on earth, suggesting that ancient methods of predicting weather, like those in Joseph's time, were based on similar observations.

Will Alexander, a former chief of the Division of Hydrology in South Africa, also studied pattern recognition. He showed that annual river flows are linked to sunspot activity, demonstrating this with data from the Vaal Dam. He found that river flows followed a twenty-one-year cycle, alternating between drought and high inflows, synchronised with double sunspot cycles. This pattern recognition is a fundamental aspect of how our brains work, helping us make sense of the world around us (Alexander, 2009).

As highlighted earlier in this chapter, the influence of Babylonian astrology and civilization had spread to Joseph's region and had a marked impact on people's understanding of the world at that time. Surrounded by the natural environment, solar activities and agricultural life, Joseph developed the ability to find patterns in his dreams.

8

Genesis 37–50 is a story about survival and adaptation.

As indicated earlier in this chapter, the first verse of Genesis 37 highlights the unstable life and nomadic existence that Jacob's family led as sojourners: 'Now Jacob lived in the land of journeys …'. The Hebrew verb *gur* used in the text means 'temporary dweller'. This suggests to us that a strong survival instinct was etched in Joseph's mind at an early age.

From childhood, Joseph's continued existence was dependent on nature. In addition, the influences of the Babylonian civilisation on his region meant that he would have acquired knowledge about the correlation of the movements of the moon and the planets with sunspot cycles and the like.

The sleeping unconscious mind dreams and arrives at symbolic visions of the future. This view, which provides an alternative explanation of how Joseph got it so right when it came to interpreting his own dreams as well as those of others, is grounded in contemporary science.

Joseph's predictions exemplify the concept of long memory, or long-term persistence, which has strategic implications in fields such as climate, hydrology and finance. Researchers from various disciplines have explored this concept, tracing its origins to the work of Harold Edwin Hurst, a hydrology engineer who studied the Nile's water flow with the aim of controlling floods and sustaining development in Egypt (Graves *et al.*, 2017).

Hurst found that natural events tend to have long stretches of high or low values, unlike random events. His findings, known as the 'Hurst phenomenon', showed discrepancies between theoretical models and real-world data. This led to the development of long-memory models.

Hurst's ideas were developed further by mathematician Benoit Mandelbrot. While working at IBM, Mandelbrot pioneered the field of fractal geometry and challenged the conventional use of bell curves in statistics. He argued that outliers are inherent to systems and should not be ignored, as they were by traditional mathematical models, and demonstrated that real-world data is often more complex and interconnected than previously thought.

Mandelbrot's ideas help explain how seemingly random events follow patterns. He applied his models to various fields, including stock market prices, revealing that price movements are not as random as previously thought. He coined a term – the Joseph Effect – for the predictable, continuous cycles he observed, such as the biblical seven years of plenty followed by seven years of famine (Tamplin, 2023; Graves *et al.*, 2017).

Mandelbrot's work emphasised the importance of understanding roughness and irregularity in natural and economic systems, which led to significant advancements in mathematical modelling, and had practical applications such as determining ideal dam sizes for water conservation, as we will see in the section that follows.

In essence, Joseph's ability to foresee the future based on observed patterns aligns with these modern scientific concepts, demonstrating the enduring relevance of long memory in understanding and predicting complex systems.

9

Why is the Joseph Effect important?

The answer is simple: the Joseph Effect suggests that patterns and cycles, rather than random events, drive financial markets and other systems. This means that periods of high prices are likely to be followed by more high prices, and periods of low prices by more low prices.

For decades, financial market theory assumed that markets were efficient, with prices reflecting all available information. The rise of social media made this idea even more appealing. However, the Joseph Effect challenges this notion by emphasising the importance of patterns and cycles over random fluctuations.

The Joseph Effect introduces predictability in market movements, which can help investors follow a disciplined investment strategy. Instead of reacting impulsively, investors can stay committed to their plans, benefitting from dollar-cost averaging and compounding, buying low and selling high when the market presents opportunities, and remaining invested during market fluctuations.

The concept also extends to technology. For instance, Tim Berners-Lee created the World Wide Web to help physicists share information. His idea evolved into the internet we use today, which has changed how the world operates. Reflecting on the thirtieth anniversary of the internet, Berners-Lee observed that the Web has evolved into a multifaceted platform, serving as a communal hub, educational institution, healthcare provider, retail space, creative workshop, professional environment, entertainment venue, financial centre, and more (World Wide Web Foundation, 2019).

Berners-Lee's vision was driven by the idea of linking information easily, allowing users to find connections between seemingly unrelated things (Berners-Lee, 2000). This principle influenced Google's approach, setting it apart from Yahoo, which relied on organising information in neat categories. Google's success lies in embracing the full capabilities of the Web, as Berners-Lee envisioned (Hern, 2019). This approach allowed Google to dominate the search engine market and innovate with products such as Gmail. By offering one gigabyte of email storage, Google anticipated falling storage costs and an exponential rise in user numbers, ultimately outpacing competitors such as Yahoo and Hotmail (Press, 2016; Indah, 2023).

The Joseph Effect also provides lessons for personal finance. Just as Joseph saved Egypt by ensuring that Pharaoh stored up grain during years of plenty, individuals can secure their financial future by saving and investing during their productive years. This prepares them for leaner times when their income may be lower. Ultimately, the solution is straightforward: you should save and secure as much as possible, building your capital consistently – the more the better. More than one millennium before the birth of Christ, Joseph advised Pharaoh that one-fifth of all grain produced in Egypt should be stored in silos for use in times of need. This principle remains relevant and applicable today.

Just as hydrologist Will Alexander showed that annual river flows and sunspot activity follow long-term patterns, so financial planner William P. Bengen proposed the 4% rule for safe retirement withdrawals, based on historical data and patterns in market returns (Bengen, 1992, 1994). This rule helps investors determine how much they can withdraw annually without depleting their savings.

Through his calculation of the safe withdrawal rate, Bengen offered a viable and useful method to address the issue of determining the necessary capital for retirement or for a future planned date, which is best illustrated through the analogy of a dam.

You will remember that Benoit Mandelbrot's mathematical models were used to determine the ideal size of reservoirs. This offers a useful analogy: we can compare the characteristics of sound financial planning to the characteristics of the ideal dam.

These are the characteristics of the ideal dam:
- It has a uniform outflow.
- It ends the period as full as it began.
- It never overflows.
- It has the smallest capacity that meets these conditions.

This analogy helps us understand how to manage our finances. The dam represents our accumulated funds, with the water level symbolising our savings. The inflows are our income and investment returns, while the outflows are our expenses. Just as a dam needs a consistent water source, we need a steady income. The goal is to ensure that withdrawals (outflows) do not deplete our savings (the dam's water level) so that our funds last as long as we live.

To build and maintain this 'financial dam', we need to do the following:
- Secure a reliable source of income, such as a job or business.
- Continuously invest and save, ensuring that our 'dam' remains full.
- Prepare for unexpected events that might affect our finances, just as a dam must account for evaporation or unexpected inflows.

Ultimately, the key is to save and build capital consistently. The more you save, the better prepared you are for the future, just like a well-maintained dam ensures a steady water supply.

The global financial services industry has adopted the 4% rule as a guideline for retirement planning, recommending it as a reliable method to ensure that capital endures (Jonathan, 2014). With an estimated safe withdrawal rate, determining the ideal amount of capital needed is straightforward. It is a matter of working backwards. For instance, if you need to withdraw R500 000 annually, you should aim to have a minimum of R12.5 million saved by the time you retire.

Ultimately, the Joseph Effect emphasises the importance of recognising patterns and cycles in various aspects of life, from financial markets to technology and personal finance. By understanding and applying these patterns, individuals and organisations can make more informed decisions and achieve better outcomes.

CHAPTER 2

THE NOAH EFFECT:
Decoding the impact of large-scale catastrophes

'… I will cause it to rain upon the earth forty days and forty nights; and every living substance that I have made will I destroy from off the face of the earth.'
– New King James Bible, *2004, Genesis 7:4*

1

It was Sukkot, the Jewish autumn holiday of thanksgiving. Things on the Israeli border with the Gaza Strip had been relatively quiet for some time. A complicated truce between Israel and Hamas had held for years, save for the occasional missile launched into Israel, which the reliable Iron Dome anti-missile system successfully repelled, preventing any damage to property or injury to citizens. The attention of the Israeli army (IDF) was focused on the country's northern border, with little concern for the south, and many IDF soldiers were on leave.

But on 7 October 2023, Hamas shocked the Israelis and the world by launching a coordinated attack from Gaza, south of Israel (Britannica, 2024). On this day, the opponent did not play according to the rules. A barrage of over five thousand missiles was fired into Israel, and the Iron Dome system was overwhelmed. The attack led to devastating carnage, igniting a brutal war as Israel moved to eliminate its adversary.

Like the Second World War and Covid-19, which brought the world to a standstill in 2020, the events of 7 October 2023 can best be described as low probability, unpredictable, chaotic and hugely disruptive. They fall under the category of events that trigger ripple effects such as fear, supply chain shocks, inflation, commodity shortages, panic and outsize price shocks in financial markets.

Such events are unpredictable, yes, but what should we do when they happen? Should we prepare for defeat, or can we find better ways to face such challenges? Should we look for opportunities in the mayhem? In my opinion, there is no better way to find guidance on how to handle such a situation than to go back several thousand years, to when Noah was the only man to save his family from the deluge.

2

When God reflected on his creation, the dramatic multiplication of his people and the resultant population increase, he realised that his people had grown corrupt, wicked, evil and violent. This is not what the Lord had intended; according to the Old Testament book of Genesis, the Hebrew book of creation, 'it grieved him at his heart' (*New King James Bible*, 2004, Genesis 6:6).

However, there was one man who had found favour in God's eyes: Noah. He was different from other men of his generation. And so God confided in Noah, telling him of the impending destruction that he planned to unleash on the earth through a flood, the likes of which had never been witnessed before. All living things would be destroyed, except for those covered by the covenant that God later swore to Noah.

God instructed Noah to build an ark of gopher wood, providing detailed specifications for its construction: 'The length of the ark shall be three hundred cubits, the breadth of it fifty cubits, and the height of it thirty cubits' (*New King James Bible*, 2004, Genesis 6:15).

The measurements are given in cubits, and you may wonder what exactly a cubit is. It is an ancient unit of length based on the distance from a person's elbow to the tip of their middle finger. Measuring in this way is like using your own body as a ruler. Typically, a cubit is about eighteen inches or forty-five centimetres, but it could vary slightly depending on the person measuring. Noah would have calibrated a rope based on this measure and used it much like a builder uses a tape measure today.

God then made a covenant with Noah: Noah would bring two (a male and a female) of every living creature on the earth onto the ark. Noah himself, along with his wife, his sons and their wives, would also be on board.

Noah was an obedient man, as God had known, and he did not disappoint. He built the ark according to the instructions he had been given. When it was ready, God told him to bring the living things on board as previously instructed (for every living thing, two of each of its kind), and warned him that all hell would break loose in seven days' time.

Noah was six hundred years old when the waters of the flood broke on the earth. As the waters rose, the ark – with Noah and his family on board – was lifted and it floated. The rains poured down relentlessly for forty days and nights, eventually submerging the hills and mountains under fifteen cubits of water. The ark, crafted with divine precision, was tossed upon the waves but remained steadfast, safeguarding its precious cargo. Meanwhile, all life outside the ark had perished: 'And every living substance was destroyed ... and Noah only remained alive, and they that were with him in the ark' (*New King James Bible*, 2004, Genesis 7:22–23).

The rains stopped after forty days and forty nights, but it took another 150 days for the floodwaters to abate.

In the seventh month, the ark rested on Mount Ararat, a destination known only to the Lord. Noah opened the window of the ark and sent out a dove to check if there was any land not covered by water, but the dove came back, having failed to land. Seven days later, Noah opened the window again and let the dove fly out; when it came back with an olive leaf in its beak, he concluded that the waters had abated. After a further seven days, he sent off the dove again, but this time it did not return; the dove was now free in the wild where it belonged, and it was time for Noah and his crew to disembark. As God had promised Noah, the floodwaters had destroyed all living things on earth except for those that had boarded the ark.

This is the story of Noah, the ark that he built and the Great Flood, as told in the Old Testament in the book of Genesis.

3

The flood story, as recounted in both the Bible and the Quran, has captivated audiences worldwide for centuries. Its themes of survival, renewal and the power of nature resonate deeply across cultures, with both Muslim and Hebrew traditions centred around the hero, Noah (Old Testament) or Nuh (Quran). It is rightfully referred to as 'the deluge': an event so chaotic and catastrophic that it was impossible to predict.

Moses wrote Genesis close to two millennia before the birth of Christ. His account of the flood (told in Genesis 6–9) is notably brief and abrupt. The narrative also does not contain a single word of dialogue.

By contrast, Abraham and Moses often engaged in dialogue with their Lord when approached by God, and in some instances even made firm objections to his instructions, as a son would in conversation with his father.

For instance, when Abraham was being tested for obedience, the conversation went as follows: 'And it came to pass after these things, that God did tempt Abraham, and said unto him, Abraham: and he said, Behold, here I am' (*New King James Bible*, 2004, Genesis 22:1).

On the other hand, Moses needed a great deal of convincing and a few miracles to persuade him to do what God wanted; he quickly assessed the complexity of the task God was asking him to perform and the dangers that lay ahead, and raised objections, as in this example: 'And Moses said unto the Lord, O my Lord, I am not eloquent, neither heretofore, nor since thou hast spoken unto thy servant: but I am slow of speech, and of a slow tongue. And the Lord said unto him, Who hath made man's mouth? or who maketh the dumb, or deaf, or the seeing, or the blind? have not I the Lord?' (*New King James Bible*, 2004, Exodus 4:10–14). However, this was not the case in Noah's story.

This noticeable absence of dialogue in the Genesis account of Noah's Great Flood prompted scholars to search for other versions of the flood story.

Flood myths are deeply ingrained in Mesopotamian culture, where the Tigris and Euphrates rivers often flooded. As Assyriologists and archaeologists have uncovered, multiple versions of these flood stories exist, all sharing striking similarities. The Great Flood became a cultural touchstone, with events often described as having occurred before or after the deluge.

George Smith was an English Assyriologist who made a major contribution to the field. While working as a banknote engraver for a printing firm, his passion for the Assyrian culture led him to spend his lunch hours at the British Museum reading everything he could find on the subject. When his unusual ability to decipher cuneiform tablets was observed, he was invited to join the British Museum (Wikipedia, 2024).

In 1872, Smith began translating a clay tablet discovered in Nineveh that described a great flood caused by the gods of Babylon to punish humanity. The tablet was encrusted with lime deposits, which a conservator removed after a few days. Once it had been cleaned, Smith found details mirroring the biblical flood story, including information about one person being instructed to build an ark and to save one pair of each species, the ark coming to rest on a mountain and the release of a dove. Overwhelmed by his discovery, Smith famously began undressing in excitement.

The announcement of Smith's discovery, made in the presence of the Archbishop of Canterbury and British Prime Minister William Gladstone, garnered significant attention due to its potential implications for the Church. The story made headlines, and a British newspaper, the *Daily Telegraph*, funded Smith's expedition to find more tablets in Nineveh. In 1873, funded by the newspaper to the tune of £1 000, Smith discovered further tablets relating to the flood story (Wikipedia, 2024). Tragically, he died of dysentery in 1876 at the age of thirty-six while continuing his research in Mesopotamia.

More recent discoveries were made by Irving Finkel, a curator at the British Museum, who spends his time deciphering ancient Mesopotamian clay tablets. Many of these cuneiform tablets record the everyday activities of the Babylonians. However, a significant discovery came with the 'Ark Tablet', a clay tablet that revealed striking parallels to the biblical flood story, offering a glimpse into the shared cultural narratives of ancient Mesopotamia.

The discovery of the tablet came about when a young man, Douglas Simmons, brought an ancient clay tablet with him when he visited the British Museum one day in 1985. It had been a gift from Simmons's father,

Leonard, who had collected clay tablets and other souvenirs while serving in the Royal Air Force in the Middle East during the Second World War. Frustratingly, Finkel was not able to convince Simmons to leave the tablet, which seemed to reference a flood, with him. It was not until 2009, twenty-four years later, that Simmons returned with the tablet and agreed to lend it to Finkel.

Finkel was thrilled by the tablet's content and called it the 'Ark Tablet'. It is central to Finkel's book, *The Ark Before Noah: Decoding the Story of the Flood* (2014). Roughly the size of an iPhone, it dates back to around 1750 BC and contains sixty lines of cuneiform. It begins with a dialogue between the god Ea and the Babylonian man Atrahasis (translated as 'the exceedingly wise'), the equivalent of Noah (Finkel, 2014: 107):

'Wall, wall! Reed wall, reed wall!
Atrahasis, pay heed to my advice,
That you may live forever!
Destroy your house, build a boat;
Spurn property and save life!
Draw out the boat that you will make
On a circular plan;
Let her length and breadth be equal ...'

The tablet includes detailed instructions for building the boat, including the use of materials such as palm fibre rope and bitumen, and tells the story of Atrahasis being instructed to bring aboard pairs of every wild animal. The flood story closely resembles the biblical account, but the ark described is a round coracle with a base area of 3 600 m² and a diameter of seventy metres, different from the oblong shape typically depicted in the Bible (Holland, 2014).

Finkel notes that references to the flood story appear as early as two millennia before the birth of Christ, long before written records. He identified three main flood stories, each with its own flood hero: the Sumerian Flood Story, the Atrahasis Epic and the Epic of Gilgamesh (Finkel, 2014). These stories share some similarities with the accounts in Genesis and the Quran.

Historical records show that the Hebrews were taken into captivity in Babylon around 600 BC (Soskice, 2014). However, by the time Genesis was written, Babylonian influences – ranging from their astronomical science and cultural practices to flood folklore – had already permeated Jewish culture.

Moses's Old Testament account succeeded in transforming the story of the Great Flood into a narrative of profound global impact. Recognising its powerful potential, the Hebrews elevated this ancient tale, imbuing it with deep interest and significance that has resonated through the ages.

4

Deciphering ancient languages to reveal the secrets of the past is an extraordinary skill. To delve even deeper into the flood story, I turned to the scientific insights of William Ryan and Walter Pitman, marine geologists from Columbia University. In their 1998 book, *Noah's Flood: The New Scientific Discoveries About the Event that Changed History*, they examined the biblical flood story through the lens of geology, offering a fascinating blend of ancient legend and modern science.

Around twenty thousand years ago, the last great glaciers began melting, causing sea levels to rise (Ryan & Pitman, 1998). In around 5600 BC, the retreating glaciers in Europe started redirecting water away from what is now the Black Sea, which was then a freshwater lake. As the Black Sea's levels dropped hundreds of feet below the Mediterranean, the dry land between them, including the Bosphorus Strait, separated the two bodies of water. As global sea levels continued to rise, the Mediterranean eventually overflowed, breaking through the Bosphorus Strait and flooding into the Black Sea with a force two hundred times greater than the flow of the Niagara Falls. This deluge mixed saltwater with freshwater, transforming the Black Lake into the salty Black Sea. It is likely that the roaring waters caused immense noise and lasted for months, devastating the region.

Ryan and Pitman described what witnessing this flood might have been like (1998: 16):

A group of distant kinsmen, haggard and terrified, came in along the shore. They described how their valley had been inundated. The waters of the

Great Salt Sea above were pouring into the lake below, turning their once peaceful valley into a wild torrent. Their villages were swept away. Days later, the rising water invaded the delta and fields. The frightened villagers fled to the hills, making sacrifices to their goddess in hopes of appeasing the gods. Petrified, they retreated from the chaos and told others of the doom they believed was unleashed by the gods.

To support their hypothesis, Ryan and Pitman analysed sediment cores from the Black Sea. They found freshwater molluscs below the sea and saltwater molluscs above it, indicating a dramatic change. Carbon dating showed that mud was deposited between 18 000 and 8 600 years ago. These findings, they believe, provide scientific evidence of the Great Flood mentioned in Genesis.

The flood story was passed down through generations, reaching Mesopotamia, where floods from the Tigris and Euphrates rivers were common. It is likely that this familiarity amplified the drama in these stories. The many versions of the flood story, from Genesis and Sura 71 to the tablets deciphered by George Smith and Irving Finkel, reflect this.

5

Noah, a man of great faith, prepared for the deluge by building an ark, thus saving his family and many other species. His story offers us useful lessons on the importance of foresight and preparation when it comes to dealing with catastrophic and unpredictable 'black swan' events, such as the Great Flood, the Second World War and the Covid-19 pandemic, which are sometimes also referred to as 'Noah Effect' phenomena.

In an attempt to understand this phenomenon, I delved into the pivotal events before and after the Second World War, uncovering how this catastrophic period reshaped the world in profound and unexpected ways.

In his study of the origins of the war, historian Alan Bullock (1971) identifies various contributing factors, including Britain and France's policy of appeasement and their failure to secure an agreement with Russia, Mussolini's alliance with Hitler, the Nazi–Soviet pact, the naivety of the Polish for believing they could keep Germany and Russia at bay and the isolationism policy of the United States. However, he maintains that the true cause of the war remains Adolf Hitler's character (especially his anti-Semitic, racist prejudices) and Germany's aggressive foreign policy.

Between 1933 and 1939, events unfolded rapidly, catching Europe and America off guard, and leading them into a war for which they were unprepared. By 1939, Hitler's expansionist policies had sparked the Second World War, the most ruinous conflict in human history.

The Second World War caused immense devastation globally, especially in Europe, resulting in millions of casualties. However, it had mixed implications for Los Angeles: when the federal government increased its defence budget, the small town almost five thousand kilometres away from America's industrialised East was transformed into an industrial powerhouse, producing warships and planes for the Allies (Arthur, 1994). This led to the establishment of steel and aluminium industries such as the Kaiser Steel Plant and the Fontana Mill. The demand for labour opened up opportunities for women, blacks and Hispanics, revolutionising the workforce.

By 1943, Los Angeles had experienced significant growth, fuelled by an influx of new residents who, in turn, encouraged their families and friends to join them. This migration created a ripple effect, steadily increasing the population as more people were drawn to the opportunities and vibrant life the city offered.

There is no better example than Lockheed Aircraft Corporation (now Lockheed Martin), which played a crucial role in the war by producing fighter planes (Lockheed Martin, 2020). In 1938, its plant was based in Burbank, Los Angeles. The company received a large order from Britain's Royal Air Force, which boosted its reputation. Following the attack on Pearl Harbor in 1941, the Burbank plant was classified as a strategic military site and camouflaged to look like a suburb. This opportunity allowed Lockheed to grow into the world's largest arms producer (NBC News, 2012).

The financial success of Lockheed is evident in its stock market performance. In 1978, shares traded at $4 each; by 2023, they were trading at $435 (Macrotrends, 2023). An investment of a thousand shares in 1978 was worth $435 000 in 2023, plus dividends.

The Second World War, much like the Great Flood of Noah's time, unleashed a wave of unpredictable and transformative changes. For Los Angeles, the war catalysed a metamorphosis that was beyond imagination.

San Francisco, today a wealthy industrial hub, was also shaped by the 'black swan' event of the Second World War. The city, over six hundred kilometres north of Los Angeles on the West Coast of the United States, grew immensely as a result of the war. More than thirty shipyards consolidated to form the world's largest shipbuilding complex, crucial to winning the war. Between 1940 and 1945, the San Francisco Bay Area produced 1 400 ships, averaging one per day (National Park Service, 2024). This industrial boom led to a population surge, and the recent tech boom has added even more people, making San Francisco the second most densely populated city in the United States after New York, with 18 451 people per 2.58 square kilometres. This high population density has led to a severe housing crisis.

In the 1950s, local authorities aimed to preserve San Francisco's character by restricting new housing developments and high-rise buildings. This decision, coupled with the Second World War's impact, contributed to the city's current housing affordability issues (Weinberger, 2016). According to Wolf Richter, a publisher of business and finance trends, house prices in San Francisco have increased by 531% (adjusted for inflation) since 1960, whereas household incomes have only risen by 91% over the same period (Richter, 2019).

6

Next I investigated the profound repercussions of Covid-19, discovering that this global crisis vividly exemplifies the Noah Effect in our contemporary world.

In December 2019, health authorities reported an outbreak of pneumonia of unknown origin in Wuhan, Hubei, China. Shortly afterwards, the genome of a new coronavirus was released and made public to the scientific community (Ciotti *et al.*, 2020). This virus, later named Covid-19, quickly spread worldwide, causing numerous deaths. Despite mandatory face mask policies, the virus continued to infect millions. When individuals died from Covid-19, their bodies were wrapped in special plastic, and funerals were limited to a small number of family members.

Covid-19 had a devastating impact on health systems and economies globally. Governments imposed lockdowns, restricting both domestic and international travel (Yi-Chi *et al.*, 2020). Health systems were overwhelmed and the numbers of deceased people were so high that undertakers struggled to manage. The lockdowns used to restrict the spread of the virus severely damaged economies, leading to business closures, job losses and widespread financial hardship. Governments had to provide financial support to many people who could no longer afford necessities.

The World Health Organization reported that as of December 2023, 772 million people had been infected with Covid-19, and nearly seven million had died, with most deaths occurring by December 2021, before vaccines became widely available (World Health Organization, 2023). Nearly seven million people died in less than three years due to a single virus, despite significant technological and medical advancements.

Like the Second World War, Covid-19 was a 'black swan' event – an unforeseen happening with enormous consequences. As the pandemic unfolded, travel ceased, airlines went out of business and supply chains were severely disrupted (Hald & Coslugeanu, 2020). A shortage of computer chips from China affected the availability of electronic equipment as well as automotive production, leading to worldwide inflation (Xiling *et al.*, 2021). Major economies struggled to control this inflation, prompting reserve banks to hike interest rates to levels not seen in decades.

The pandemic starkly revealed the world's vulnerability to unpredictable events. As the virus spread with alarming speed, governments struggled to implement risk mitigation strategies in time. In 2020, humanity, ill-equipped to mount an effective defence, confronted an invisible and elusive enemy. The profound impact on society underscored just how unprepared and exposed we truly were.

7

Scientific investigations into the flood story, such as those by marine geologists Ryan and Pitman, and the mathematical models of Benoit Mandelbrot, provide modern interpretations of the ancient deluge. These studies explore the historical and hydrological significance of extreme events, known today as Noah Effect phenomena (Walter, 2014; Graves *et al.*, 2017). When researchers try to create a scatter graph for chaotic events such as these, the many outliers make it impossible to fit the data onto a smooth curve, meaning that traditional mathematical methods cannot predict them. This highlights the importance of the Great Flood, which inspired the concept of the Noah Effect – a phenomenon where past chaos continues to influence present random events. These Noah events often lead to what is called the 'Joseph Effect', named after the biblical story of Joseph's seven years of plenty followed by seven years of famine.

The Covid-19 pandemic was a prime example of a Noah Effect event, bringing winners and losers. Pre-pandemic, branded-goods companies and software firms were favoured stocks. During the initial lockdown phase, before the Pfizer vaccine was announced on 8 November 2020, people relied heavily on deliveries and software. Consequently, Amazon shares rose by 79% and Netflix shares by 59%, while the real estate and energy sectors suffered (*The Economist*, 2022). Office occupancy plummeted, and banks faced defaults and reduced margins due to lower interest rates. This level of disruption is characteristic of a Noah Effect.

Between 2020 and 2022, the tech sector experienced varied performance: Apple shares soared, while Facebook and Meta lost significant value (The Economist, 2022). Nvidia, a microchip designer, saw its stock spike by 166%, while Intel's stock slumped. As vaccines were rolled out and governments regained control, supply chain disruptions from prolonged lockdowns led to global inflation. Major economies struggled with rising inflation, prompting aggressive interest rate hikes to control it. For example, South Africa's prime interest rate, which had been lowered to 7% in 2021 to support economic recovery, was hiked to 11.75% by May 2023.

Lightstone Properties reports that the exceptionally low interest rates from mid-2020 to late 2021 allowed new buyers to enter the market but also led to overextension. By comparing the number of buyers in May 2021 to those selling by May 2023, Lightstone calculated an 80% level of distressed sales (Moneyweb, 2023). In the same article, First National Bank reported that 23% of sales driven by financial pressure remained elevated, surpassing the historical average of 18% since the fourth quarter of 2007.

During periods of low interest rates, people qualify for bigger loans and so tend to buy bigger homes, but high interest rates make mortgages unaffordable, leading to rental demand. Those who buy their homes when interest rates are low and do not have a financial buffer face foreclosure when interest rates increase. While this scenario represents a financial disaster for some, it creates opportunities for others to buy distressed properties at lower prices.

It is illustrative to look at the performance of the Cape Town property market following the Covid-19 pandemic. The Cape Town market has shown sustained growth, with house prices rising 141% between 2010 and 2022, the highest increase in South Africa (Statistics South Africa, 2023). The city's limited supply of land for development keeps both demand and prices high. Recent statistics reveal that the Western Cape (including Cape Town) now leads the country in terms of the number of building plans that have been approved (Pam Golding Properties, 2023). However, estate agents lament the low housing stock compared to the burgeoning demand (Fourie, 2023). While the impact of high interest rates between 2022 and 2024 has been less dramatic in Cape Town than in other major cities, it has nonetheless disrupted the momentum of property prices.

It can be advantageous for investors to buy property at times when interest rates are high, as opportunities for bargains may arise. Investing wisely means acquiring properties at prices below their fundamental value. Although unpredictable, Noah Effect events create such opportunities.

The sustained rise in Cape Town's property prices prompts a compelling question: are these soaring values grounded in solid economic fundamentals, or are they merely fuelled by market hype? Cape Town's competitive fundamentals are backed by its inclusion in PWC Africa's 'Cities of Opportunity' report, in which it is benchmarked against major global cities such as London, Berlin, New York, Singapore, Kuala Lumpur, Paris, Toronto, Mumbai, Sao Paulo, Hong Kong, San Fransisco, Los Angeles, Beijing, Moscow and Shanghai. The comparison is based on a set of key performance indicators that include the following criteria: the city's role as a gateway; its health, safety and security status; sustainability and natural environment; demographics and quality of life; transportation and infrastructure; economic influence and the ease of conducting business. The report highlights Cape Town's strengths, including its transport system, business-friendly environment and natural beauty. Despite inequality stemming from the country's past, Cape Town is seen as having strong fundamentals and potential for future growth (Williams, 2017).

In summary, Cape Town's property market has demonstrated remarkable resilience and growth post-Covid-19, driven by limited land supply and strong demand. As one of South Africa's top-performing markets, it offers unique investment opportunities, particularly during periods of high interest rates. With competitive fundamentals recognised globally, Cape Town stands out as a vibrant, promising destination for future growth.

8

As we have journeyed through ancient flood stories, scientific discoveries and modern-day catastrophes, it has become clear that the Noah Effect is more than a tale of survival – it is a profound lesson in human resilience and adaptability. From Noah's ark to the economic ripples of the Second World War and the global upheaval of Covid-19, these events remind us that while we cannot predict the future, we can prepare for it.

The Noah Effect teaches us that amid chaos, there is always an opportunity to rebuild, innovate and thrive. Just as Noah constructed an ark to weather the storm, we too must build our own arks – be it through foresight in investments, adaptability in crises or innovation in the face of uncertainty. The stories of the past and the data of the present both point to a timeless truth: those who are prepared, who anticipate the unpredictable and who remain resilient in the face of adversity will not just survive but emerge stronger.

As we look to the future, let the Noah Effect be a reminder that even in the darkest of times, there is a path forward. It is in our hands to find it, to steer our course and to emerge from the storm with renewed purpose and strength.

PART II

THE STRENGTH OF THOUGHTS:
INVESTING SIMPLIFIED

CHAPTER 3

SUCCESSFUL INVESTING:
The power of thought

'Hast thou the soul of a free man or the soul of a slave?'
– George S. Clason

1

The terms 'now', 'now-now' and 'just now' typically signify an immediate action in all English dictionaries. Yet their usage in daily speech can significantly alter their meaning, often implying a future action. This notion counters the teachings of our school days, when delaying tasks was discouraged. Procrastination, a common human behaviour, can hinder success if not managed.

This chapter delves into personal tales that reveal insights into human nature and financial acumen, with a focus on the benefits that come with taking speedy action rather than procrastinating. It also warns investors of the dangers of changing their investment strategy in the face of challenging events and crises. Investors who resist the temptation to make panicked decisions when markets are volatile are rewarded for their level-headedness over the long term.

Among these narratives, I sought to highlight a distinctive story, one that stands in contrast to the rest. Julia epitomises this unique perspective. Her first appearance on Talk Radio 702's *Money Show* when she was twenty-seven and her subsequent annual discussions about her financial journey every July for the following decade make her story a focal point of this chapter. At the time, I found her input so valuable that whenever I missed an episode, I would seek out the podcast to catch up on her insights. Julia's journey is the centrepiece of this chapter, offering a rich exploration of individuality and investment behaviour.

2

James Coddington is a businessman based in Auckland, New Zealand. He is the founder of a technology business, Joy Business Academy, whose mission is to disrupt traditional training methods (Nadkarni, 2020). When conventional training methods are used, it takes a long time for young people to acquire the skills needed to be considered for employment. The aim of Coddington's business is to train people in a fraction of the time it normally takes, and thus to plug the skills shortage in the industry. Technology is the basis of Joy Business Academy. The company provides experiential learning through simulations, virtual reality and game learning.

Coddington, who made his first million dollars in his late twenties, is a believer in the saying 'You can't save yourself to riches.' But this saying is often misconstrued. He clarifies its meaning by explaining that a person must improve their earning potential before they can make meaningful savings. This entails continuous learning and upskilling. You cannot save what you do not have. His life experiences have taught him not to put too much faith in long-held financial myths. Coddington suggests that to get ahead, you need to value your money and invest it wisely. Start by investing in yourself, and when you have some extra funds, place them in a safe investment that you trust will grow. This could be property, blue-chip shares, art or gold.

Despite his successes over the years, Coddington concedes that he has made many poor financial decisions. One that still haunts him is a choice he made in his final year of university – passing up the opportunity to buy an acre of waterfront land on the newly formed Lake Dunstan in Cromwell (Central Otago) for $30,000. Instead, he chose to spend the money on an expensive, but highly enjoyable three-month skiing trip in Whistler, Canada. He prefers not to think about how much that piece of land is worth now (Nadkarni, 2020). However, he was young and probably felt that his future was too distant for him to need to worry about investing in land at the time. He procrastinated, and this decision proved to be a painful mistake.

Coddington's experience is all too common, yet one might not expect such folly from someone who has been canonised. However, even saints are not immune to the pitfalls of procrastination: the famous Saint Augustine also suffered a bout of procrastination at some point during his early adult life (Andreou & White, 2010). Augustine acknowledged the internal conflict between his soul and body, recognising that they had been adversaries since the beginning of time. In his *Confessions*, Augustine recounted how, after years of indulging in sexual pleasures without love, he vowed to return to Christianity, praying for chastity and self-restraint, but adding, 'only not yet'. Despite his deep disdain for his current lifestyle and his sincere desire to change, he kept postponing any real change until 'tomorrow' (Poliquin, 2018).

Procrastination is known as the thief of time. Some people procrastinate on occasion, while others do it more persistently. Does it help to know that you are not alone in suffering occasional lapses of procrastination? Or is that knowledge cold comfort?

3

Dietmar Gunther* called me on a Wednesday afternoon. He was guardedly excited. 'I have been given the keys to a new house that I must sell. I have known the clients, a couple, for almost fifteen years, and I sold them the house myself about eight years ago. It needs work, but you must see it. Panther Street. Great location. You fix it how you normally do, and it will sell fast.'

Dietmar was my real estate agent. Now happily retired, he had decades of experience in real estate and was a specialist in the area. Dietmar was different from most estate agents. He sold properties on behalf of clients and picked up fixer-upper bargains when they became available. His renovation skills were beyond compare. When Dietmar bought a property in need of tender love and care, he would renovate it until it looked new, attending to all details with what I teasingly referred to as his 'German efficiency'.

*Not his real name.

Dietmar was a German immigrant who had arrived in the country in his late twenties. His English was fluent, but his accent betrayed his German heritage. Nostalgia meant that he drove a German BMW SUV, bought meat from the German butcher close to Bedfordview, dined in German restaurants and served his clients complimentary German sweets on Sunday show days. He had made his fortune in real estate.

When Dietmar called, I always had to put everything down, listen to him and then immediately arrange to view the property on offer. This time he already held the keys, so I made an appointment to view the house after work the same day. The owners had emigrated to Australia and so it was vacant.

The house was in the unassuming tree-lined Johannesburg East suburb of Kensington, established at the beginning of the twentieth century by Max Langermann, who planned the layout of the streets and gave them British names such as King Edward, Nottingham, Derby and Leicester, with all the streets ordered alphabetically.

Katoomba Street was named after a warship that had played a significant role in English history. The British Royal Navy had dispatched a squadron of battleships led by the colonial cruiser HMS *Katoomba* to protect the coastlines of British colonies Australia and New Zealand, which arrived triumphantly at the port of Sydney in 1891 (Australian National Maritime Museum, 2023). Estate agents of English origin recited this history with an air of nostalgic pride, including such details in their profitable small talk during show days on Sundays, while subtly persuading clients to buy the property in question and settle in the suburb.

The layout of the streets was completed in 1903. The houses have typically English architecture – both Georgian and Victorian styles are common – and are popular with English-speaking folk. Bay windows, Oregon floors and Oregon doors are typical features. In most cases, the condition of the doors is very good; Oregon is durable. Decades ago, the preferred décor style in the suburb meant that most doors were painted with an oil-based paint, which served to preserve the underlying wood perfectly. The wooden floors lay safely under ageing carpets, which protected the wood from water damage and the elements.

Renovators usually sanded the old paint off the Oregon doors, removed the old carpets and sanded down the Oregon floors. Serious renovators hired seasoned wood and floor artisans who would give the Oregon wood the correct treatment, varnishing it to a high-gloss, gleaming finish. Once its facelift was finished, the house would exude an incredible marketing appeal.

Many of the houses were handed down from generation to generation. Built in the jacaranda-lined streets around the ridge of the Langermann kopjes, they were well constructed and remained structurally in great shape. However, most of them were in need of rejuvenation when the property boom of the late 1990s attracted immense interest in the suburb, and so many property owners and renovators embarked on the renewal of their houses.

The basic architectural design of the houses was largely left untouched to retain the heritage feel of the area, but the kitchens and bathrooms were usually upgraded. In addition, bathrooms were added, the houses were repainted according to the latest colour trends, and many other aesthetic changes were made to increase the curb appeal of the properties. Real estate enthusiasts termed the modernisation process the 'Chelseafication of Kensington' in a nostalgic reference to the affluent West London suburb of Chelsea. The formal English word for the process is 'gentrification'.

By the time I met with Dietmar at the property, he was already excited about the prospects for this oldie. He had figured out the best layout and other possibilities for the renovation, and wasted no time advising me on what he thought was the best approach to revamp this character home. I always had my own ideas about how to tackle a renovation, but my approach was inevitably driven by my accounting background; I tended to drop anything that attracted higher costs, or find a less expensive way of doing it.

Dietmar knew the market very well, and so I listened patiently to him as he showed me the house. Once we had completed the tour, he warned, 'I give you two days to come back to me. You must tell me in two days if you are interested. You are the first person I called to show the house. If you do not take the house, I am going to buy it myself and fix it.' I was already familiar with this line, which Dietmar frequently used in our dealings.

This was a Wednesday. I went off to do my homework and assess the feasibility of the project. For some reason, I initially doubted Dietmar, silently questioning if he was right about the best way to refurbish the house because I feared it would result in exorbitant costs. Knocking down so many walls to create additional space always costs money; could I expect the selling price to compensate me for these costs? Always wary of overcapitalising, I called in a few of my usual team of artisans – the builder, the electrician and the plumber – to obtain urgent input for my cost estimations. I also checked property platforms for the latest property sales in the area, as I normally do.

This was in 2012, when the housing market was recovering from the slump caused by the 2008 global financial crisis; I had become much more cautious in my dealings and needed to do more calculations to convince myself before making a decision. I had a decent job that I valued, with a reputable employer. Renovating houses was a passionate side hustle that I was determined should never create conflict with my employment. I was doing well enough flipping homes to finance private school fees for my children and later to pay for them to study at overseas universities. However, this hobby – including whatever feasibility study was required for the project – was only to be done in my spare time. That week, my boss had given me an urgent work assignment that demanded many hours to complete. I had to work long hours late into the night. Soon I was out of time.

I dithered. I did not call Dietmar until Monday, missing my ultimatum by two days. I did not even consider calling him to ask for more time: there is a good reason why the Germans have a reputation for efficiency. When I called Dietmar at last, his first reaction was to chuckle mockingly. He had given me preferential treatment by allowing me to view the house before anyone else. I had not called by the agreed date, and so he had exercised his option. He had proceeded with the deal, signing an offer and concluding the purchase of the property for himself. Since the clients knew him and the house was vacant, they were only too happy to allow Dietmar to take immediate occupation and begin the renovations.

Whenever Dietmar was busy with a renovation, I always visited the property to check on his progress and learn a few things; he was a master in this trade. With the fervour of a true craftsman, Dietmar would assess the finished product, his eyes tracing every line and curve. 'When it comes to quality, it's the small details that matter,' he'd declare with gusto, pointing out each subtle nuance that met his exacting standards. So a week later, I was back at the property, keen to see if he was indeed knocking down all those walls as he had advised me to do. And yes, I found out that he was doing exactly that. The home was now a construction site. Dietmar was no time waster; in just one week, several walls inside the house had disappeared, with only the supporting walls remaining, and on this blank canvas, it was possible to see clearly how his renovation plans would transform this old house. There was a new space for an ensuite bathroom and added space for the kitchen, and a lovely flow from the open-plan living areas to the kitchen and the patio.

Two months later, after the house had been renovated and was ready to go back on the market, Dietmar sold the property for more than double what he had paid for it. And it could have been me! I could have been the one making a tidy profit. I could have secured the opportunity without committing outright in case my calculations proved that the project was not worthy of my time. I should have insisted on a 'conditional' clause in the offer to purchase. But procrastination had taken over. I had blinked, and on this one, I had lost. Every fool must learn. Fortunately, other opportunities continued to come, and I never gave up.

4

In 2007, twenty-seven-year-old Julia* made her first appearance as a guest on Bruce Whitfield's radio show, *The Money Show*, which was broadcast on Cape Talk and Radio 702 every weekday evening for more than twenty years (Primedia Broadcasting, 2024).

Whitfield was introduced to this remarkable young lady by another weekly guest on his show: Warren Ingram, co-founder of financial services firm Galileo Capital, who had been Julia's financial advisor (Whitfield, 2021). His twenty-minute profile of Julia was so popular that he asked her

---

* Not her real name.

to return to the show in July every year for the following ten years or so (Whitfield, 2018).

It was stories such as Julia's that drew listeners to *The Money Show*. The concept of an ordinary person saving enough from their monthly income to attain financial freedom at a young age was both inspiring and eye-opening for those eager to discover what it truly takes to achieve independence. The audio recordings of all the shows were made available online as podcasts, allowing interested listeners to enjoy them at their convenience.

'Counsel in the heart of man is like deep water; but a man of understanding will draw it out.' (*New King James Bible*, 2004, Proverbs 20:5)

Julia had always been an inquisitive person who noticed the fine details, with nothing of importance escaping her attention. Just short of thirty years old, the young management consultant had noticed her aunt's lifestyle, which she could not help envying.

Her aunt enjoyed the finer things in life: in addition to her stylish clothes and upmarket car, there was an aura of assuredness about her that indicated a level of financial security that contrasted markedly with the financial precariousness experienced by other members of the family.

A road trip from Durban to Johannesburg with her aunt just before the 2008 global financial crisis changed Julia's life.

Julia's financial discipline was meticulous, extending even to her choice of vehicle. She drove a used Opel Corsa Lite, a car she had owned for years – a decision that was far from arbitrary. This small hatchback, with its well-proven 1.4-litre fuel-injected petrol engine, was a masterstroke of practicality. Despite its modest size, the engine delivered more torque and horsepower than many sedans with larger 1.6-litre engines (*Car Magazine*, 2006). The Corsa Lite was designed for urban efficiency, making it an ideal companion for navigating city traffic. It boasted an impressive acceleration, reaching zero to a hundred kilometres per hour in just twelve seconds. But it wasn't only about speed; the car's stopping power was equally remarkable, with a stress-driven braking time of 3.2 seconds, ensuring a smooth and safe ride for both driver and passengers.

Where the Corsa Lite truly shone was in its fuel efficiency. Consuming just 6.7 litres per hundred kilometres – equivalent to about fifteen kilometres per litre – it was a wallet-friendly choice that aligned perfectly with Julia's savvy approach to spending. For someone who valued every dollar, this car offered the perfect blend of performance, efficiency and reliability, proving that even the smallest details, such as vehicle choice, played a crucial role in her path to financial freedom.

In a further attempt to cut travelling costs, Julia lived in a rented apartment close to work. However, she always had the feeling that there had to be a better way to do things if she was to make real progress towards her goal. Nobody could advise her to cut costs because in that department, she was doing better than everyone else.

The road trip from Durban to Johannesburg is six hundred kilometres long. The route runs along one of the finest freeways in South Africa, connecting the economic heart of the country, Gauteng's Johannesburg, with the popular tourist destination and commercial port of Durban, the capital city of KwaZulu-Natal. I have always had good driving experiences on that N3 freeway, which make for easy conversation in the car. I engage cruise mode, take my foot off the pedal and enjoy the journey while my automobile purrs quietly along. To spice it up, there are several fine stops along the N3 that are ideal for a break, to refuel or have a quick meal.

Julia wanted to ask her aunt a simple question: how did she afford nice clothes, a great car and dream holidays? The trip from Durban to Johannesburg provided a good opportunity for a productive discussion between aunt and niece, and Julia did not waste this chance.

Her aunt's answer was equally simple: investing made everything possible for her. But Julia's aunt had a question of her own: what was Julia's goal for her life?

Julia wanted to be financially independent by the age of forty. Earning an annual salary of R350 000 – at the time (2007) quite a decent salary for her age – Julia had saved R60 000. During that drive, her aunt offered to introduce her niece to her financial advisor. Julia wasted no time and did not procrastinate. She had a goal that she intended to achieve.

She met with her new financial advisor and agreed to follow a plan. Her monthly income was to be divided into thirds. The first third would go towards income tax. (There is nothing certain in the life of human beings except for death and taxes; we are certain to die, and we will always be obliged to pay the taxman, whether we are alive or dead.) The second third would go into investments, and the last third would cover her living expenses. Each third was equally important. This was the basis of the plan.

In over a decade of working, Julia's income grew five times. However, she was not satisfied with her earnings as a young professional. Management consultancy involves the imparting of intellectual knowledge to clients. Consultancy firms traditionally run training workshops to keep staff abreast of the latest knowledge and competitive with rival firms. This was the environment in which Julia worked. She made it her business to keep honing her skills, displaying an eagerness to learn and do better. In time, she was rewarded with strong career growth. Every promotion was accompanied by a salary increase; in a single decade, her salary grew until it was five times greater than it had been. In addition to the investment advice from her aunt and her new financial advisor, Julia had conceived of another significant pillar of success: growing her earning potential by improving her skills and so achieving higher remuneration.

Julia's model for investment reflected her character. She invested in a range of low-cost index-tracking funds every month without fail, regardless of how the markets were performing. She kept to her plan. By 2017, her portfolio was sitting at an admirable R4.7 million. When Whitfield hosted Julia again in 2021, her investments had been diversified in different index and exchange-traded funds (ETFs), and their value had grown to R6 million. During those years, she fell in love, got married and started a family, and so had been faced with all the normal challenges that confront young people in this position, including additional expenses. But with the exception of one withdrawal of R141 000 to pay for renovations to the family home so that it accommodated her growing family and the purchase of a more suitable car, she did not succumb to the temptation to dip into her accumulated investment kitty. That was the only withdrawal she made. When the investment markets were not performing well, and inflation and interest rates were high, Julia aggressively increased her monthly mortgage bond repayment, and the loan balance was on its way towards zero.

From her debut on *The Money Show*, Julia quickly captivated audiences, earning admiration for her unwavering financial discipline and laser-focused determination. Not content with simply increasing her income, she adhered relentlessly to her savings plan, a commitment that soon earned her the fitting moniker of 'Supersaver Julia'.

The impact of compounding on Supersaver Julia's investment journey is clear. She was twenty-seven when she started. She did not procrastinate. She started at an early age, and the power of compounding gave sustained momentum to her financial discipline and persistence. Assuming that the markets will deliver an average return of 10% every year, financial calculations indicate that without another cent being added to her capital, her funds should accumulate to R15 million by the time she turns fifty and to R39 million by the age of sixty. However, we know that curveballs happen and roadblocks are occasionally encountered along the road of life (for instance, Covid-19 caused turmoil in markets as recently as 2020). Joseph and Noah Effects can detract from or help with the accumulation of savings (see Chapter 1, 'The Joseph Effect', and Chapter 2, 'The Noah Effect' for a detailed explanation of these two phenomena). Life happens and there is no forecasting what individuals will encounter in their lives. The most important thing to learn from Julia is that it's possible to accumulate capital when the right plan is crafted. It must be added, however, that strong financial discipline is essential, and that people who want to accumulate wealth must resist procrastinating and start early.

5

Between 2007, when Julia embarked on her ambitious savings marathon, and 2020, the world endured two seismic shocks: the 2008 global financial crisis, triggered by sub-prime mortgages, and the unprecedented Covid-19 pandemic. As the world reeled from these upheavals, investors everywhere fretted over the potential impact on their portfolios. While the pursuit of financial freedom is a common aspiration – a longing for respite from the relentless grind of daily life – Julia's goal was far more specific: achieving financial independence by the age of forty. Given the tumultuous landscape, it is not far-fetched to imagine that Julia harboured anxieties about the stability of her hard-earned progress. So, how did she navigate the choppy waters of these crises and stay on course towards her goal?

'Though the waters thereof roar and be troubled, though the mountains shake with the swelling thereof. Selah.' (*New King James Bible*, 2004, Psalms 46:3)

The sub-prime mortgage crisis was caused by the reckless lending of banks to individuals with weak credit ratings and the fact that regulatory authorities in the United States allowed the practice to persist uncontrolled. This phenomenon continued over many years, especially in the decade leading up to the 2000s, when securitisation and trading of mortgage loans led to the creation of a financial product (the mortgage-backed security) that was traded by financial services companies. A rapid, unsustainable increase in house prices followed, causing a property price bubble.

Between 2004 and 2006, the US Federal Reserve Bank increased interest rates from 1.25% to 5.25%, a development that tipped the financial markets over the edge (Duignan, 2023). It was a disaster that had been a long time in the making. The bubble was destined to burst; when this happened in 2007, it caused a crisis of enormous proportions and a lending freeze by banks. House prices collapsed below the value of loans secured against the properties. Since the sub-prime loans had become securitised, the mortgage-backed securities traded in global markets caused the rest of the world to be engulfed by the crisis; as the saying goes, 'When America coughs, the world catches a cold.' The crisis hurt those who had become dependent on debt to acquire property: interest rates rose, and the poor and middle class were crushed by debt, leading to widespread foreclosures and dispossession. Recession followed, and millions lost their jobs. The financial crisis that followed was catastrophic.

The other shock to the economy was caused by a virus. The Covid-19 pandemic, which started in China, saw hundreds of millions of people being infected by the virus at a speed no one could have imagined or predicted. Millions of people perished across the world. The ensuing global lockdown caused havoc to global economies as economic activities around the world came to a standstill. Many businesses collapsed and never recovered after the pandemic, leading to job losses and immense suffering. In South Africa, businesses and retrenched staff applied for Covid-19 relief from the state.

The fall from grace of what was once a blue-chip JSE-listed company on the eve of the Covid-19 lockdown in 2020 was a sign of things to come

(Mahlangu, 2020). Edcon, the ninety-one-year-old retailer that owned Jet and Edgars, had already been struggling under debt for years before the pandemic. The company did not have sufficient cash to survive the unforeseen lockdown announced by the President of South Africa on Sunday 15 March 2020 and implemented with immediate effect.

Edcon had spent several years grappling with financial challenges, striving to stay afloat (Smith, 2020). In 2019, the business, perceived as too big to fail, had received a R2.7-billion lifeline bailout from the Public Investment Corporation. The lockdown was the last straw. On the Thursday after the lockdown took effect, Edcon CEO Grant Pattison called a conference to address creditors who supplied the retail business (Hogg & Wessels, 2020). Choking with emotion, Pattison broke down and cried. Edcon could cover its salary bill, but there was insufficient cash to pay creditors.

I listened to the audio clip of Pattison's announcement on talk radio. It was extremely depressing. Fortunately, the clip did not receive much more airplay. There was no sense in causing further anguish to audiences tuning in to the radio, desperate for positive news. By June 2020, 22 000 Edcon employees had been served with retrenchment notices.

Stock markets across the world tanked during both of these global shocks, causing despair and panic among investors and retirement funds. As a retirement fund trustee of what has now grown into a R5-billion stand-alone fund, I remember their devastating effects only too well. I was an employer representative trustee on a board of eight trustees (four employees elected and four appointed by the employer). The board of trustees had to report back annually to fund members during those years of dreadful returns with a minus in front of the percentages.

As a board, we met several times before the annual general meeting (AGM) in 2009 to put together a suitable communication strategy for members. It was important to prevent panic among members and to encourage them to remain focused on the long term. We needed to implore members to avoid distractions caused by temporary shocks.

This was easier said than done. The questions from members attending the mid-2009 AGM in the aftermath of the 2008 financial turbulence revealed investors' concern and anxiety, especially in the case of those close to retirement age. The 2008 crisis brought the Johannesburg Stock

Exchange All Share Index (JSE ALSI) to almost 50% of its high (it fell from 33 191 in May 2008 to 17 814 in November 2008, a period of six months [*MarketWatch*, 2008–]), and it took three years for the index to find its way back to levels prior to the financial crisis.

It was a difficult time for investors and a nervous time for the trustees sitting in front of fund members congregated in an auditorium for the fund AGM. On this occasion, attendance was understandably much better than in previous years. Members wanted to learn about the implications of the economic mayhem on the fund performance. Trustees, the principal officer of the retirement fund and investment consultants huddled next to each other in the front row, as if seeking safety in numbers as they waited for questions from the floor.

One such challenging question from the floor was the following: 'May I urgently transfer my share of the fund to the capital protection portfolio, even though this request falls outside the almanac dates reserved for changes?' Now, this course of action would result in transferring the member's share of the fund at its lowest values and locking in the loss, while simultaneously parking the funds in a cash portfolio – resulting in lowered risk, but also yielding returns too low to beat inflation.

Fortunately, the board of trustees had prepared the principal officer well to handle challenging questions such as this one. He adhered to the principles of the AGM communication strategy as agreed upon by the board of trustees, responding in simple terms:

> Imagine your pension fund as a carefully tended garden. Over the years, we've planted a diverse array of seeds – stocks, bonds and other investments – each chosen for its potential to grow and yield fruit. In a stable environment, this garden flourishes, providing us with a steady, predictable harvest.
>
> However, just as a garden can face sudden storms and harsh conditions, so too can the market experience periods of volatility and downturns. Think of the recent crash as a severe storm that has swept through our garden. During such times, it might seem like the plants are wilting and the garden is struggling. But remember, these are temporary conditions, not the end of the story.

Our strategy is akin to the careful tending and pruning we do after a storm. We assess the damage, make adjustments, and focus on nurturing the resilient plants that can weather the storm and thrive in the long run. We have chosen a diverse range of investments precisely because it helps us withstand and recover from such market turbulence.

Just as experienced gardeners know that storms are part of the cycle and trust in the eventual recovery, so too do we remain confident in our long-term strategy. The fundamentals of our investments remain strong, and we continue to manage the fund with the same care and prudence that has guided us through past challenges.

In essence, while we acknowledge the current volatility and the recent downturn, our focus remains on the long-term growth and stability of your investments. The storm will pass, and our well-tended garden will continue to yield rewards over time.

The effectiveness of a message often hinges on the messenger delivering it. Our principal officer, impeccably dressed yet conservative enough to blend in, exemplified this truth. He spoke with a measured cadence, deliberately slowing down at key points, as if to ensure no one was left behind. As he paced across the podium, his eyes swept the audience, locking onto those engaged in the proceedings. The board could not have chosen a better person for the task. His presence, supported by the full board of trustees seated in the front row, seemed to instil a quiet confidence among the members, their expressions conveying what they were feeling: 'We can trust these people with our money.'

6

Displaying nerves of steel, Julia was also not tempted to make rush decisions during the turbulence caused by the 2008 global financial crisis and the Covid-19 pandemic. She allowed the power of dollar-cost averaging to intervene, and kept her capital invested. (Dollar-cost averaging is an approach in which the investor regularly invests additional amounts without attempting to time the markets [in other words, not waiting for a time when markets are speculated to be favourable].) Stock markets fluctuate over time; market movements are often volatile. When stock prices are low, the same rand amount will purchase a larger number of additional mutual units in the index funds, creating a good opportunity that offsets the effect of buying when prices are elevated.

The table that follows illustrates how this strategy works and its benefits. The example assumes that an investor, Jacobie, puts away a fixed amount every quarter, investing into an ETF, a mutual in which she will be allocated units, or what is called a share of the fund. She invests R10 000 per quarter, which accumulates to R40 000 over the four quarters.

Table 1 Illustration of dollar-cost averaging

Period	Market price	Amount invested	Units bought	Total units owned	Amount invested	Units bought	Total units owned
		Jacobie: Dollar-cost averaging			Rudolph: Lump-sum investing		
Quarter 1	20.00	R10 000	500	500	R40 000	2 000	2 000
Quarter 2	12.50	R10 000	800	1 300			
Quarter 3	20.00	R10 000	500	1 800			
Quarter 4	25.00	R10 000	400	2 200			
TOTAL		R40 000	2 200	2 200	R40 000	2 000	2 000
Value of investment by Q4		R55 000 (2 200 × 25)			R50 000 (2 000 × 25)		
Capital gain		R15 000			R10 000		

As a comparison, it is assumed that another investor, Rudolph, invests a lump sum of R40 000 at the beginning of the period. The total amount of capital invested (that is, R40 000) is the same in both cases, but Jacobie has bought 2 200 units, while Rudolph bought 2 000 units. Jacobie is in a better position by the end of the fourth quarter, with 200 more units owned than Rudolph, translating to R5 000 more in value invested. Dollar-cost averaging benefits from the price movements and market volatility during the period.

Taking advantage of dollar-cost averaging, Julia stayed invested and persistently added a third of her monthly salary to her investments.

Supersaver Julia was selfless in sharing her experiences of growing her savings from almost nothing to R4.7 million over more than ten years and compounding to R6 million by 2021. Every one of those years, Julia shared what she had learnt on Bruce Whitfield's radio show.

Julia opted to seek the knowledge of those who knew more about money than her. We must seek expert knowledge about bricks from a bricklayer; that is the correct approach. But not all advice is good; some advisors are driven by sales incentives and commissions, while others are armchair or dinner-table experts. For this reason, Julia should receive full credit for maintaining control over her investment approach.

Julia used debt to buy her family home. However, she respected debt enough to know that as much as it is an enabler, it must be paid off as quickly as is practically possible to reduce the amount of interest paid to the bank over the term of the loan. In many instances, the return from investments is less than that from savings achieved by paying off interest on debt. Julia owns her car outright, with no debt. Debt is useful for possessions that appreciate. It is preferable to own a home and avoid the payment of rentals to a landlord, as these payments do not result in any ownership of property.

It was a privilege to hear Julia's insights during her annual appearances on the show. Her zest for life and vibrant energy came across strongly, although listeners might have been forgiven for thinking at first that she was a frugal person uninterested in the finer things in life. However, she endeared herself to listeners by sharing that she ate out regularly and loved travelling (she went on at least one international holiday every year). All that was built into her financial plan – the third of her monthly income earmarked for expenses. She was human after all, a young woman driven by an unwavering ambition to live life on her own terms, embracing the freedom she so deeply craved.

7

Much of this chapter has reflected on Julia's discipline and single-mindedness. Another thing that remained constant throughout her radio appearances was her strong preference for index funds and ETFs, both of which have grown in popularity over the years, particularly in the early 2000s.

Mutual funds, also called 'unit trusts', are pooled investments to which individual investors contribute. Individuals own a portion of the pool, also referred to as 'units'. The pool is invested in shares, bonds, money markets and the like. Investors receive a return on investments based on the performance of the mutual fund, less fees, of course.

There are two categories within mutual funds: actively managed funds and index funds.

- The goal of actively managed funds is to outperform the stock market benchmark. They require intense decision-making by portfolio managers because investing in them involves constant stock-picking, selling and buying. The fees charged by active managers are quite high, as they must recover the costs associated with the active investment style.

- Index funds involve investments in portfolios that mirror a specific share index or a portion of a share index (for example, the JSE Top 40). Index funds are passively managed and aim to match the performance (investment returns) of the chosen stock market index. The fees for investments in index funds are much lower than those for active funds due to the different investment style.

Julia is not alone in her faith in index funds; many other people share similar views. Magda Wierzycka, the outspoken CEO of Sygnia Asset Management, believes that index-tracking funds are more cost-effective and perform better than actively managed funds. She notes that while individual active managers might sometimes outperform market indices, they rarely do so consistently, especially when their higher fees are taken into consideration.

Two key issues come to the forefront: investment returns and the costs associated with investing. Investors use the total expense ratio to compare the cost efficiency of different funds. This is calculated by dividing the cost of running a fund by the value of assets managed by the fund.

In 2015, Wierzycka published a review of expense ratios in which she analysed a sample of eight funds (Allan Gray, Investec IMS, Momentum, Glacier [Sanlam], Fairbairn Capital, ABSA AIMS, Sygnia and 10X) (Wierzycka, 2015). Of the eight, only 10X and Sygnia were passively managed; the rest were active funds. The two passive funds had the lowest expense ratio (10X at 1.03% and Sygnia at 0.45%), while the actively managed funds were tied at 1.79%. In the sample, the range was therefore 0.45% to 1.79%.

Passive funds are considerably more cost-efficient than actively managed funds, as proven by Wierzycka. There are good reasons for this. Investing with the aim of delivering returns that beat the market is a costly exercise (Ellis, 2012). In addition, beating the market is the exception rather than the norm, especially when we consider the riskiness of that approach. Here is the irony, however: people are quite cost-conscious when buying consumer products. For example, there is one thing that most people do when they dine out. On receiving the bill, presented in a leather-bound waiter's billfold, together with complimentary peppermints, they begin the traditional audit of the bill. Some pull out a pen and spectacles and start ticking off each line, occasionally calling the waiter over to complain about an unfamiliar charge on the bill. Most often, there is nothing to raise an issue about, and they settle the bill with an air of satisfaction, having completed what they view as an important task.

The consensus is that one should always check in case the restaurant has made an error. The real aim of this scrutiny is to pay the correct cost of what has been consumed. I cannot argue with this principle; it is good to think like that. But a person who wishes to make more significant savings has two more effective options: the first is to stay home and cook up a storm, and the second is to dine out, but to select a restaurant that offers good food at reasonable prices.

Another common practice is shopping around and comparing prices online. Consumers are quick to brag about having found a bargain in a promotion, especially one that has escaped the attention of their colleagues. However, this cost-saving mindset is usually thrown out of the window when people are choosing where to invest their hard-earned money. This behaviour is an example of what is known as 'loss-aversion bias': the placing of a higher weighting (bordering on revulsion) on losses and a lower weighting on potential gains.

Most are familiar with the compounding effect when it is applied to investing and growing the nest egg. However, the destructive effect of compounding costs is seldom discussed. There is what appears to be a subtle tendency to encourage investors to 'focus on performance and only performance' on the assumption that higher investment returns more than offset investment fees paid (Crane, 2006).

Most investors see investment fees as inconsequential when selecting asset managers. The commonly held view is that the superior returns of active management offset its higher costs. This assumption is incorrect. This relegation of investment costs as a minor matter has been peddled successfully over the years by those providing financial advice (Crane, 2006; Haslem, 2004). Consequently, the mutual fund industry tends to avoid competing based on price. Frustratingly, asset management firms receive payment for their fees first, before anything is paid out to investors, even when a fund's performance is weak or negative. That is the contract. At that point, it is too late to complain about the costs. Wise investors avoid such a state of affairs by comparing the total expense ratios of various fund managers before committing to an investment.

Economics Nobel prize-winner William F. Sharpe wrote an article titled 'The Arithmetic of Investment Expenses' for the *Financial Analysts Journal*. Using simple language, he explained the concept of the terminal wealth ratio. This ratio measures the impact of investment expenses on invested capital over a specific period. Sharpe noted that the higher the real rate of return on the underlying assets, the higher the terminal wealth ratio will be. This is because higher returns increase the final value of the earlier contributions more than the later ones (Sharpe, 2013). The calculation was based on two funds: one with a total expense ratio of 0.06% and the other with one of 1.12%.

The wide expense ratio spread used in Sharpe's calculation compares with the one that Wiercycka published in 2015 for her sample of eight asset managers (0.45% to 1.79%), which displayed a significant disparity between active and passive funds. Sharpe did his arithmetic and calculated the terminal wealth ratios. The probability of a low-cost fund delivering a higher terminal wealth in thirty years' time is much greater than for active funds, even when the gross returns are the same. Sharpe determined that a frugal investor who opts for low-cost passive funds stands an even chance – about 50/50 – of having over 20% more money available for retirement compared to someone who invests in active funds. While a long-term investor might find a high-cost asset manager who can outperform benchmarks enough to cover their fees, the truth is that active management fees are extremely high compared to readily available passive options. The maths vindicates Julia in her decision to stick with index funds. The simplest things are often more effective than more complex strategies, even though most people believe otherwise.

Julia's story displays the opposite of procrastination, the human trait that afflicts most of us. Many people can give an account of how procrastination caused problems in their lives. Charlie Munger is not one of them.

In early November 2023, a journalist from the *Wall Street Journal* sat down with ninety-nine-year-old Munger, Warren Buffet's business partner for almost five decades, for what we now know was to be one of his last interviews. Financial journalists seized every opportunity to tap into the insights of one of the sharpest investment minds of all time.

When asked how ordinary people should invest, Munger responded that most people should probably just invest in index funds. Passive funds are a sensible option for those who do not want to spend much time thinking about investments and do not have any special skills in picking stocks (Fox, 2023).

Even at his advanced age, Munger could vividly recall his childhood, conjuring up images of intimate moments shared with his grandfather, during which the older man imparted invaluable lessons that Munger eagerly absorbed. Although this wisdom was learnt during a life of endless hardship, Munger's grandfather often reflected that with hindsight, the challenges he had faced were actually manageable. In the moment, however, they had been incredibly tough.

One of the lessons Munger remembers learning from his grandfather is this: procrastination is the enemy; it prevents people from seizing life's rare opportunities. He further observed that a deep-seated fear of using debt often intensifies prevarication and procrastination, adding that leverage is key in the appropriate circumstances.

Munger's advice to readers of the *Wall Street Journal* was crystal clear: when life offers you a genuine opportunity – one that does not come around often – you must act decisively. He likened it to being invited to the pie counter only a few times in life. When that moment arrives, it is foolish to settle for a small slice. The challenge, of course, is knowing when the time is truly right, which is not easy. However, the worst outcome is letting fear or hesitation cause you to miss out altogether. Even legendary figures such as Warren Buffett have only had a handful of these moments, and their success hinged on recognising them and taking a bold step forward. Remove just ten of those pivotal moments from Buffett's journey, and his record would be unremarkable.

The lesson here is clear: when life offers you a chance, don't just nibble; take a hearty bite, for the extra risk is often minimal compared to the potential gain (CNBC News releases, 2023).

8

Shades of later: Now … now-now … just now …

Language is not only a medium for communicating between humans; it also reflects the culture of a people. In the South African lexicon, citizens use linguistic quirks such as 'now', 'now-now' or 'just now' when talking about when they will do something. Foreigners and tourists visiting South Africa or dealing with South Africans for the first time often find the use of these words both amusing and confusing. The phrase 'just now' is expected to intimate urgency, intent and instant action; that is the universal meaning of these words. But in the South African context, the linguistic quirks turn out to mean 'varying shades of later', or even 'gimme a break, I have much more important stuff to do'.

Putting off those things you can do today and promising yourself that you will attend to them at a later date is a bad habit. It is one of the main reasons why so many people across the globe reach old age without having accumulated the money they need to live comfortably, even after many years of working. The extent of the problem differs between countries, but the difference is only in the scale. According to the National Treasury of South Africa (2014), only '… 6% of South Africans are able to maintain their lifestyle and replace their income fully at retirement'. A large share of the responsibility for this uncomfortable statistic may be attributed to the scourge of procrastination, which bedevils humans.

Julia's investment journey reveals several psychological factors that are crucial in the realm of investing:

- Procrastination awareness: Successful investors are often those who recognise and combat procrastination. By creating a plan and adhering to it, they take proactive steps towards their financial goals.
- Autonomy in decision-making: Even when seeking expert advice, it is key to maintain control over investment decisions. This autonomy allows investors to stay aligned with their personal risk tolerance and financial objectives.
- Cost-consciousness: Being mindful of investment costs and their impact on net returns and capital growth is a sign of a savvy investor who understands the long-term implications of fees.
- Long-term perspective: Investors who are able to maintain a long-term view, like Julia, are better equipped to weather market volatility and avoid reactive decisions based on short-term market movements.
- Emotional stability: Keeping calm during a financial crisis is a testament to an investor's emotional resilience. This resilience is essential; without it, investors will not be able to adhere to their investment strategies during turbulent times.
- Consistent investment strategy: Persistent investment, especially utilising strategies such as dollar-cost averaging, helps in smoothing out the risks of market timing and can lead to more stable returns over time.

In essence, the psychology of investing involves a blend of self-awareness, strategic planning, emotional control and consistent execution. Julia's example shows us that success in investing is not just about knowledge and timing but also about psychological readiness and behavioural discipline.

This chapter has featured the experiences of a few people who went on to be successful beyond measure, but who always remained wary of procrastination.

Just before she turned thirty, Julia fought this human failing by putting together a plan that she stuck to. She sought financial advice from experts, but she also kept control over her investment decisions, navigating two global financial crises along the way. Julia is fussy about the negative effects of investment costs on net returns and capital growth, maintains a long-term view of investing and keeps calm during financial crises. She invests persistently to take advantage of dollar-cost averaging.

It must be possible to avoid the prospect of being excluded from that 6% statistic of retired people who are able to support themselves financially. Julia is proof of this.

CHAPTER 4

FEAR OF MISSING OUT:
Money, markets and smart investing

'There is nothing so disturbing to one's well-being
and judgement as to see a friend get rich.'
– Charles Poor Kindleberger

1

For every action, there is an equal and opposite reaction. Every object persists in its state of rest or uniform motion in a straight line unless it is compelled to change that state by forces impressed upon it. For a constant mass, force equals mass times acceleration.

The three statements in the previous paragraph are the three laws of motion that Isaac Newton formulated in the seventeenth century. If you did physical science in high school, you may be familiar with the laws of motion. But if you do not recognise them, it really does not matter. A brilliant scientist and mathematician, Newton formulated the laws of gravity and motion, made major contributions to our understanding of optics and invented calculus. In short, he laid the basis for our understanding of the workings of the universe. His talent and genius were acknowledged during his lifetime. You would expect such an accomplished man to remain rational, regardless of the circumstances in which he found himself.

Newton was born on Christmas Day in 1642 at Woolsthorpe Manor, almost two hundred kilometres north of London, three months after the death of his father. Born prematurely, he was a tiny, delicate baby. As one of his relatives recounted in the old English of the time (Westfall, 1994: 7):

> … when he was born he was so little they could put him into a quart port
> & so weakly that he was forced to have a bolster all round his neck to keep

73

it on his shoulders & so little likely to live that when two women were sent … for something for him they sate down on a stile by the way & said there was no occasion for making haste for they were sure the child would be dead before they could get back.

As a result of his precarious health, his baptism was delayed until 1 January 1643, which is often mistaken as his date of birth.

Newton was financially secure from the moment of his birth. He inherited his paternal estate as well as his mother's paternal estate, together with various additional estates that his mother acquired during her second marriage. However, his stepfather, a wealthy clergyman almost three decades older than his mother, refused to allow Newton's mother to bring her young child to live with them when they married, and so he was brought up by his grandparents. In spite of his difficult childhood, though, there is no doubt that Newton's inborn talent and desire to learn and invent gave him the impetus needed to make an incredible contribution to the development of humankind.

Described by those who grew up with him as 'a sober, silent, thinking lad' (Westfall, 1994: 13), Newton remained an introvert throughout his life (The Newton Project, 2024).

Once he had finished his schooling, Newton was admitted to Trinity College at Cambridge University. After completing his undergraduate and post-graduate studies, he was elected a fellow of Trinity College. Two years later, he was appointed professor of mathematics at Cambridge. He remained at the university for almost thirty years (Isaac Newton Institute, 2024).

While maintaining his appointment at Cambridge, Newton accepted the position of warden at the Royal Mint. He later became Master of the Mint when the position became available in 1699. (Today, those positions are known by the titles of chief operating officer [COO] and chief executive officer [CEO] or Reserve Bank Governor, respectively.)

As warden (or COO), Newton is believed to have mastered the operations of the Mint by meticulously studying every document related to coinage and the governance of such a vital institution. His attention to detail was often described as nearly obsessive. He studied old accounts of the Mint in order to understand payments for services, the costs of the melting pot and even how many times the pot could be used.

Upon his appointment as Master of the Mint (governor) in 1699, Newton approached his responsibilities with his characteristic thoroughness and was handsomely rewarded for his diligence. In addition to an annual salary of £500, the Master of the Mint was entitled to a bonus that depended on the extent of activity at the Mint. For example, in 1701, a year of heavy coinage, Newton earned £3 500.

The years at the Royal Mint made Newton a wealthy man, ensuring a life of abundance, even in the costly environment of London (Westfall, 1994). Newton took his responsibilities as warden and later as Master seriously. He distinguished himself as a capable, tough and shrewd administrator of the Mint, improving its efficiency from the precarious state in which the previous leadership had left it.

In 1703, Newton was elected President of the Royal Society, another position of great influence. The early years in London had taught Newton a few lessons about political life and what leverage it can yield. As Master of the Mint and President of the Royal Society, he had become a 'personage of consequence' (Westfall, 1994: 248). His newly acquired political connections brought him closer to the royal centre of power, Her Majesty, the Queen. In 1705, the Queen of Great Britain, Anne, knighted Newton, honouring him for his achievements and giving him the right to use the title 'Sir'.

That Sir Isaac Newton was an incredibly intelligent human being will never be in doubt. The scientific discoveries he made, the laws he formulated, and all the complex mathematical and physics formulae behind these laws all bear testimony to this fact. However, his standing in England was based on far more than his scientific and mathematical accomplishments.

In addition to his earnings as Master of the Mint, Newton also had a family inheritance. As a result, he needed to find viable devices in which to invest in order to build his capital. In light of his other successes, it would not be unreasonable to assume that Newton would bring the full power of his rationality to bear when making investment decisions. However, as we shall see, this was not always the case.

2

In 1720, there was widespread euphoria when the South Sea Company offered to take over Britain's national debt. Investors and speculators bought and traded in the company's shares, and soon the trade turned into a frenzy (Carswell, 1960). The shares, which were trading at just over £128 a share in January 1720, had spiked dramatically to a price of £1 000 by August. The company's directors became increasingly desperate to shore up and sustain the share price at that lofty level, and so, on 30 August, they announced their intention to recommend a dividend of 30% for the financial year (1720), plus a guaranteed dividend of 50% over the next ten years.

The declaration of a higher dividend payout is known for its signalling effect: it is a message to shareholders and investors informing the market that a company is confident of its balance sheet. Modern-day listed companies are known to employ the signalling effect of dividends to influence the share price of their companies. However, the elevated levels of dividend payouts promised by the South Sea Company on 30 August 1720 raised eyebrows. Investors who held scrip in the company were not convinced, as recent operating profits did not justify such levels of dividend. Players in the market began to pay closer attention to the company's real value.

Archibald Hutcheson, a respected economist, analysed the South Sea Company's financials with the objective of deriving a valuation. He concluded his report by pointing out that there were too many unknowns: in the absence of key variables such as past profits, current profits, and projected future profits and cash flows, it was not possible to perform a satisfactory valuation of the company's shares. The report cast doubt on the company's performance and prospects.

Those who had doubted the promises of the South Sea Company's directors now had reason to believe that they had been right all along. Confidence in the company quickly turned to alarm and panic, leading investors to rush to sell the stock. By December of the same year, the share price had crashed to £124. Underpinned by corruption at high echelons of government, speculator behaviour caused the volatility, creating a bubble, which resulted in the inevitable crash. Many investors were ruined.

One investor who had considered the South Sea Company worthy of investment was Sir Isaac Newton. On 20 April 1720, Newton sold all the South Sea shares that he had acquired in previous months. He made a 100% profit of £7 000, quite a large sum at that time.

Newton should have taken his profit and walked away from all dealings with the company. However, the mania surrounding the South Sea Company during that spring was too much for him to ignore. A few weeks later, Newton was seized by an impulse to invest even more capital in South Sea shares.

By that point, the share price had risen much higher than when Newton had first bought shares, fuelled by the speculative and frenzied crowd behaviour of investors. Following the crash in December 1720, Newton lost £20 000. As he said at the time, 'I can calculate the motions of the heavenly bodies, but not the madness of people' (Kindleberger, 2000: 31).

Irrational behaviour is a human trait that is often exacerbated in crowd situations. If Newton had remained invested in the South Sea Company from the time of his initial investment instead of selling his shares in April 1720, he would have watched the share price spike and return to its January value by the end of the year without any loss of capital. Instead, he allowed the chaos and noise of the crowd to overpower his initial instincts.

Newton was far from the only intelligent man to behave irrationally when it came to the South Sea Company. Another distinguished player in the financial services sector – in fact, a banker – discounted his professional instincts and joined the frenzy by subscribing to South Sea shares worth £500 in August 1720, when prices were close to their peak. In explaining his irrational course of action, the man later said, 'When the rest of the world are mad, we must imitate them in some measure' (Kindleberger, 2000: 122).

3

Allen Funt, whose name is synonymous with the birth of reality television, began his journey with a fine arts degree from Cornell University. His academic curiosity led him to participate in a 1934 study using a two-way mirror to observe infants' eating behaviours, revealing distinct differences when they were fed by their mothers versus by nurses. This early encounter with observational study foreshadowed Funt's innovative approach to entertainment (Holmes & Jermyn, 2004).

Following the outbreak of the Second World War, Funt's path took a detour when he joined the US Army's Signal Corps in 1941. There, he crafted audio messages for infantrymen and produced morale-boosting radio programmes. It was during this time that Funt pioneered *The Gripe Booth*, a radio show inviting soldiers to air their grievances. However, the intimidating red recording light often silenced previously outspoken soldiers. Ingeniously, Funt disconnected the light, capturing unguarded conversations that were both candid and entertaining (Holmes & Jermyn, 2004).

These experiences – the two-way mirror and *The Gripe Booth* – planted the seeds for what would evolve into Funt's groundbreaking show, *Candid Microphone*, which debuted on ABC Radio in 1947 and transitioned to television as *Candid Camera* in 1948. The show's ingenious concept of filming unsuspecting individuals in humorous scenarios resonated with viewers, securing its place on television for an astonishing five decades, including a seven-year stint on CBS, where it became the seventh highest-rated show in the United States during the 1960–61 season.

Bradley Clissold, a scholar with a PhD in modern British literature and film, attributes the enduring appeal of *Candid Camera* to the Cold War-era's surveillance anxieties. This cultural backdrop, Clissold argues, fuelled the American public's fascination with the show's voyeuristic charm (Holmes & Jermyn, 2004).

Candid Camera captivated audiences around the world, filming over a million people in its hidden-camera escapades. Memorable segments such as the 'Face the Rear' elevator prank showcased Allen Funt's genius in orchestrating social experiments. In this iconic episode, an unsuspecting individual, unaware of the hidden camera and the actors involved, succumbs to social pressure and conforms to the odd behaviour of facing the elevator's rear (Rakoff, 2000). This simple yet powerful experiment revealed the humorous side of human nature and the instinct to conform.

Another classic episode took place at a New York City postbox, where a man engages in conversation with what he believes to be a sentient postbox. As the postbox falls silent whenever a passerby approaches, the man's increasing desperation to elicit a response and so to affirm his sanity is both amusing and telling (Maas & Toivanen, 1978). Funt's commentary accentuates the humour of the situation, capturing every nuance of the participant's reactions.

These episodes, while entertaining, also subtly commented on the human condition, exposing our natural responses to unusual situations and the lengths to which we go to avoid social discomfort. Funt's work with *Candid Camera* not only pioneered reality television, but also held up a mirror to society, revealing the power of conformity and the often-overlooked complexities of human behaviour.

In another episode, Funt's ingenuity is on display at a local dry cleaner, where a sign reads: 'Today is Wednesday; please walk only on the black squares' (Rakoff, 2000). Without question, customers hop from one black tile to the next, as if playing a game of adult hopscotch. Funt's voice-over likens their actions to a playful dance, yet the underlying message is profound: we often conform to authority without hesitation.

This tendency to follow the crowd or obey commands can have darker implications, as history has shown, from the obedience in Nazi Germany to the herd mentality that fuels financial market frenzies. *Candid Camera* not only entertained but also invited criticism and reflection. Some viewers, including one who wrote a notable critique in *The New Yorker*, highlighted the way in which the show exploited people's innate trust and decency for laughs, often leaving them in undignified situations.

Through these vignettes, *Candid Camera* did more than make us laugh; it made us think about our actions and the power of conformity in our lives. Funt's hidden camera antics revealed a simple truth: despite our complexities, humans have a surprising willingness to follow the script, even when it is laid out on the floor of a dry cleaner's shop.

4

Do humans share similar behaviours with other mammals? Our ancestors certainly found sheep attractive for domestication due to their versatile utility. Traditionally, sheep are prized for their wool, pelts, meat and milk, with almost 25% of current sheep breeds retaining this multi-purpose nature (Nowak *et al.*, 2008).

Archaeological evidence suggests that sheep were domesticated between eight and ten thousand years ago, and today, nearly two thousand breeds exist (Nowak *et al.*, 2008). The relatively docile nature of sheep compared to other mammals made them one of the first animals to be tamed. As herbivores, they spend their time grazing in pastures.

Sheep are more intelligent than commonly believed. They possess specialised neural mechanisms in the right temporal and frontal brain lobes that help them recognise familiar human faces for up to two years. They respond to food calls, can solve problems and learn names, and can even carry packs (King *et al.*, 2012). Sheep have a 'gregarious' social instinct (Landsberg & Deneburg, 2014), bonding closely with other sheep, especially relatives, and exhibiting strong flocking behaviour. The collective odour of the flock creates an olfactory signature, contributing to group cohesion. Farmers know that separation from the flock is stressful for sheep, often causing them to become highly vocal or withdrawn.

This flocking behaviour, found in insect swarms, schools of fish and herds of mammals, is believed to have evolved as a defence mechanism. As a prey species, sheep benefit from flocking, as it allows for better detection of predators. When faced with danger, sheep will flee together in unison, following a leader. Interestingly, sheep do not display hierarchical structures, but leadership emerges from independent individuals initiating group movements.

Polish-American psychologist Solomon E. Asch's concept of the individual as 'a minority of one against a unanimous majority' (Asch, 1956) highlights a parallel between sheep and human behaviour. Just as sheep exhibit flocking behaviour, humans often conform to group decisions, even when those decisions contradict personal instincts. This herd behaviour, resembling that of animals, can be observed in various contexts, including investing. Investors with a herd mentality tend to buy shares when prices are high, driven by the majority's enthusiasm, and ignore the wise counsel of buying low and selling high. This fear of missing out, or 'FOMO', as it is called today, drives them to follow the crowd, even if it means making illogical decisions.

In summary, both sheep and humans exhibit strong tendencies towards group behaviour, driven by instincts for safety, acceptance and conformity. Understanding these behaviours can provide valuable insights into our own actions, particularly in situations involving collective decision-making.

5

James B. Maas, a renowned psychologist and writer, spent nearly five decades at Cornell University. From 1968 until his retirement in 2011, Maas incorporated episodes of Allen Funt's *Candid Camera* into his introductory psychology courses. Funt, who passed away in 1999, bequeathed his extensive archive of films, videos and recordings from *Candid Microphone* and *Candid Camera* to Cornell. Although these episodes were produced for entertainment, Maas found they had enough experimental quality to illustrate human behaviour effectively (Maas & Toivanen, 1978). The sequences were meticulously planned and the behaviours of the people were accurately recorded, much like situational experiments conducted by psychologists. This valuable inventory of films has become an important resource for psychologists researching human behaviour.

Maas's empirical analysis of *Candid Camera* episodes highlighted people's conformity behaviour and tendency to follow authority blindly. Psychologists refer to this phenomenon as the 'power of the situation', where social settings, subtle situational forces and manipulation by others influence people's actions and emotions. Solomon Asch (mentioned in the previous section) conducted similar situational experiments in 1956 to investigate social influences. Asch's study revealed a psychological tendency for individuals to uncritically accept group ideas, best described as conformity. Like sheep, people follow others, and become stressed and panicky at the prospect of being isolated from the herd.

This conformity phenomenon is a scientifically proven characteristic of humans. Recognising it is the first step towards addressing the challenge. Group pressure is powerful and often irresistible, but awareness of its force is crucial in confronting and neutralising its effects. In financial markets, herd behaviour among investors significantly influences the prices of stocks, commodities, currencies and other financial products.

Charles Kindleberger's book *Manias, Panics, and Crashes* chronicles historical financial crises from the seventeenth century to the modern era. Kindleberger explains how mob psychology drives the herd: people start rationally, but gradually lose touch with reality, succumbing to the fallacy that the whole is different from the sum of its parts. This leads to market failures and financial crises caused by asset bubbles.

During bull markets, investors fear missing out as they hear about others' profits. Initially, patience prevails, but eventually, greed takes over, leading investors to follow the herd. This often results in stretched share valuations and ignored advice to buy low and sell high. When the asset bubble bursts, many lose money. Ponzi schemes thrive on this desperation for high returns, ignoring the warning that if something seems too good to be true, it usually is.

Kindleberger's book teaches us that financial crises are largely due to human behaviour. Despite historical precedents, investors often buy into the hype, believing this time things will be different (Kindleberger, 2000). Financial analysts and asset managers perpetuate this belief, discarding traditional valuation methods and changing narratives. Resisting the fear of missing out is easier said than done, as Funt's elevator episodes demonstrate the strong instinct to conform to the group, regardless of logic.

To combat herd mentality, it is essential to have a clear investment strategy. Objectively sticking to a long-term plan can help individuals avoid blindly following the crowd. In times of unwarranted optimism or crippling pessimism, maintaining a clear head and objective assessment is crucial. Volatility demands a thick skin to deal with the noise.

6

Herd mentality is not confined to individual investors; even institutional investors such as retirement and mutual funds are susceptible. After all, they are run by people. As a trustee of a retirement fund, I gained first-hand insight into their operations.

Trustees are required to undergo training to prepare them for their responsibilities, although they may not be experts in all areas. To bridge this gap, boards hire specialists to help manage the fund and fulfil their members' goals. In addition, there are regulations designed to safeguard the governance and investment activities of the fund by imposing restrictions on the types of investment permitted.

Given these regulations and safeguards, it is natural to wonder whether this means that the folly of herd behaviour is avoided. Unfortunately, even those we trust for expert advice can sometimes lead us astray.

In 2014, our board of trustees gathered for a routine investment meeting, expecting the usual update on global and local financial markets. But our investment consultants had something different in mind – a new opportunity they believed was crucial for us to consider. They urged the board to invest in African equities, arguing that Africa was poised to outperform other emerging markets over the next decade.

The consultants were persuasive, armed with projections of high earnings growth aligned with robust GDP forecasts across many African economies. What seemed to seal the deal was their mention of increased interest from heavyweight investors – US venture capitalists, pension funds and other institutional players – who were beginning to flock to the continent. It sounded like a promising way to boost our returns, and the board decided to adjust our strategic asset allocation, tweaking our investment policy to include a small slice of African equities.

Thank God it was a tiny slice. The Africa portfolio turned out to be a disastrous investment. When commodity prices, especially oil, plummeted, the portfolio's performance never recovered. Eighteen months later, we instructed our consultants to liquidate the portfolio. But even with such a small allocation, the process was agonisingly slow: many of the African holdings were illiquid, forcing us to sell in small parcels over time.

Looking back, the warning signs were there. The African market was relatively new and untested, and the surge of interest from US funds and pension funds had created a herd mentality. We were caught up in it, following the perceived credibility of others instead of scrutinising the risks ourselves. It was a humbling lesson in the dangers of following the crowd.

7

The urge to react to news and market sentiment is not limited to ordinary investors. Analysts and fund managers are just as prone to similar behaviour when faced with what appears to be important news.

Associated Press (AP), a respected American news agency, is a not-for-profit organisation that runs like a cooperative. Headquartered in New York City, AP has created a reputation for separating fact from fiction since it opened its doors in the nineteenth century.

At 1.07 p.m. on 23 April 2013, a tweet from the handle @AP said, 'Breaking: Two Explosions in the White House and Barack Obama is Injured' (Selyukh, 2013). The market took heed. This was a disaster with serious implications for market sentiment. Market prices went on a roller-coaster ride and crashed. According to Reuters, an estimated $136.5 billion was wiped off the S&P 500 in ten minutes: 'On the floor of the Chicago Mercantile Exchange, traders quickly traded on the tweet, selling S&P futures and buying Treasury 10-year futures' (Selyukh, 2013).

Shortly after the tweet was released, the White House Press Secretary reassured Americans that there had been no explosions at the White House and the President was fine. AP immediately retracted the tweet with apologies because it was false. The tweet was the result of a hack on its Twitter account. Fortunately, in this case, the markets recovered as soon as the news was confirmed as false, but this example highlights how vulnerable the markets and their investors are.

Investment firms use algorithms known as 'high-frequency trading systems'. These algorithms comb through social media, analysing tweets and posts from industry leaders and other sources, and gauging market sentiment, which is a key driver of investment decisions. High-frequency trading systems use machine learning and artificial intelligence to detect and weed out information from unreliable sources, but the impact of the AP tweet incident proves that such systems are not perfect. They still fall victim to human misinformation.

The story of Capitec Bank is another legendary example. Listed on the JSE in 2002, Capitec had always wanted to disrupt the domination of the big South African banks (FNB, ABSA, Standard Bank, Nedbank and Investec). In hindsight, the approach that Capitec adopted seems simple: it decided to exploit a gap in the market. Capitec insisted on keeping a low-cost base; a low-cost flat organisational structure made this possible.

In banking, the cost-to-income ratio is an important metric. While other South African banks averaged a cost-to-income ratio of 56%, Capitec's was far lower, at 38% (Koornhof, 2022). This differentiator meant that Capitec could offer its banking services at much lower fees than all the other South African banks, making Capitec's services much more affordable than those of other banks. Customers voted with their feet and the bank's financial performance grew in double digits every single year.

The markets rewarded Capitec: between 2002 and 2022, the market price of its shares increased 46% per annum (during the same period, the JSE index grew by 13% per year); an investment of R1 000 in Capitec in 2002 would have been worth R2.26 million by 2022.

In 2018, however, the fundamental basis of Capitec's success story was under threat. A report published in January 2018 by US international investment research company Viceroy Research labelled Capitec a 'wolf in sheep's clothing' (Viceroy Research, 2018). Viceroy reported that following its research and due diligence, it had concluded that Capitec was 'a loan shark with massively understated defaults masquerading as a community microfinance provider' (Viceroy Research, 2018). The report concluded that it was only a matter of time before the bank reached a net-liability position (that is, bankruptcy), likening this seeming inevitability to the recent insolvency crisis of African Bank. Viceroy implored the Reserve Bank to act urgently and place Capitec under curatorship.

The Financial Sector Conduct Authority (FSCA) investigated the substance of the Viceroy report, finding its conclusions to be unsubstantiated and based on false assumptions and information (Ciaran, 2021). Meanwhile, the report had caused a 25% crash in the share price of the bank.

The FSCA investigation discovered that Viceroy had benefitted from the crash through profit sharing of proceeds arising from its private client, who had taken a short position on Capitec shares. There was sufficient evidence to prove that Viceroy had been deliberate in its actions and it was fined $3.5 million by the FSCA. However, the effect of the fake news on innocent investors was devastating, and it was alarming to know that this false news had emanated from what should have been a reliable source of information.

8

More than 60% of the adult population relies on social media platforms for information. Platforms such as Twitter (now X), Instagram, LinkedIn, Facebook and Sina Weibo enable users to share information online (Bouri *et al.*, 2019). Consequently, the responsibility for quality control has shifted from journalists to platform users, raising the possibility of false content being disseminated. This phenomenon is explained by rumour theory, which suggests that people often share information without verifying its accuracy. As a result, the potential for unnoticed false information is high.

Nicolas Pröllochs and Stefan Feuerriegel, funded by the German Research Foundation (and with the permission of Twitter), conducted research compiling an extensive data set of Twitter rumours from its inception in 2006 until 2017 (Pröllochs & Feuerriegel, 2023). This data set included 126 301 cascades corresponding to 2 448 rumours, and involved 4.5 million retweets by approximately three million users. (In social media networks, rumours or shared information follow a propagation path known as a 'cascade'.) The data revealed that each rumour generates multiple cascades, leading to viral retweeting chains. Pröllochs and Feuerriegel found that sharing behaviour differs between true and false rumours, with false rumours propagating more deeply as a result of crowd effects. You might think that crowds would enhance quality control, but the opposite is true: false rumours tend to go viral to a greater extent than true rumours. Platform users do not throttle false rumours, but instead conform to the resharing habits of their peers, exhibiting herd behaviour, or the fear of missing out.

Businesses have recognised the marketing potential of online herd behaviour. In 2020, companies in the United States spent approximately $38 billion on sponsored content on social media platforms to attract

86

clicks and drive traffic to their websites, demonstrating positive commercial outcomes (Mattke *et al.*, 2020).

Historically, herding behaviour and FOMO have also influenced investing decisions, particularly during financial market crises. One notable example is the Dutch Tulip Mania of the seventeenth century (Kindleberger, 2000). Tulips became highly fashionable and extremely valuable, with a single tulip bulb becoming an acceptable dowry by 1610. This craze led ordinary people to speculate in tulips, inspired by the fortunes made by professional farmers. Middle-class and poor families mortgaged their homes to buy large volumes of tulips, hoping to resell them at higher prices. New tulip varieties fetched even higher prices, leading to a speculative bubble between 1633 and 1637. As is common in manias, logic was abandoned as individuals followed the herd. When the bubble burst suddenly in 1637, Dutch families were left in a state of financial ruin.

These examples illustrate the significant impact of herd behaviour on both the dissemination of social media information and financial markets, emphasising the importance of critical thinking and cautious decision-making.

9

They called him 'the Wolf of Crypto'.

In 2021, a thirty-two-year-old pest control entrepreneur named James Gale decided to make his ambition of trading cryptocurrencies a reality. In June of that year, he launched the cryptocurrency Koda in a flashy ceremony in London. The event was designed for maximum publicity, attracting celebrities, entertainers, broadcasters and even porn stars, with Lamborghinis lining the streets outside the launch venue. Gale embodied the image of a knowledgeable crypto businessman, confidently stating, 'I plan to make everyone involved in the project millionaires. I'm going to make people's dreams come true. But for me, in the not-too-distant future, I won't just be a millionaire; I'll be a billionaire' (Borrel, 2023).

Gale warned investors about the risks of the crypto market, advising the use of caution where potentially dubious cryptocurrencies were concerned. He emphasised the dangers of 'rug pulls' and popularised the term 'slow rug pull', a tactic where a new crypto company promises great returns, only to disappear and leave investors in financial ruin. Unlike many cryptocurrencies where the creators are anonymous, everyone knew that James Gale was behind Koda, which resolved the issue of trust. In contrast, the founders of Bitcoin remain anonymous under pseudonyms such as 'Satoshi Nakamoto'.

Gale's approachable persona helped to ease investors' concerns. He quickly gained the title of crypto expert, and Koda trended immediately after its launch. When Pete Gilbert was interviewed for the BBC programme *The Wolf of Crypto* (the podcast was released in August 2023), he explained how the launch persuaded people to buy Koda coins (BBC Radio, 2023). The fear of missing out prompted many to invest. Gilbert, who owned the Potters Arms pub in Winchmore Hill, north of London, became Koda's ambassador. The pub even offered workers the option of receiving their bonuses in Koda coins. One employee, fifty-year-old Jade Darby, believed Koda was a life-changing investment, hoping to use her earnings to buy property and refurbish her stables.

Initially, Koda seemed promising. Weeks after its launch, Koda was worth £0.00041 per coin, and three months later, it had grown to £0.0014, an increase of 251%. Gale's promises seemed conservative as Koda's performance vindicated its glossy launch. At the Potters Arms, Gilbert hosted crypto nights to promote Koda, and Koda staff attended to help patrons purchase the currency. However, Koda's rally came to an abrupt halt in November 2021, when the crypto market, including established currencies such as Bitcoin, slumped spectacularly (Borrel, 2023). Another crash in May 2022 saw some cryptos bounce back, but Koda never recovered, losing 99% of its value and devastating the investments of Winchmore Hill residents. Life savings were lost, relationships were broken and one man even committed suicide. In just a few months, Koda created a trail of destruction and broken hopes.

The cryptocurrency market continues to grow, with fourteen leading cryptocurrencies constituting 68% of the market capitalisation (Bouri *et al.*, 2018). Bitcoin, which broke ground in 2009 with blockchain technology, inspired numerous other cryptocurrencies. Despite their popularity, cryptocurrencies remain an unregulated asset class, lacking consensus on valuation methodologies. Institutional investors, such as retirement funds, are restricted by regulations from investing in these risky assets. Consequently, many crypto investors are young individuals who rely on social media and online forums for investment advice, which increases the potential for herd behaviour driven by fear of missing out. This speculative nature makes crypto markets extremely volatile.

In the world of cryptocurrencies, the term 'whale' refers to big crypto holders with at least ten thousand coins. But why are large crypto investors called 'whales'?

Whale watching is a thrilling pastime, drawing tourists to coastal regions where they can witness the awe-inspiring presence of whales. On the Northwest coast of America and Canada, humpbacks and orcas grace the waters, while in Hermanus, near Cape Town – known as the land-based whale-watching capital of the world – visitors can observe migrating humpbacks and Bryde's whales from the shore (Hermanus Whale Watchers, 2024). These majestic creatures, particularly the humpbacks, embark on incredible journeys, migrating up to almost nineteen thousand kilometres between the food-rich Antarctic seas and the tropical waters where they breed and raise their calves (Robbins *et al.*, 2011).

The sight of a pod of whales is both overwhelming and exhilarating. Their massive size and acrobatic displays, particularly breaching (when they propel themselves out of the water), leave spectators in awe.

Just as whale watchers are drawn to these enormous creatures, like their namesakes, crypto whales possess significant market influence, moving through the financial seas with a power that can both thrill and terrify onlookers.

Whale-watching apps allow users to follow these traders' actions, encouraging herd behaviour among investors. Pump-and-dump schemes are common, where coordinated efforts artificially inflate prices before the assets are dumped on unsuspecting buyers (Hamrick *et al.*, 2021). Social media platforms such as Telegram and Discord facilitate these schemes. As a result of the inherent risks, financial advisors typically recommend only investing amounts that do not constitute a significant portion of their clients' portfolios.

In August 2023, the US Court of Appeals ruled that the United States Securities and Exchange Commission (SEC) had improperly denied an application from Grayscale Investments to create a Bitcoin ETF, calling the rejection 'arbitrary and capricious' (Livni, 2023). This decision led to a crypto market rally. The SEC reconsidered and approved Bitcoin ETFs in early January 2024. This means that investors can now own shares in funds containing Bitcoin, rather than storing the cryptocurrency in online wallets. However, SEC Chair Gary Gensler cautioned that ETFs do not eliminate the risks and volatility associated with Bitcoin (Yaffe-Bellany, 2024).

In conclusion, while the allure of cryptocurrencies continues to attract many, the market's speculative nature and lack of regulation pose significant risks. Understanding these dynamics and maintaining a cautious, informed approach is crucial for investors navigating this volatile landscape.

10

Allan Gray asset managers are ranked in the top five in South Africa based on the total value of investments under management. The company believes that the philosophy guiding how it invests the capital entrusted to its portfolios is best described as a valuation-based investment approach. This differs from value or growth philosophies, for example. Other asset managers follow similar or different investment philosophies.

One investment philosophy used is termed 'deep value investing'. The information that follows illustrates the philosophy of John Biccard, a respected South African deep value portfolio manager who works for Ninety One (formerly Investec) (Planting, 2020).

Biccard identifies as a value investor, which is his preferred approach. However, he acknowledges that it is also possible to profit as a growth or momentum investor, suggesting that the key is to determine the style that suits the individual best and stick with it consistently, avoiding switching between different strategies. He advises that it is important for an investor to understand their strengths and weaknesses, develop a solid plan and adhere to it consistently over the long term, which means committing to the same investment style for at least ten years.

Asked whether a poor performance in an investment selection would make him change his approach, he responded that he would not stop, but would keep going. According to him, investors must do the necessary work, including analysis and calculations, before making investment decisions. For instance, if an investor bought a share at a sufficiently low valuation, it does not matter if the share price halves; the investor should buy more. And if the share price halves again, they should continue to buy more (Van Niekerk, 2022).

Biccard, who was interviewed by Moneyweb in 2022, has been at Ninety One for over twenty years, and is currently the portfolio manager of the Ninety One deep value fund (formerly the Investec deep value fund). The company provides a fund fact sheet that explains its investment philosophy on the landing page of the Ninety One Value Fund: the fund aims to provide capital growth over a long period (Ninety One Value Fund, 2023). The company's definition of a long period is at least ten years. It invests in shares that trade at values below their net asset value. These shares are neglected by most investors and traded at discounted values.

This investment approach provides a practical example of Benjamin Graham's 'margin of safety' in action – it would take a total crash in a share for an investor to sustain serious loss if the price paid for the share had been lower than its attributed asset value. Graham believes that by avoiding overpayment for an investment, it is possible for an individual to minimise the risk of their wealth disappearing or suddenly being destroyed (Graham, 2006).

Between 2010 and 2020, the Ninety One deep value fund entered a period of sustained poor performance – a phase that could easily have broken the resolve of Biccard, its portfolio manager. But Biccard, ever the contrarian, refused to waver in his investment philosophy.

As a board trustee of a R5-billion retirement fund, I had a front-row seat to this unfolding drama. Our fund had 15% of its assets tied up in the Investec Value Fund, as Ninety One was then known. Before 2010, the returns were satisfactory, but as the years progressed, our concern grew. Each quarterly report delivered the same disheartening news, with returns remaining stubbornly below those of other equity asset managers.

The tipping point came in late 2013 during an investment committee meeting. Our consultants presented a risk–return scatter graph, and there it was: the Investec Value Fund, represented by a lonely red dot, was perilously close to zero on the return axis, yet far to the right on the risk spectrum. It was a stark, undeniable image of the fund's struggles.

While acknowledging the fund's adherence to its deep value strategy, our consultants suggested we monitor it for another quarter. But the board had reached its limit. 'How do we face the members at the next AGM with these numbers?' one trustee asked, voicing what we were all thinking. The decision was made: 15% of our equity portfolio would be pulled from the value fund and reallocated to a momentum asset manager.

This was not an isolated incident; many value funds saw similar outflows during those tough years. Yet Biccard remained steadfast, driven by his conviction in the long-term merits of his approach, despite the prevailing winds.

In a 2022 interview, John Biccard used the example of Impala Platinum, a mining company listed on the Johannesburg Stock Exchange, to illustrate how his contrarian investment approach can yield significant results. Over the past five years, Ninety One has made substantial profits from Impala, he confided, but their strategy was far from conventional.

When Impala's stock initially traded at R300, Ninety One did not buy. Instead, the company waited as the share price declined steadily over six or seven years. It was not until the stock hit R80 that Ninety One began buying. As the price continued to fall, eventually bottoming out at R20, Ninety One kept buying, gradually lowering its average purchase price to around R35 or R40.

This approach, known as 'averaging down', seemed risky to many, and some critics even thought it was reckless. However, within two years, Impala's share price surged from R20 to R200. This dramatic turnaround meant that Ninety One's investment strategy – initially seen as a gamble – resulted in a return of ten times its original investment. Biccard's example highlights how going against the crowd can lead to remarkable success, even when the strategy appears questionable at the outset.

In August 2023, Tiger Brands was the top holding in the Ninety One Value Fund, representing 9.5% of the total investments under management

(Ninety One Value Fund, 2023). Tiger Brands had performed poorly in recent years when compared to the market. It had been rated a leading South African food company for many years, but poor business decisions and hard times had caused financial analysts to lose interest in it. The reason why most financial analysts did not believe in Tiger Brands was obvious: the company's earnings had fallen consistently (60% from 2017 levels) over the years (Van Niekerk, 2022). So why does Biccard continue to hold the shares in the Ninety One Value Fund? What does he see in the company that makes him differ from his financial services peers? When asked this question, his response was again testament to his stubborn conviction, which is supported by independent analysis. Biccard points out that it is likely that it will take years before Tiger Brands reaches a point where its value is unlocked, requiring patience that many investors lack. However, when the earnings eventually start to grow again and the price-to-earnings ratio expands, investors will see significant returns.

Biccard demonstrates the determination and conviction required by an investor faced with the collective thinking of the crowd. He has enough successes under his belt to prove the worth of his investment philosophy. The landing page of the Ninety One Value Fund alerts investors to the fact that when compared with the JSE All Share Index, periods of outperformance for value funds are short and sharp. In 2019, the Ninety One Value Fund delivered a spectacular 35% return. It is such returns that keep Biccard believing in his contrarian approach. His example provides hope that with a degree of determination as well as independent information-gathering and analysis, it is possible to resist the urge to follow the crowd when everyone else behaves like sheep. Biccard does not follow the herd.

11

In all financial manias and crises, some investors remain rational, while others behave irrationally. Destabilising speculators who buy shares when prices are high and sell when they fall belong in the latter category. The sage advice 'Buy low and sell high' remains a cornerstone of wealth creation, a concept that is explored in depth in this chapter. The chapter has outlined the financial ruin caused by irrational investment behaviour and invited the reader to consider how a rational investor might succeed in emerging unscathed and wealthier from a mania-fuelled bubble.

In 1720, when investors – including Sir Isaac Newton – lost thousands of pounds as a result of the South Sea Bubble, one rational participant thrived, emerging with a fortune. Reflecting on the tumultuous months of the crisis, this investor concluded that the additional rise above the true value of capital is merely imaginary; one added to one will never equal three and a half. Hence, all fictitious value must ultimately result in loss for someone. The prudent course of action, the investor surmised, was to divest early, allowing the proverbial Devil to ensnare the laggards. This investor's rational response to the crisis allowed them to resist the temptation to follow the crowd in 1720, instead buying low and selling at the peak. The shiver down my spine when I read this text indicates its impact and requires no further explanation.

Financial crises have occurred throughout history, and the types of investor involved remain the same. The driving forces are the fear of missing out, or FOMO, and the human tendency towards herd behaviour.

An observation by English journalist and businessman Walter Bagehot about a financial crisis in 1814 is as relevant today as it was then. He described the frenzy as affecting even those far removed from commercial concerns – people such as clerks, labourers and servants – who risked their savings, meant for old age and sickness (Kindleberger, 2000: 29). The great speculators went bankrupt, the middling ones faced a precarious existence and the poor dupes lost their little hoards, becoming dependent on charity. By the time the delusion had dissipated, it had left a trail of financial devastation in its wake.

'But God hath chosen the foolish things of the world to confound the wise; and God hath chosen the weak things of the world to confound the things which are mighty.' (*New King James Bible*, 2004, 1 Corinthians 1:27)

Is it better to follow or to lead? Individuals form groups, and when faced with decisions, each person must determine the best course of action for them. However, the allure of aligning with the majority often proves irresistible. History shows that financial crises unfold in similar patterns. This chapter highlights instances where individuals succumbed to FOMO and groupthink, disregarding their instincts and knowledge, often resulting in their financial ruin. Conversely, some individuals have mastered the art of tuning out the noise and so being able to make independent, prudent investment decisions. These individuals profit during market euphoria by adhering to principles such as buying low and selling high, dollar-cost averaging, maintaining a margin of safety, and adopting a long-term approach to mitigate panic and anxiety.

CHAPTER 5

THE LANDLORD OF SEATTLE AND OTHER PEOPLE'S MONEY

'If you don't owe, you don't own ...'
– Lorenza Arango Vasquez

1

Why does debt affect people so differently?

During my time as a retirement fund trustee, I learnt that pension funds have a key role beyond maximising retirement benefits for their members. Fund trustees oversee a broad spectrum of responsibilities, from the exhilarating thrill of making investment decisions – something I found immensely enjoyable – to the more mundane tasks, such as managing the distribution of death benefits.

Employees must balance their immediate financial needs with planning for their future security. While our provident fund did not lend directly to members, it did offer a unique service: members could borrow from approved loan providers, with their loans guaranteed against their retirement fund contributions, provided they met certain affordability criteria. The maximum loan amount was limited to 40% of their fund credit. This arrangement offered security to the loan providers and shielded members from the high interest rates typically charged on the open market. However, the fund's rules strictly limited these loans to home purchases or improvements.

I took advantage of this facility to convert two outbuildings at my family home into charming garden cottages, successfully paying off the loan within five years. This investment not only enhanced the value of my property, but also created a steady stream of rental income. Reflecting on my experience, I considered it a fitting example of the typical borrower's journey, with no reason to believe otherwise.

As trustees, we often debated this policy. Concerned that members might misuse loaned funds for non-essential purposes, we revised our service contract with the loan providers, requiring them to send inspectors to verify that the loans were being used as intended.

Despite our best intentions as fund trustees, our attempts to guide members towards the strategic use of debt ultimately proved unsuccessful. Each time inspectors contacted members to arrange a visit to review their building projects, they were denied access. The annual inspection reports consistently showed low compliance, which troubled us – especially since members were charged an inspection fee for each loan. Initially, we blamed the loan providers, believing they had not tried hard enough. We even summoned their executives to explain themselves. But after they had left, one trustee offered a different perspective: 'Are we being paternalistic by insisting on inspecting members' personal projects? We may be accused of playing "Papa". Yes, the loans are guaranteed, but only against the member's fund credit. If a member defaults, they bear the loss.'

This insight shifted our thinking. We realised that our approach might be overreaching, so we removed the inspection clause. That experience taught me a valuable lesson: when debt, financial circumstances, discipline and temptation converge, the outcome varies widely from person to person.

In the grand theatre of wealth creation, debt plays a role that is both empowering and perilous. Like a dancer in a complex ballet, leveraging requires a delicate sense of balance – one that teeters between the allure of increased profits and the stark reality of potential losses. Investors, drawn by the promise of gain, might be tempted to embrace as much leverage as possible. However, true wisdom lies in adopting a more measured approach.

Leverage is like a double-edged sword: in a thriving market, it can carve out monumental successes, but when the market stumbles, that same leverage can inflict devastating losses. The savvy investor practises moderation, understanding that sensible use of leverage can yield substantial rewards – rewards often overlooked in the exuberance of a market upswing.

Determining the right amount of leverage is a complex and nuanced task, requiring a careful assessment of risks. When venturing into new, unstable or high-risk opportunities, the pursuit of maximum returns can be incredibly dangerous. Caution becomes the guiding principle, and survival hinges on maintaining a 'margin of safety', a concept championed by the esteemed Benjamin Graham (2006). The level of risk inherent in the assets under consideration should dictate the degree of leverage employed; the higher the risk, the less leverage should be applied. While this cautious approach may limit potential gains, it also shields against financial ruin in challenging times.

This chapter explores the strategic use of debt by both ordinary and extraordinary individuals, particularly in the realm of property investments, by examining the stories of three people or groups of people: a young landlord in Seattle, a determined woman who built one of New York's largest real estate agencies from the ground up, and small-scale cocoa farmers in the Colombian countryside. Equally significant are the stories and lives of countless individuals who could benefit from using debt more wisely.

2

Todd Baldwin is a young American born in 1992 who lives in Seattle. When he was a child, he watched his mother, a dedicated family woman whom he loved very much, struggle to make ends meet while taking care of her family. A single mom with three kids, she needed to juggle four jobs to balance the family budget.

At the age of twelve, Baldwin looked for jobs to help his mother. He recalls his first job shovelling manure, for which he earned $3 per hour. This experience shaped Baldwin's approach to life from an early age.

Baldwin is a millennial, a member of 'Generation Y', as it is called, but he is different from most of this generation. He became a millionaire before the age of thirty; he crossed the net worth psychological barrier of one million dollars at the age of twenty-five (McNair, 2023a; Elkins, 2020). In 2020, he was profiled on CNBC's *Millennial Money* series.

After dropping out of Western Washington University, Baldwin worked as a commercial insurance salesman earning $50 000 per year. Through sheer hard work, he doubled his salary in a few months.

Baldwin married early. When he was twenty-three, he and his wife Angela went looking for an apartment to rent. However, rentals in Seattle are exorbitant, so the couple decided to purchase a property instead of renting. They bought their first property for $506 000 in 2015, putting down a deposit of $19 000 from their savings.

Baldwin used his credit card tactically. He made payments for essentials against the credit card and paid off the balance by the end of every month. The credit card facility improved his credit rating, and the bond application was approved without incident.

Now, Baldwin is aggressively frugal: 'We are super frugal,' he says, referring to himself and Angela (Elkins, 2020). The couple shared a 2009 Ford Focus for many years and succeeded in spending very little on a daily basis (their monthly grocery budget is $25). In addition, Baldwin is unorthodox. As soon as they had bought the first house, the couple discovered that they could earn rental income by bringing tenants on board (this practice is called 'house hacking'.) They rented out bedrooms that they were not using; even after paying the monthly mortgage instalment, they had surplus cash left over from the rental income.

Nine months later, the couple used mortgage finance to buy another house. Then the process acquired its own momentum and scaled. By 2020, the couple owned six properties, all of which they rented out. They maintained a good credit score, paying the monthly mortgage instalments without fail.

Baldwin's model is to rent by the room versus single occupancy tenants. Understanding that his house-hack model might not suit everyone, Baldwin suggests enduring any difficulties while young, noting that it is easier to have room-mates at twenty-two than at forty-two (Elkins, 2020).

Baldwin's approach is far from scattergun when it comes to selecting what property to buy. The house must meet five critical characteristics:
- a good bedroom-to-bathroom ratio
- sufficient parking for the tenants
- the location should show evidence of going through a positive transition (for example, new businesses or new grocery shops opening in the area)
- low or no homeowners' association fees (levies)
- good public transport in the area.

Baldwin attributes his success to his strict, focused, objective adherence to his criteria. He states that he would not consider purchasing a house unless it met all five critical characteristics, rejecting any that met only four out of five (Elkins, 2020).

'For unto every one that hath shall be given, and he shall have abundance: but from him that hath not shall be taken away even that which he hath.' (*New King James Bible*, 2004, Matthew 25:29)

How did the Baldwins manage to survive on a monthly grocery budget of only $25? The couple did not have children in 2020 when they were profiled in the *Millennial Money* series, but that could not explain the minimalist budget.

The answer is that they made use of a strategy called 'secret shopping' to earn money and save money on daily expenses.

Baldwin started secret shopping when he was in college and needed cash. He desperately wanted to take Angela out on a date. As a young man, he wanted to impress her; he knew that first impressions matter. After a great deal of research, he discovered that it is possible to get free food and free entertainment.

Businesses and manufacturers are always keen to know how their products are doing in the marketplace. Companies also want to know whether their employees are performing as expected. Once they have this information, firms know what changes to make to align with the markets and the competition, and to improve profits. Baldwin found out that companies hire mystery shopping firms to find independent contractors like him to pose as regular customers at their establishments, buy a specific product or service, and then report on their experience.

In 2020, the Baldwins earned a monthly average of $415 from secret shopping, getting paid to do activities that they would have done anyway, such as eating out or watching movies. This explains how they managed to survive on a monthly food budget of $25 and gives meaning to a phenomenon known as the 'Matthew Effect': those who have found wealth shall continue to receive more. The Matthew Effect is named after a Bible verse in the book of Matthew.

It was not by luck that Baldwin stumbled upon his wealth; it was by persisting and working hard, and by using the tools – including mortgage financing – that are available to all humans. In short, he became wealthy because of his tenacity, grit and discipline.

Baldwin has kept his sales job, improving his skills enough to find his annual salary rising to $150 000 by 2020. He has also used his after-work time effectively.

There is a single-mindedness about the couple. They save an aggressive 80% of their income every month, most of which is reinvested into real estate; the balance goes to conventional retirement funding. In 2020, their real estate portfolio comprising six properties was valued at $4.4 million and they owed $3.1 million in mortgages, the costs of which are paid by rentals from tenants. (For example, the couple bought a duplex in a suburb just outside downtown Seattle in 2019 for $900 000 and shared their home with tenants. Their monthly mortgage bill was $4 700 and they received $4 500 in rental income, so almost all their financing costs on the property were paid.)

The couple's net worth was inching towards $1.5 million by 2020, but Baldwin has always held loftier ambitions. He learnt early in life not to follow the crowd and not to copy friends or family, but to be his authentic self, believing in and betting on himself all the time.

At the time of the 2020 interview, Baldwin was driving a Ford Focus. He swore that he would not buy a more expensive car until he had achieved certain important milestones, at which point he would probably buy a Tesla Roadster. He added, 'I want it because it's the fastest car in the world. I've got a lot of places to be and zero time to waste' (Elkins, 2020). He aims to have built a portfolio of six thousand apartments by the time he turns sixty. This young man is not one to procrastinate.

There is a subtle dimension that underpins Baldwin's model: his real estate investments are all in the Seattle area. This is important. The properties are all within a short radius of each other, which makes them easily accessible and manageable. Real estate letting is viewed as passive investing, but there are some fundamental considerations that should not be missed. By staying within the Seattle metropolis, Baldwin avoids being an absentee landlord. This allows him to promptly address any issues that arise at his properties, ensuring that his tenants remain satisfied. He also keeps up with any developments in the area because he is actively engaged in the community; if a neighbourhood is deteriorating, he knows before it is too late, so he can sell the property and move elsewhere. When profitable developments become available, he immediately pounces and takes advantage of them.

Baldwin has come to understand that time is life's most precious commodity, one that must not be squandered. His journey reflects a deep passion for real estate. By the age of thirty, he had already established a solid foundation for his future, leaving little doubt that he will reach his life's goals. Remarkably, it was debt that enabled him to achieve financial independence.

3

Douglas Boneparth, a prominent American entrepreneur and the president and founder of Bone Fide Wealth, has emerged as a leading voice in personalised financial advice tailored to millennials.

Born in 1987, Boneparth is himself a millennial, which adds a unique resonance to his expertise. The landing page of Bone Fide Wealth LLC proudly proclaims, 'New York City's Financial Adviser for Millennials' (Bone Fide Wealth, 2024), emphasising the company's commitment to serving younger generations while subtly excluding older ones. Yet I find Boneparth's financial guidance refreshingly straightforward and universally applicable, as it fundamentally centres on the timeless principles of effective money management.

Speaking of debt in an interview on CNBC's *Millennial Money* show, Boneparth said, 'When paying off debt interferes with seeing the big picture, it's too much …. Those who treat debt as a cardinal sin are likely being too extreme in their view.'

There is a good reason why most people fear debt: they know someone close to them who struggles with debt, fails to meet their monthly debit orders and is always anxious about money. Feelings such as these may cause people to maintain a negative attitude towards debt, which feeds through generations from parent to child. An American study done in 2019 by

The Ascent found that 28% of people surveyed think about the money they owe every day (Hecht, 2019).

Boneparth suggests that debt should be seen as a normal part of life, not as a sign of financial irresponsibility. Borrowing for homeownership or education should be considered an investment in an individual's future. Using debt (such as a mortgage or a student loan) may be the only means available for a person to buy a home or to finance their studies. When it is used in the right way, debt is very useful.

The conceptual framework of accounting defines an asset as follows: 'A resource controlled by the entity as a result of past events and from which future economic benefits are expected to flow to the entity' (International Accounting Standards Board [IASB], 2018). From this definition, it follows that good debt results in future economic benefits (to be specific, net cash inflows).

A home provides more than just shelter; it offers a financial advantage when purchased with a mortgage. Instead of paying rent, the borrower makes monthly instalments to the bank, which include both interest and capital repayment. Over the typical loan term of twenty years, these payments gradually reduce the loan balance until the debt is fully eliminated, and the opportunity cost of rent is saved. However, this benefit diminishes if the home is in a price bracket higher than the borrower can afford.

In contrast, an investment property generates rental income from tenants, which can offset the monthly loan repayment. When rental income exceeds loan costs, a surplus is created, turning the property into a true asset with tangible economic benefits.

On the other hand, expenditures on items such as vacations, big-screen televisions and luxury cars result in outflows, since these items depreciate and do not generate income. Borrowing for such purposes is considered bad debt because it does not lead to asset creation, but rather requires ongoing cash outflows for maintenance.

The use of credit cards for consumption (for instance, to pay for vacations or luxury goods) can be particularly perilous. The interest on credit card debt can be up to three times higher than the standard prime interest rate, and if the user only pays the monthly minimum, they end up paying high interest over extended periods for items that depreciate or are consumed quickly. However, credit cards can also be used in a more empowering way. By using a credit card for necessary purchases only and paying off the full balance every month without fail, the user can establish a good credit record. Within six months, this practice can lead to an improved credit score.

4

This section gives an illustration of how debt can be used to advantage by focusing on a local woman who is building her rental portfolio in much the same way as Todd Baldwin.

Thirty-five-year-old Joanna has accumulated savings in mutual unit trusts over the years and the balance has grown to R1 035 000. She has now decided to invest the cash in an investment property.

Following the Covid-19 pandemic of 2020, reserve banks across the world were forced to hike interest rates to combat stubborn levels of inflation. These higher interest rates made the property market soft; potential buyers realised that their buying power had been greatly reduced. It was a buyers' market in which sellers were finding it hard to sell their properties, and Joanna wants to take advantage of the situation.

While property hunting in the sought-after greater Sandton and Fourways suburbs of Johannesburg, Joanna finds a two-bedroom, two-bathroom apartment listed on property platforms at R900 000 and success-fully negotiates a sale price of R800 000.

The first option is to buy the apartment for cash. The conveyancing and bond registration costs are R26 000 (because it is a cash deal, she will only have to pay transfer costs). Thus the full cost of acquiring the property will be R826 000 (capital employed). The balance of Joanna's cash, R209 000, will remain in her unit trust accounts and she will receive rental income of R10 500 per month for the apartment.

In this option, the total capital invested by her in the property is R826 000, which is equal to the capital employed because this is a cash option. There will be a monthly net cash flow of R8 700 (R10 500 – R1 800) from rental less monthly costs such as levies and rates; annualised, this amounts to R104 400. The annual return on invested capital will be 12.6%.

The second option is to split the R800 000 into five and use it to make down payments (20% deposit) on five properties. Since each property costs R800 000, Joanna will have to borrow R640 000 per property from the bank to finance the purchase. She is dogged and will diligently look out for the right properties in good locations that all cost the same price of R800 000. The transfer and bond registration costs will amount to R47 000 per property, which Joanna will pay from the cash in hand. The full cost to acquire each property will be R847 000, with a registered bond of R640 000. The prime interest rate is 11.75% and the loan term is twenty years. The repayment will be R6 935 monthly; additional costs (municipal rates, insurance and levies) will total R1 800 (the tenant will pay the electricity and water bills). As in the first option, the rental will be R10 500 monthly.

To make the deal more lucrative for her and more affordable for tenants, Joanna will aim to find two tenants to share each apartment since all of the properties come with two bedrooms and two bathrooms. Joanna's net cash flow will be R1 765 (R10 500 – R6 935 – R1 800) per month; annualised, this amounts to R105 900 for the five apartments. The total cash flow into Joanna's pocket will be R8 825 per month, enough to build up a reserve to cover maintenance and repairs, which will be required from time to time. This translates to an annual return of 10% on Joanna's invested capital. However, the balance sheet is king: by splitting her cash and leveraging the properties with debt, Joanna has secured five properties in her real estate portfolio. The total value of Joanna's real estate portfolio will be R4 million (R800 000 × 5), with a total debt of R3.2 million, which will be paid off by her tenants' rentals over twenty years.

Ignoring the impact of inflation on house prices over the twenty years, Joanna will have a fully paid-up property portfolio of five apartments with a value of R4 million if she follows the second option. If, on the other hand, she chooses the first option and opts to use the cash at her disposal to buy just one property with a value of R800 000, she will have only one apartment but no debt.

Admittedly, this is a simple example used for illustrative purposes. In the real world, some calculations could be more complicated depending on specific circumstances, variables and permutations, but the principles remain the same.

A common mistake made by many people in calculating the annual return is to use the wrong capital amount as the denominator in the calculation.

I distinguish between two capital amounts: the capital employed and the invested capital.

The capital employed combines the debt and owners' equity. In the case of the cash option described above, no debt is involved and the capital employed is R826 000 (price plus conveyancing costs). In the leveraged option, the total capital employed is R847 000 for each property. However, this approach is quite incorrect.

The correct method for calculating the annual return is to use the invested capital instead of the capital employed. The invested capital for the cash option remains R826 000, as that is the cash Joanna withdraws from her unit trust to pay for the property. The invested capital for the leveraged option should similarly be the cash that Joanna withdraws from her unit trusts for the down payment, plus the cash paid to the attorneys for the transfer and bond registration (R160 000 + R47 000 = R207 000) for each of the five properties. When we divide the net cash flow by the invested capital, we get the annual return. In this case, the annual return is 12.6% for the cash option and 10.2% for the leveraged option – a marginally better return for the cash option but without scaling. As a collective (portfolio of five units), the leveraged option achieves more for Joanna and the total monthly rand value of the cash flow exceeds the cash option.

The wealth created at the end of twenty years through leveraging is an important factor for Joanna to consider: the second option of using debt to purchase five properties will yield a property value of R4 million in Joanna's balance sheet (without adjusting for house inflation over the years) compared to only R800 000 with the first (cash) option.

In this example, I have not considered the tax benefit of debt – interest paid on the loan is deductible against rental income for tax purposes.

One of the primary appeals of real estate is capital growth, as property values tend to rise over time. In sought-after areas such as Sandton and Fourways in northern Johannesburg, property prices are likely to outpace inflation in the medium to long term. Joanna's strategy capitalises on this potential by purchasing in a depressed property market, particularly when interest rates have increased sharply. In this buyer's market, she can negotiate and secure properties at below-average prices – effectively buying low and creating a margin of safety. As the interest rate cycle eventually improves, her portfolio stands to appreciate significantly.

Joanna's aim is to create wealth. She will be fifty-five when the five properties are paid off. Table 2 summarises the illustration.

Table 2 Scaling and leveraging effect of debt

RAND	Cash option	Leveraging debt option – 20-year term
Purchase price of apartments	800 000	800 000
Number of apartments bought	1	5
Total value	800 000	4 000 000
Transfer costs (@ R26 000 per unit)	26 000	130 000
Bond registration costs (@ R21 000 per unit)	–	105 000
Total acquisition costs	826 000	4 235 000
Deposit paid 20%	–	800 000
Invested capital (transfer, bond registration, deposit and purchase price paid)	826 000	1 035 000
Owing – debt on acquiring the apartments	–	**3 200 000**
Monthly rentals	10 500	10 500
Monthly outflows per unit (levy, rates and insurance)	1 800	1 800
Bond instalment (@ interest rate of 11.75% p.a.)	–	6 935
Net cash flow per apartment	8 700	1 765
Net cash flow for collective portfolio per month	8 700	8 825
Annual net cash flow (without adjusting for inflation and tax benefits of debt)	**104 400**	**105 900**
Return on invested capital	**12.6%**	**10.2%**
Scaling (number of properties acquired)	**1**	**5**
Owing – debt – at the end of 20 years (end of repayment period)	–	–
Annual net cash flow after 20 years (without adjusting for inflation, when both options are debt free)	**104 400**	**522 000**
Balance sheet contribution of apartments (without adjusting for inflation) – end of 20-year repayment term based on original price ignoring selling costs	**800 000**	**4 000 000**
Balance sheet net after 20 years – including unused cash (R209 000) in the cash option (R1 035 000 less R826 000) – without adjusting for inflation over the 20 years	**1 009 000**	**4 000 000**

5

Barbara Corcoran's struggle with dyslexia made reading and mathematics difficult for her during school, forcing her to develop creative ways to navigate her challenges without letting them hinder her progress. Decades ago, dyslexia was poorly understood, and one can only imagine the barrage of insults she is likely to have endured, both at school and at home. Yet individuals born with this condition often learn early on to cope with unkind remarks, and Corcoran was no exception. Her resilience and ingenuity led her to become a celebrated real estate entrepreneur and self-made millionaire.

Remarkably, Corcoran began her journey at the age of twenty-three in 1973 with just $1 000, which she borrowed from her boyfriend, using the cash as working capital and setting up a real estate agency office. She earned commission finding tenants for clients and managing their apartments.

Does it follow logically that saving money will make you wealthy? This is the question asked of Corcoran when she was a guest on CNBC *Make It* show in 2023 (Jackson, 2023a, 2023b). She has a unique perspective on life: she responded to the question by saying, 'I'm just not a believer in saving money … I've never saved a dime my whole life' (McNair, 2023b). Instead, Corcoran advocates for spending and investing. Her approach involves dressing well, looking the part, working hard and using credit to leverage real estate investments.

With her first commission in 1973, she purchased an expensive wool coat, which she still believes to be the best investment she has ever made. She spent $320 on this coat, retiring her old navy-blue pea coat from New Jersey, which had become a liability. The new wool coat made her feel confident and helped her exude the image of a successful realtor. She wore it for the next four years, attracting clients who began to take her seriously, and commissions started to flow in steadily. However, her growth came from spending, investing and leveraging debt.

Corcoran's business philosophy embodies a refreshing perspective on wealth creation. Rather than fixating on frugality and the minutiae of cutting costs, she champions the pursuit of new opportunities to amplify income. This approach elegantly distinguishes between the cautiousness of saving and the boldness of investing. At the heart of her strategy lies a commitment to hard work and the calculated use of credit, transforming real estate into a powerful engine for growth and success.

Corcoran's method is a testament to the idea that fortune favours those who dare to take strategic risks. She built her business into one of the largest real estate brokerage firms in New York before selling it to another real estate brokerage firm for $66 million thirty years later.

6

But what is it about debt, apart from its leveraging and scaling benefits? What makes debt such a viable option for economic activities? Lorenza Arango Vasquez of the Institute of Social Studies in the Hague, Netherlands was keen to investigate this question, and so she visited small-scale farmers in Colombia. What she found was beyond anything she had expected.

Colombia has been known for its drawn-out internal conflict since the 1960s. In 2016, a peace accord between the Revolutionary Armed Forces of Colombia (FARC) and the government ended the fifty-year-old conflict (Vasquez, 2020). Some bands of the FARC guerilla movement broke away and became dissidents. Although the breakaway factions comprised conflict-hardened bush fighters who subsequently embarked on new forms of violence and abuse in remote areas of Colombia, conditions in the rest of the country had improved. The violence had become isolated and much more contained, allowing farming communities to resume activities on their land. Families who were displaced years ago during the violent conflict returned to their properties. Small-scale cocoa farmers were confident enough to plan and make their farms increasingly productive without fearing the return of the decades-long violence and conflict.

As part of the land restitution process, the Colombian Institute of Agrarian Reform granted subsidies to these families to acquire agricultural plots, offering to cover 70% of the total cost, with the balance to be paid through loans from the Agrarian Bank. The Agrarian Bank also offered loans to finance the working capital requirements of small-scale farmers. Credit immediately became a part of life for the cocoa farmers, as they needed funding to be productive.

Vasquez travelled to the municipality of El Carmen de Chucurí, located in the north-east of Colombia, spending three months with small-scale cocoa farmers in 2016 and a further two months in 2018. Most of the municipality's twenty thousand inhabitants live in rural areas (Vasquez, 2020). The municipality is in a geographical area that is favoured with fertile soils and abundant water resources. Rural cocoa farmers have increasingly made good use of nature's gifts to cultivate cash and food crops. They have embraced debt to improve production.

Vasquez was intrigued by how debt shaped the lives of these farmers. She aimed to uncover whether their actions reflected the subtle yet powerful influence that debt can exert over a person's choices and behaviours. The cohort of interest was a group of farmers who had a long history of being in debt.

In search of deep perspectives on debt and debt relations, Vasquez conducted extensive interviews with the farmers and spent time with neighbours, acquaintances and shopkeepers of the cohort who knew them well enough to comment.

For most of the farmers, interest-bearing debt was a novelty. They now had to project and budget for future cash inflows and spending, and prioritise debt payments. Most had to cut down on their food, clothing, housing and schooling costs to avoid defaulting on debt payments.

Vasquez collated the results of the surveys into separate categories. She called the first of the categories the 'disciplining of mindsets'. These are some of her findings:

- One farmer from El Centenario village explained in August 2018 that prior to taking on interest-bearing debt, he worked solely to meet his family's daily needs. Earnings from a single day's work would be used to buy food for that night's dinner, and there was no thought for the next day. However, once he had gone into debt, he knew the bank would not wait, which forced him to make a mindset adjustment.
- Another farmer from El Centenario village mentioned in July 2016 that for him to save money for loan payments, his family had to live on a dirt floor.
- In July 2018, a farmer from El Carmen noted that any bank debt requires sacrifice. When production is low, the entire family must forgo

many things. Discipline is necessary, as even buying a set of clothes might become impossible due to the need to repay the bank. This means children cannot always be given certain items that they need, as doing so would disrupt the family's financial balance.

- Finally, in July 2016, a farmer from El Carmen described how the municipality transitioned from coffee to cocoa as a result of warmer weather.

Cocoa, being a strong economic activity with monthly yields, quickly became an important source of income in the principality. The production of cocoa, a cash crop that is tied to the availability of credit in the rural municipality, has become the dominant farming activity in the area. As a result, much less hectarage is now given to other crops, such as cassava, plantains, avocados and citrus fruit, which constitute the farmers' staple diet. The exposure to external markets, which determine the price of cocoa, leaves farmers vulnerable to inevitable price volatility. They have learnt to hedge the risk of low prices by increasing production.

Globally, cocoa production is dominated by small-scale farmers, a reality that makes it critical to use new methods to guarantee increased yields. The introduction of clones in cocoa cultivation resulted in production increasing from five hundred kilograms per hectare per month to approximately three thousand kilograms, a fivefold increase. The use of clones is a departure from traditional methods, which demand organic cultivation practices but are much less productive per hectare. Cloning produces uniform plantlets that are healthier and high-yielding, and effective for intensive production in small-scale farming.

Farmers attribute the improvement of the community's financial welfare to credit lines. Credit made it possible to scale production on the plots.

The farmers' responses to Vasquez's questions confirm their shift from a subsistence lifestyle to contemporary entrepreneurship:

- In June 2016, a female cocoa farmer from El Carmen noted that the land did not yield enough profit to keep up with credit.
- According to a male cocoa farmer from El Carmen in August 2016, the only choice was to keep growing cocoa; failing this, falling into default was inevitable, leaving them in a difficult situation.

- In August 2018, another male cocoa farmer from El Centenario village stated that without debt, farmers could not own anything, and they had to become indebted to progress.

The price of cocoa reached a high of $3 per kilogram in 2016, falling to $1.20 in 2017. It recovered to $1.50 in 2018, but was still below the level required for farmers to meet the repayment of their interest-bearing debt. To earn enough to repay their debt, some small-scale farmers took on temporary work, labouring on neighbouring farms. This side hustle, which became a necessary strategy to cover income shortfalls and balance their budgets, required long hours of work to achieve targets and the excessive work routine placed a huge physical demand on bodies.

Vasquez collated another set of results from her survey interviews into a separate category that she termed the 'disciplining of bodies'. The farmers' responses illustrate this phenomenon:

- A male cocoa farmer from El Carmen explained in July 2016 that if a task typically takes ten days, he completes it in seven by working longer hours without rest. This allows him to use the remaining three days to earn extra money to pay the bank. By working more efficiently and intensively, he can pay off his debt.
- A male farmer from El Toboso village shared in June 2016 that after injuring his foot and being unable to work, he developed a gastric ulcer due to stress as he worried persistently about missing loan payments. The bank was relentless, calling multiple times a day to demand payment.
- In August 2018, another male cocoa farmer from El Centenario village noted that before having bank debt, he could afford to miss a day of work without consequences. However, with debt, he had to work continuously, without falling ill or getting tired, to meet repayment deadlines.

This chapter offers a nuanced view of debt, emphasising its psychological impact on individuals. It suggests that debt is not a one-dimensional financial tool, but has complex psychological implications that can influence a person's financial decisions and overall well-being.

Here are some key psychological aspects of debt as highlighted in the chapter:

- Debt as a double-edged sword: Debt is portrayed as having the potential to be both beneficial and detrimental. This duality can lead to cognitive dissonance, where individuals must reconcile the risk of economic strain with the potential for financial growth.

- Good versus bad debt: The distinction between 'good' debt (that which is used to acquire things that appreciate in value or generate income) and 'bad' debt (that which devalues or strains finances) reflects the importance of strategic financial planning and the psychological comfort that comes from making informed borrowing decisions.

- Behavioural influence: Debt can significantly affect behaviour, potentially leading to stress or satisfaction, depending on how it is managed. The psychological burden of 'bad' debt can lead to anxiety and a sense of being trapped, while 'good' debt can provide a sense of progress and investment in one's future.

- Decision-making: The chapter underscores the importance of discernment in borrowing practices, suggesting that psychological factors play a crucial role in deciding when and how much to borrow.

The responses from the cocoa farmers in conversation with Vasquez draw a familiar reaction from many of us, especially those who have made use of debt. The only difference is the circumstances – city versus rural farming – but the experiences are no different. Debt has a disciplining effect that pushes people to perform at levels well above the norm. Debt keeps humans on their toes.

Debt has been used by businesses for centuries. The disciplining effect of debt is a phenomenon that has been argued to be one of the key reasons why businesses use debt in their capital structure to fund growth (Jensen & Meckling, 1976). The experience of the cocoa farmers of Colombia demonstrates that what works for firms works for individuals as well.

The story of El Carmen de Chucurí illustrates the disciplining effect of debt, which favours those who put credit to productive use. With debt, the farmers became the owners of their plots and the means of production.

This is not intended to encourage reckless borrowing. In this case, the positive effect of debt on individual productivity has had the ripple effect of boosting regional economic growth.

Market highs and lows are experienced by all businesses. The price of cocoa has for the most part remained below $3.50 per kilogram since the 1980s (Peng, 2024). Cocoa farmers experienced a crash in cocoa prices in 2017 from a high of $3 to $1.20 per kilogram.

West Africa (Ghana and Ivory Coast mostly), which dominates global supply of cocoa, was hit by droughts attributed to climate change (higher temperatures) at the turn of the new millennium. The result has been a decline in cocoa production in West Africa. Ghana and Ivory Coast contributed 70% of world cocoa at the peak of their production, but it was forecasted that they would contribute a much reduced share of 53% by 2024 (Schroth *et al.*, 2016).

The deficit in world production was estimated at 374 000 tonnes in 2024. In 2022, the price of cocoa started to increase steadily. By 2024, the cocoa price had skyrocketed to a high of almost $10. In May 2024, it was just below $8 per kilogram. At the new highs, the price is three times greater than the highest price achieved since the 1980s. In addition to supply issues, financial markets – the intricacies of the futures markets, bets, hedges and the behaviour of markets – are to blame for the increase.

Colombia farmers are set to raise production to benefit from the supply issues caused by climatic conditions in West Africa (Sanchez, 2024). Could this be the moment for these farmers to leverage debt for expansion? Will the soaring prices translate into a windfall for them?

For cocoa farmers, these are indeed exciting times. A prolonged period of persistently low cocoa prices has given way to a new cycle of high prices. Experts predict that these elevated prices will endure, driven by dry season temperatures that impact on water availability – unless cocoa farmers adopt adaptation strategies such as planting shade trees. This pattern of cyclical pricing is reminiscent of the 'Joseph Effect', the phenomenon named after the biblical story of seven years of plenty followed by seven years of drought, which is discussed in depth in Chapter 1.

Fortune, as they say, favours the bold and relentless. If all the farmers in El Carmen de Chucurí continue to work their land in 2024 and beyond, the sustained high cocoa prices could offer them the chance to reduce their debt and significantly increase their net wealth.

'If you do not owe, you do not own.'

PART III

MINDSETS: BREAKING BOUNDARIES AND BARRIERS, AND REDEFINING LIMITS

CHAPTER 6

AGEING GRACEFULLY, LIKE A JACARANDA IN BLOOM

'The jacaranda flames on the air like a ghost
Like a purer sky some door in the sky has revealed.'
– Douglas Stewart

1

Plants, trees and animals tell stories about the lives of humans: stories of love, loss and human endeavour. The jacaranda tree holds a special place in botanical gardens in warm sub-tropical regions such as South America, southern Africa and Australia. Festivals are held in Australia when the jacaranda blooms. In South Africa, the blooming of the jacaranda has given rise to popular folklore.

The jacaranda grows in warm, temperate, sub-humid conditions and is indigenous to two South American countries, Argentina and Brazil. Jacarandas were brought to South Africa from Brazil in 1888 (Henderson, 1990). Two trees were planted at Myrtle Lodge in Sunnyside, Pretoria in 1888.

The jacaranda tree grows fast, reaching a height of between fifteen and twenty-two metres. Its double-compound fern-like leaves measure an average of three hundred millimetres in length. The leaflets, measuring ten millimetres by two millimetres, are shaped almost like a diamond. The tree is mostly deciduous; the leaves turn yellow during winter and begin to fall off the tree, leaving it leafless in spring. The jacaranda produces a profusion of mauvish-blue, tubular flowers, almost thirty millimetres long, arranged in a showy formation of large clusters. The trees have a long lifespan, often exceeding a hundred years.

The jacaranda blooms spontaneously and delightfully, with the flowers appearing earlier than the leaves. In Grafton, a town north of Sydney, Australia, a jacaranda festival is held every year in late October in similar fashion to the *hanami* cherry blossom festival in Japan (Museums of History New South Wales [NSW], 2015).

As stunning as the blooming is, the jacaranda sheds its flowers in equally spectacular fashion. A few weeks after the blooming, the number of fallen petals matches those remaining suspended on the tree. Abscission, the scientific term used to describe the shedding of leaves and flowers as the tree gets rid of organs that are no longer needed, protects the tree from water loss (Srivastava, 2002).

The persistent shedding of leaves and flowers during those few weeks in October can be a source of frustration to homeowners struggling to keep their gardens tidy. However, the niggly day-to-day matter of cleaning the yard is forgotten thanks to the aesthetic delight of the flowers in their customary purple haze (Henderson, 1990; Museums of History New South Wales [NSW], 2015; Srivastava, 2002).

What is it in the botanical life cycle of the jacaranda that draws people to the tree? Does blooming serve as a reminder of the arrival of a milestone?

This chapter is not about botany or landscaping. Instead, I explore the stages of life, from youth to maturity, drawing a parallel to the blooming cycle of the jacaranda tree. I use the inspiration of this exciting tree and its blooming flowers to explore the stories of real people – some famous, others unknown or forgotten – who dared to challenge age stereotypes and achieved spectacular successes.

2

One popular piece of examination folklore in South Africa involves the jacaranda. As students at university during October, we would fondly say, 'The jacarandas are falling!' It was a rallying cry among students, a warning that examinations were around the corner. It was time to finish blooming and produce fruit.

Most people earn a living by going to work or running an enterprise. The skills and wealth they accumulate along the way are like a student going to class and completing homework and assignments in preparation for the examinations.

Every day that passes, the age clock keeps ticking; time, the great equaliser, changes our bodies and mindsets in ways that we may sometimes like, but at other times do not welcome. As we approach the age of fifty, we move into a time commonly referred to as 'midlife', implying that a certain level of maturity, skills and wisdom has been acquired over the years. It is a time of blooming, just as a jacaranda blooms in summer.

On the other hand, midlife is also a time when doubts creep in. Writing for the online newsletter 'Sixty + Me', Penelope Whiteley argues that people tend to take one of two distinctly different approaches when they turn fifty (Whiteley, 2017):

- Some take a positive, confident and proactive approach to ageing, embracing their age with pride, energy and a zest for life.
- Others take a passive, possibly negative outlook towards getting older, characterised by a state of resignation and a lack of enthusiasm.

Whiteley advocates developing a positive attitude, which means carrying yourself with style and confidence. Her advice to dress in a way that makes you feel fabulous underscores the importance of self-presentation and how it can influence your self-esteem as well as the way you are perceived by others.

Writing for *The Guardian*, Jess Cartner-Morley echoed Whiteley's sentiments, even taking them a step further. According to her, dressing well is not about being extravagant or eccentric to the point of discomfort or embarrassment, but rather about finding a style that makes you feel good about yourself and uplifts your spirits (Cartner-Morley, 2022). This, in turn, can positively affect how others perceive you and interact with you: they are likely to celebrate your presence and your vibrant attitude towards life. What this suggests is that views shaped by common age stereotypes must be challenged.

This idea of adopting a vibrant, positive attitude to life and ageing brings us to the story of Ray Kroc and two brothers: Richard ('Dick') and Maurice ('Mac') McDonald.

3

Today, McDonald's is one of the most globally recognised brands. It is known for its clean premises, professional operations and virtually instantaneous production of fast-food meals, using a system that has revolutionised how fast-food restaurants operate. The franchise is found in most countries across the world.

In 1986, *The Economist* created The Big Mac index, which is based on the price of a Big Mac burger in different countries and aims to measure whether currencies are priced at the right level. For example, when *The Economist* published the updated Big Mac index in 2024, it showed that the rand was undervalued when compared to the US dollar. *The Economist* has revealed that it never intended to make the Big Mac index a precise gauge for the alignment of currencies, but instead offered it as a light-hearted tool 'to make exchange-rate theory more digestible' (*The Economist*, 2024). However, the index has found its way into mainstream economics textbooks and the curricula of business schools.

The Big Mac index is a testimony of the power of the McDonald's brand. But without the part played by three remarkable individuals in its early history, McDonald's would not be what it is today.

Raymond Albert Kroc was born in 1902 in Oak Park, Illinois to parents of Czech descent whose principles on raising children prioritised discipline, good manners and good behaviour (Love, 1986; Stewart, n.d.). Kroc, who inherited his father's love of baseball, learnt to play the piano as a child. At school, he discovered a passion for debating and joined the school's debating club.

Kroc's best memories of his schooldays involved his time in the school's debating team, where he excelled. On those occasions when audiences responded to his debating prowess with a standing ovation, he felt free and in his element. However, Kroc did not enjoy school and preferred to earn money doing odd jobs and selling lemonade, all the while scheming how to put his dreams into action.

When the United States entered the First World War in 1917, Kroc had a convenient reason to drop out of school. He lied about his age and enlisted, hoping to join the war and fight for his country. However, the war ended just before he was shipped overseas.

Kroc knew from his debating days that he had two important natural talents: the ability to think quickly and the skill of being able to convince people that his point of view was correct. These are the skills of successful salespeople, and so he looked for a job as a salesman.

Kroc's first sales job was for the Lily Tulip Paper Cup Company, where he spent fifteen years selling paper cups, rising to the position of regional sales manager. However, his ambitions meant that he was never easily satisfied.

Fifteen years selling paper cups did not make Kroc wealthy, but they gave him valuable industry contacts and a strong reputation as a salesman during one of the most difficult periods in American history, the Great Depression (1929–39).

Kroc was approaching the age of forty when an industry contact, Earl Prince, introduced him to a new milkshake multimixer that Prince had invented. Prince offered Kroc the opportunity to become his business partner. The multimixer was a game changer: its five spindles reduced the time needed to make milkshakes while multiplying the number of milkshakes made. As a result, customer waiting time was reduced to a fifth of the original time.

Kroc transformed himself from a paper-cup salesman into a businessman with a stake in the Prince Castle sales company, obtaining exclusive marketing rights for the multimixer. The new device shook up the market and proved to be a hit, with Prince Castle selling up to eight thousand multimixers in a good year.

However, market dynamics in the United States shifted in the years following the Second World War and competition for market share increased as the pace at which business was done grew dramatically. Sales of the multimixer began to drop every year, until the company was in a desperate situation and Kroc was close to financial ruin.

As his multimixer business faltered, Kroc surely faced moments of doubt and discouragement, but giving up was never in his nature. As fate had it, a small restaurant in San Bernardino, California called and placed an order for several multimixers in 1954. Kroc was befuddled: an order for that number of mixers meant that the restaurant was making between thirty-five and forty milkshakes at a time. In all his years as a salesman, he had never come across a restaurant that was so busy. Kroc concluded that there must have been a mistake, which he should immediately check out and have corrected. When he called the restaurant, the proprietor, Dick McDonald, answered the phone and calmly confirmed that the order was correct.

Whenever Kroc smelt money, he could not rest until he had found a way to take a bite of it. He immediately added a visit to the intriguing restaurant to his travel itinerary, travelling from Chicago in the East to San Bernardino on the outskirts of Los Angeles on the West Coast, almost three thousand kilometres. He wanted to see for himself how it was possible for that small restaurant to sell so many milkshakes. This was 1954 and Kroc, now fifty-two years old, was still scheming and dreaming, and making the most of each new opportunity, just as he had at the age of fifteen.

4

Brothers Dick and Mac McDonald had made a pact that they would both be millionaires by the age of fifty. Moving from New Hampshire to Hollywood, they took up employment as stagehands. By the early 1930s, they had earned enough money to open a movie theatre in Monrovia, but business was slow and they were not making a profit. Despite concessions from the landlord, they hardly turned over enough to pay the $100 monthly rental.

Running a business during the Great Depression was tough. However, as is often the case, those who actively engage in trading often encounter new opportunities along the way. We could say that they create their own serendipity. This was the case for the McDonald brothers.

The brothers noticed a hot-dog stand across the street from their cinema that appeared to be one of the few businesses making a profit in the neighbourhood. They closed the movie theatre and acquired a hot-dog stand. It turned out that their market was primarily racetrack patrons, a seasonal cohort that depended on the racing season. In addition, the population in Monrovia was too small to generate sufficient turnover to share among competing businesses in the area.

The brothers moved to San Bernardino, California, which offered much better business prospects since there was a large working population. Instead of a hot-dog stand, they now wanted to open a drive-through restaurant. To pursue their more ambitious project, additional capital was necessary, prompting them to seek loans from various banks. They had to contend with many rejections; one bank after another declined their application, but the Bank of America eventually approved a loan of $5 000 (the equivalent of $115 000 today) and their dream of opening a drive-through restaurant was realised in 1940.

This investment changed the lives of the McDonald brothers. The restaurant was soon making a profit of $50 000 per year ($1.15 million today). The McDonalds suddenly found themselves in the ranks of the San Bernadino wealthy. They paid $90 000 for a mansion – one of the biggest houses in the city, built on top of a hill – which they shared.

Despite their new wealth and status, the brothers remained humble. However, in 1948, with the money still pouring in, they became concerned that complacency would set in. As Dick McDonald recalled, 'We just became bored. The money was coming in, and there wasn't much for us to do' (Love, 1986).

By that time, new operators were imitating their business model and competition was growing: their business was no longer the only drive-through restaurant in town. The McDonalds served a wide range of food and beverages, with a menu comprising hot dogs, hamburgers, lemonade and milkshakes. The clients were teenagers and young men. Attractive young women (known as 'carhops') served the food. This business set-up had worked well during the early years. However, the McDonald brothers were enterprising businessmen who were always reviewing their business model. They realised that the same factors that had contributed to their recent success were now becoming a liability. The business was doing well, but drastic changes were necessary to take it to the next level.

To begin with, flirting and groping were unavoidable in the carhop model. Carhops spent a great deal of their time brushing off the unwanted amorous advances of ill-behaved young men. The brothers wanted a family-friendly business model and speed of service was not negotiable. As Dick recalled, 'Our whole concept was based on speed, lower prices, and volume … we were going after big, big volumes by lowering prices and by having the customer serve himself. My God, the carhops were slow. We'd say to ourselves that there had to be a faster way … our intuition told us that they [customers] would like speed' (Love, 1986: 14).

In the fall of 1948, the McDonalds closed their hugely profitable restaurant for three months while they implemented a complete overhaul of the business.

First they decided to drop the carhops. It was hoped that this would eliminate drinking and smoking on the premises and make the restaurant more appealing to families.

They also reviewed the menu, concluding that the wide range of items offered too many choices, many of which contributed little to the bottom line. Each item was analysed to determine if it should be kept on the menu and the menu was slashed from twenty-five items to nine. This purging left a much simpler and more manageable range of menu items.

One observation that had a far-reaching influence on strategy was the realisation that 80% of the restaurant's business was generated by hamburgers. The fact that the appliances used to make hamburgers were easy to clean and that hamburgers took less time to prepare than other food items pushed them up to the top of the pecking order.

Having concluded that the hamburger was the central theme, the brothers cut the price of a hamburger by half, from a competitive thirty cents to just fifteen cents. This was an unprecedented tactic.

The next innovation was the conversion of the kitchen into an assembly-line-type production. In those days, kitchen equipment was not designed for mass operations, so the McDonald brothers had to design equipment that craftsmen would manufacture specifically for their business.

Within a year of reopening, the restaurant operated like an assembly plant, with the new 'Speedee Service System' in action. The building was an unusual octagonal shape, with windows from roof to counter. In a further departure from tradition, the commercial kitchen followed a 'fishbowl' design, allowing customers to have a full view of the preparation of their orders as they were cooked and packed. It was as if the business was saying, 'We have nothing to hide here; it's all clean.'

It was Dick who designed the golden arches, which remain the signature feature of McDonald's to this day.

The McDonald brothers had wanted to build a fast-food restaurant that appealed to families, and they had achieved this aim: as the first counterman in the revamped store recalled, 'The kids loved coming to the counter … They would come with two bits in their fists and order a hamburger and a coke. They would see Mama in the car, but they also could feel independent. Pretty soon, it sinks that this is great for the business …' (Love, 1986: 16). Kids loved the McDonald's experience and their parents followed. Winding queues during peak periods were the norm.

No other restaurant in the city was as popular. McDonald's became a legend in California. By the mid-1950s, the drive-through restaurant was turning over annual revenue of $350 000 and net profit of $100 000. Dick and Mac McDonald were splitting profits of $100 000 between them every year.

The spectacular success of the McDonalds' restaurant is what brought Ray Kroc the salesman to San Bernardino in July 1954. By then, the McDonalds had bought ten multimixers, along with replacements and spares. Kroc was intrigued: what could a hamburger outlet possibly be doing with ten multimixers? He found out when he visited the restaurant.

5

When Kroc arrived at the restaurant at noon, he found almost 150 customers eagerly queuing and being served. He ordered a hamburger, fries and a drink, and was shocked but impressed when the food appeared almost instantly.

Kroc, who had been given his school nickname – 'the dreamer' – for good reason, could not contain his excitement when he witnessed the long queues of people waiting to be served at the restaurant and the speed with which service was delivered. He immediately saw the massive franchising opportunities that the business offered and wanted in. The meeting between Kroc and the McDonald brothers that followed brought about a spectacular change to the fate of each of the three men as well as that of the McDonald's business.

Although the brothers' previous franchising experience had been a disaster, they accepted Kroc's proposal of a franchising partnership. Because the McDonalds had burnt their fingers before, they forced Kroc, who would sell McDonald's franchises, to sign a strict contract. The price of each franchise was $950. Kroc would receive 1.4% of the profit for each sale, with the McDonald brothers receiving 0.5% of the profit.

If the price of a franchise was set at levels reflecting the value created by the McDonald brothers' unique business model, 1.4% would generate a decent amount of income for Kroc. The brothers' share of 0.5% of the profit of each sale represented a solid passive income stream for them. In addition, they were free to focus on the original restaurant, continuing to split an annual profit of $100 000.

But with only 0.5% at stake, the brothers had little incentive to invest further efforts in the franchising enterprise and they soon became what may be described as fat and content partners. They were doing well in every respect; for instance, they swapped their Cadillacs for newer models annually. In contrast, Kroc, driven by his ambition to grow the franchise business from coast to coast, worked incredibly hard. However, the 1.4% share was not enough to keep him afloat. Although he was selling high volumes of franchises, he was slowly being driven towards bankruptcy.

Kroc's frustration and disgruntlement with the McDonald brothers festered over the years from 1955, when he first started selling McDonald's franchises. He and his wife had drifted apart as he invested more and more time in the business, and in 1961, his marriage broke down. The divorce made Kroc even more bitter. However, despite evidence that his 1.4% share of the franchise profits left Kroc financially distressed, the McDonald brothers stuck to the contract and refused to renegotiate its terms.

Financing whiz Harry J. Sonneborn approached Kroc with a new business model. He pointed out the fact that it was the real estate that made every franchise opportunity operable: every drive-through restaurant operated from a building and a plot of land (more about this later). Even Kroc, with his clever brain, had not grasped this insight or its consequences.

Kroc's attorneys and his new financial advisor helped him find loopholes in his contract with the McDonald brothers. In 1961, the conflict erupted into a corporate fight, which resulted in a hostile takeover of the McDonald's empire. Kroc did not have the cash to buy out the brothers, so with the help of his advisors, he raised enough finance from banks to do so. The brothers negotiated hard, wanting to end up with no less than $1 million each after tax. The final settlement was $1.35 million for each of the brothers. A royalty of 1% of the business profits in perpetuity was promised to the brothers in a handshake agreement that Kroc never honoured.

The relationship between Kroc and the McDonald brothers was punctuated by ruthless business practices and instances of dishonesty. For example, Kroc took the credit for coming up with the concept of the golden arches, which had been designed and built well before he met the brothers. In addition, Kroc named his first franchise 'McDonald's Number 1', even though it was actually the ninth store, and Kroc failed to honour his royalties handshake agreement with the McDonald brothers.

Both parties displayed the formidable streetwise behaviour that they had acquired over the years, illustrating how the real business world operates. The success of many large business empires can be attributed to their assertive marketing strategies and readiness to seize opportunities, even if that means sometimes resorting to unethical practices. This perspective implies that the drive for growth and dominance in the market can lead companies to push the boundaries of ethical behaviour (Hazera, 2017; *The Founder*, directed by John Lee Hancock, 2016). It is a far cry from the case studies taught at business schools, where success is often romanticised.

6

The McDonalds brothers, children of Irish immigrants, had grown up in poverty. Their father was a shoe factory worker who was retrenched during the Great Depression. Having made a pact with each other to be millionaires by the age of fifty, they had founded the McDonald's corporation and invented the efficient 'Speedee' cook-and-serve system that revolutionised the fast-food industry. Their story is testament to their desire to escape a life of mediocrity, which fuelled their journey of endeavour.

The brothers had brought a New England frugality to their business; they did not have the benefit of an inheritance. Biographers have branded them as unambitious because they did not grow their successful enterprise to its full potential. By contrast, biographers usually cite Kroc as a prime example of an ambitious man, highlighting the way in which he made McDonald's into the franchise and the corporation that the world knows today, a business with a global presence and widely recognised branding. However, to say that the two brothers lacked ambition would call for a change in the meaning of the word 'ambition'. These two men, both workaholics, did not have a family background in the food industry, but they innovated and invented a completely new way to prepare and serve food quickly, and at a price no one believed possible.

In his review of the 2016 movie *The Founder*, Alejandro Hazera asks the question, 'Who was the Founder?', and then answers his own question: '… McDonald's today (if it still existed) would be a small franchise of fast-food restaurants in southern California. However, without the "seed" that was planted by the McDonald brothers, especially the efficient cook-and-serve system, Kroc would have remained an over-the-hill milkshake machine salesman' (Hazera, 2017).

Having excelled in debating at school, Kroc had learnt at an early age that he could bring people round to his point of view. He was not one to be comfortable with small achievements, but at fifty-two, he was a struggling milkshake-multimixer salesman. Nonetheless, the thought of slowing down or accepting an undefined fate never crossed his mind.

At fifty, many people start to rationalise, concluding that the distant horizon of their youth has become the present reality, leaving little room to pursue the ambitions they once held as children. The stereotype of ageing people is entrenched; it is in movies, books, television shows, stand-up comedy, social media and so on. But at what age can a person be considered to be old?

Of the people surveyed by employment services firm LiveCareer in 2022, 43% said that they perceive anybody over the age of forty as old. If you happen to be fifty years old, 69% of the people you work with are likely to consider you old (Hyken, 2022). However, Kroc and the McDonald brothers did not subscribe to this belief.

We should not underestimate the skills and wisdom that can only be acquired over many years. There is a significant distinction between acquiring information and gaining wisdom. Through persistent endeavour, Kroc and the McDonald brothers had accumulated substantial business knowledge by the time they reached their fifties. Put in today's context, this view emphasises the belief that true understanding and the ability to apply knowledge in meaningful ways go beyond what can be learnt through quick searches or online videos.

Kroc continued to look for opportunities and knock on doors, even when some were slammed shut in his face and others only opened halfway. He travelled across the United States selling franchises. Through his persistence, he discovered what has become McDonald's fundamental business model: real estate. You sell the franchise, become the landlord to the new franchisee and collect rent regularly – a steady income, much like an annuity. The McDonald's Corporation has perfected this strategy, which is simple if it occurs to you. (Kroc only became aware of this idea when Harry J. Sonneborn approached him.)

The McDonald brothers were in a similar age group to Kroc when they first met him in 1954. The three men had something else in common: they had all experienced the difficult economic conditions imposed by the Great Depression and had built up strong CVs operating businesses over a long period. Their business experience was peaking; it was an asset that they were ready to exploit. All of them ended up becoming millionaires, starting with the McDonald brothers when Kroc bought them out of the partnership in 1961. Kroc became a legendary billionaire in the decades that followed, a fact that sometimes obscures the many years of hard work that he endured to achieve his success.

There is one other thing that puts all three men in the same category: they all did well. Ray Kroc, along with Dick and Mac McDonald, exemplified the fact that at fifty, a person's skills, experience, and wisdom are at their peak, and it is these qualities – not a fixation on age – that should shape attitudes at this stage of life. This is the point of this chapter. Skills are honed on the job over the years and through study. When the jacaranda flowers start to fall – when people reach midlife – some of the blooming flowers remain on the tree to produce fruit, while others fall to the ground and are wasted.

This begs the question: Why retire and let all that knowledge and wisdom go to waste? The average age of the 38 700 CEOs employed in the United States in 2022 was fifty-two (Hyken, 2022). The average age of CEOs on the Fortune 500 list is fifty-seven, and several CEOs on the list are between the ages of seventy-one and ninety-one (Hyken, 2022). Nelson Mandela became president of South Africa at the age of seventy-five after spending twenty-seven years in prison. Joe Biden and Donald Trump were seventy-eight and seventy years old respectively when they became President of the United States, and each of them campaigned hard to win a second term in the 2024 elections.

American venture capitalist and investor Alan Patricof is co-founder and chairperson of Primetime Partners. He is a successful businessman, but what draws my attention most strongly to him is Patricof's attitude towards fitness and life. At the age of eighty-eight, he was the oldest entrant in the 2022 New York City Marathon, one of 47 839 participants. He completed the marathon in eight hours and fifty minutes, raising over half a million dollars for the Alzheimer's charity, CaringKind. As Patricof says, 'Why do people climb mountains? Because they're there and they're challenging …' (CaringKind, 2022). It is a state of mind born out of desire and will.

7

Louis* drove a company car, lived in a company bungalow and enjoyed free membership at the company golf course. He was on the head office payroll (reserved for the most senior mine staff), with details of his remuneration kept secret from the prying eyes of the local payroll office staffers, who were notorious for indiscreetly leaking salary information. He wore suits when most mine staff came to work in shorts. He carried himself well, and over

---

* Not his real name.

the years, many younger people had turned to him for career inspiration and mentorship.

Shabanie Mashaba Mines, based in the hot and arid Lowveld region in the south of Zimbabwe, was the world's sixth largest producer of asbestos before the use of asbestos fibre was banned worldwide. A subsidiary of the British-headquartered multinational Turner & Newall, it was an extraordinary mine where over fifteen thousand people worked. Some of these were directly employed by the mine, while others were employed by contractors hired to provide services to the mine. The town of Shabanie was built around the mine; in many senses, the mine *was* the town. The population in the province depended on the mine.

My first job was at the asbestos mine. Reporting to the Group Internal Auditor, I was assigned to the large mine stores division, where Louis, the chief storekeeper, was instructed to take me under his wing and mentor me for three months.

Louis had worked in the mine his whole career, rising to the senior management position of chief storekeeper over a period of forty years (the titles for mine workers are unique to the industry). He was meant to have retired almost five years before, but as a result of his long service and exemplary track record, his contract had been extended. Management was aware of Louis's predicament: he was not prepared for his retirement.

Living in a mine – as I experienced for myself – was an incredible experience. To attract and retain employees of a high calibre, the mine offered free housing, which it maintained at no cost to its staff. Staff also did not have to pay membership fees to belong to the five-star mine club or the golf club. They had access to top amenities such as a private hospital and excellent medical doctors as well as good private schools with top-quality teachers. Senior staff could use the holiday homes owned by the mine; all they needed to do was make a booking in advance. Thus, employees were given every incentive to remain employed by the mine and so maintain their pleasant lifestyle.

As for young single people joining the mine, the experience was outstanding. I was allocated apartment number 12 at the Men's Residence complex. It was a well-appointed, fully furnished apartment on the first floor with views across the mine. The bed was already made up with linen when I arrived with a suitcase full of clothes and a Sony shelf stereo. The mine provided everything else.

Men's Residence was serviced by a cafeteria, manned by chefs and waiters, that offered three-course meals seven days a week, and a dedicated laundry staff who took care of our laundry needs. These facilities were provided by the mine at a very small, inclusive rental pegged at a level just below the taxable threshold in arrangements agreed with the Revenue Service. Mine employees really were given the royal treatment.

Asbestos prices were high and the quality of the chrysolite asbestos fibre, a variety considered safer than others at the time, was excellent; the mine was productive, cost-efficient and well run. A consistent annual output of 140 000 tonnes per year was enough to make the mine the sixth largest asbestos producer in the world. The mine did the best it could to attract and retain staff, and its profitability meant that the comforts it offered were affordable. The trade-off was achieved through lower disposable salaries for staff. The model worked well for the mine, and the prestige attached to being a staff member of the mine was immense.

Many of the people working in the mine behaved like spoiled children, but it was great while it lasted. Louis was one of those staff who enjoyed this artificial lifestyle. For him, life was blissful. As a senior employee, he stayed in one of the mine suburbs reserved for employees at his grade: Chinda [Asbestos] Heights, on the top of the kopje, was where the mine executives lived. There, Louis lived with his family in a large four-bedroomed bungalow on a one-acre plot, which was fully maintained by the mine and included a garden service.

However, time ran out fast for Louis, as it did for many others employed by the mine. By the time he turned sixty-five, the mine's retirement age, he had not yet become a houseowner. If he had to move out of the mine accommodation upon his retirement (which was inevitable), there would be nowhere he could accommodate his family without having to pay rental costs for the first time in his working life.

The mine owned a large ten-tonne Nissan UD truck dedicated to transporting the personal belongings of employees when they retired and had to vacate their mine houses. One of the truck drivers told me several stories of his experiences during such assignments, when he had to drive departing staff to their new homes.

During one of these removal outings, the driver had to relocate Elijah, a retired senior employee, formerly a respected mine shift boss. Elijah had joined the mine after school as an apprentice miner. This was one of the most respected apprenticeship programmes run by the mine; such apprenticeship positions were greatly sought after in the country.

Once Elijah, a bright, diligent miner, had completed the apprenticeship, management took note of his abilities and groomed him for promotion. He rose through the ranks and was assigned a mine house in which he lived for decades.

On the day of the move, Elijah asked the driver to stop and offload his cargo after travelling almost three hundred kilometres towards what seemed like a wilderness, with only the occasional small, scattered village apparent. There was no house in sight, so, showing his disbelief, the driver asked if this was a mistake or if they were lost. Elijah simply told him not to worry and said that he would be all right. 'Just leave me here,' he added.

The cargo was offloaded, and the bewildered driver – with a deep sense of foreboding – returned to the mines to relate his experiences to his supervisors. The tale soon became a popular topic of gossip in the mining community.

Louis now dreaded the possibility of facing a similar fate, as his extended contract was close to its end.

I was a very young man, joining the mine shortly after completing my honours degree at university. Louis, an elderly man past his retirement age, viewed me as a threat. At my age, I was oblivious to the dynamics at play. Soon, however, I began to pick up the vibes from the grapevine. (Like most small towns that thrive on gossip, the gossip in mining communities is legendary. Word travelled faster than on today's social media and the entertainment value of gossip weighed more than the need to fact-check the information.)

The news that the grapevine picked up was that Louis had been involved with con men who had offered him fake emeralds. The story sounded credible because of the proximity of the Sandawana Mines, which were only eighty kilometres away. The hype about the emeralds mined here created what seemed to Louis like a chance to make a quick buck. However, nothing was further from the truth.

Desperate to make money, Louis fell for the con story and lost most of his pension. He was left with a jam jar full of broken green glass cut into small pieces in shapes resembling emeralds.

Keen to recoup his losses, Louis kept the jam jar with the worthless glass pieces, somehow managing to seal it. He approached me one morning, telling me that he had been introduced to an employee at the Sandawana Mines who, with help from security contacts at the processing plant, had succeeded in walking out with a jar full of the precious stones. Having no idea where or how to sell the emeralds, the employee hoped that Louis, a man of stature in the mining community who had good contacts, would be able to sell the emeralds to one of the big dealers. The man had concluded his pitch with the words, 'And that is where you come in, sir.'

Louis must have felt flattered. That is how scammers work. As the grapevine later found out, he had offered the thieving employee, whom he had seen as a white knight at his time of need, a large sum of money for the stones, hoping to make a killing when he offloaded them to the dealers at a higher price. However, Louis had lost everything in the deal and now wanted to recoup his losses. He hoped to tap into any inkling of greed in my soul, and expected that I would offer to buy the stones from him.

To be honest, the thought did occur to me, but a whole jar of precious stones seemed too good to be true. I quickly asked Louis to give me a day to get in touch with some unspecified important people. Some of my friends at the mine, who were geologists, helped out by showing me a quick test that I could use to determine if the stones were in fact emeralds.

The next day, I met Louis after work and used the scratch test my friends had shown me to test the emeralds. I had an immediate answer: the 'emeralds' were worthless pieces of glass.

This experience with Louis shocked me to the core. I found it worrying that a grown man of his age could humiliate himself by falling prey to such a scam. But Louis was desperate. An elder, more senior man at the mine stores complex took me into his confidence when I shared my experience with him and alerted me to the dynamics at play.

There was a lesson to be learnt from Louis's situation. The artificial life of an employee at Shabanie Mashaba Mines lured people into a false sense of security. While the mine offered many perks, the cost of providing these perks was offset by the low disposable salaries paid to mine workers. The salaries were much lower when compared with corporate city employees. That is how the mines looked after the bottom line. There is no free lunch.

Employees enjoyed the prestige of working in the mine and excellent job security, but with the low disposable income that they received, they found it almost impossible to put aside enough for their retirement or to invest money to create wealth. The years passed, but still these employees did not own homes of their own. They also had no material investments in their names except for pitifully small retirement funds (a contribution calculated on a small salary cannot miraculously build substantial wealth). Unfortunately, complacency crept in as the years went by, and most employees never gave a moment's thought to what would happen when they had to retire and leave the mine.

Believing that the situation was tantamount to modern-day slavery, I made the decision that once I had acquired the necessary training in this large, complex mining company, which would be valuable on my CV, I would leave. I did not want to be sucked into a sense of artificial comfort. And so, after two years, I left for the big city, where I competed with other young people of my age in a fast-paced environment. I accepted that Shabanie Mashaba Mines had to mind its bottom line and that its modest pay scales guaranteed its primary objective; however, I decided that I also needed to take care of my own business.

This cautionary experience convinced me that there must be steps a person can take to avoid ending up in a situation such as the one in which Louis found himself, and to ensure a secure and fulfilling retirement.

8

Squirrels are found in all habitable continents except for Australia. There are 287 species of squirrels (*National Geographic*, 2017). They fall into two main categories: tree squirrels, which make nests in trees, and ground squirrels, which dig tunnels and burrows underground. All species are known as industrious animals and people view them as mischievous, perhaps because of their mannerisms, beady eyes and abrupt behaviour. In urban areas, they are found in parks and sometimes stray into gardens.

Squirrels are not only focused on eating, but also demonstrate impressive cognitive and social skills. They prepare for the cold winter, when they hibernate. Most people have known that fact since high school. However, it was always assumed that squirrels – as animals – were driven by mere instinct. The caching of food, nuts and the like was deemed a random act of foraging.

Mikel Delgado and Lucia Jacobs of the Department of Psychology at the University of California, Berkeley were not content with long-established consensus scientific views. They wanted to investigate the complexity of the behaviour of squirrels. Delgado and Jacobs did not have to travel far for their study: fox squirrels are part of the mammal population at the University of California campus.

Hoarding of food is a common practice among animals. Larder hoarders keep their food stash in one spot and guard it. Scatter hoarders stash food in different locations. Squirrels are scatter hoarders. As Delgado and Jacobs conclude, 'Scatter-hoarding animals face the formidable challenge of creating diverse, ephemeral cache distributions whose location they can remember accurately enough to retrieve later. It has been well established that scatter-hoarding animals can remember the locations of caches they make, but they must also remember the contents of a cache' (Delgado & Jacobs, 2017). Scatter hoarding is a fascinating strategy because it involves distributing resources across multiple locations rather than concentrating them in one place. This approach ensures that even if some of the caches are lost or stolen, others will remain accessible, providing a reliable food supply during tough times.

Squirrels are sophisticated creatures. They solve complicated problems. The behaviour captured here provides a useful analogy for capital accumulation, preservation and the don't-put-all-your-eggs-in-one-basket approach. Admirably, squirrels solve the question 'Do I eat this nut now, or do I store it for later?' (Delgado & Jacobs, 2017).

A person's fifties are not the time to reflect on years gone by. Instead, what is required is rapid action to take advantage of the increased earning capacity that comes with valuable skills accumulated over the years. A plan of action for wealth creation should start as soon as individuals are old enough to earn an income. For some, this could be as early as their teens, but for most, it happens in their twenties. It is much easier to build wealth from an early age, but Kroc demonstrated that persistence and determination sometimes result in success later on in life.

9

Unfazed by the passage of time, the jacaranda tree continues to bloom year after year. Through the natural process of abscission, it faithfully sheds its flowers and leaves with each changing season. In its quiet persistence, the jacaranda holds stories of people – some joyful and memorable, others haunting and sad.

For many, midlife is a time when it feels like the jacaranda flowers are beginning to fall. Depending on an individual's personal journey over the decades, their fifties could turn out to be a great life stage. If they have been in formal employment, it is likely that their remuneration has grown steadily over the years. Compounding has a positive effect on a person's salary as well as on their investment income. Their mortgage balance is likely to be close to nil, and their children have probably almost finished university or college. In this scenario, everything has worked out according to plan: the person understands that once they turn fifty, the jacaranda flowers will surely fall. What was once the next milestone on a distant horizon is now reality.

In this scenario, if the person has successfully navigated their way through the obstacles of life over the years, emerging with a sufficient accumulation of wealth, they have earned the right to be defiant and look forward to retirement. It is similar to the feeling of having survived a relegation battle in the Premier League or having won promotion to the top-tier league.

The fifties often arrive very quickly. It is a time when skills and wisdom are reaching their peak. It is never too late to put together a rescue plan;

better late than never. You can increase your earning potential by building a skill set that is sought after by industry and others, developing side hustles, putting aside a much higher proportion of your earnings and building capital, and investing through mutual funds and other asset classes such as real estate. It is also important to protect whatever capital you earn. Avoid desperate strategies such as pyramid schemes and scams that promise unusually high returns; what seems too good to be true most often results in serious loss.

Certified financial planners and financial advisors serve an important role in building wealth. However, I assign financial advisors and planners to the category of a defensive strategy. Planners and advisors can only work with the capital that a client brings to the table. The responsibility for generating income and improving income streams cannot be delegated. Generating income is the personal business of the client; in the words of the great investor Benjamin Graham (2006), it is the client's 'bailiwick'. A complete strategy should comprise both defensive and aggressive strategies.

In my opinion, a comprehensive strategy should look something like this:

- Create a financial plan (or update your old one).
- Develop additional income sources.
- Downsize your housing.
- Keep your children's university or college expenses in check.
- Live below your means.
- Manage debt wisely.
- Be smart with your retirement savings.
- Make the right decisions about insurance.
- Invest with an eye on risk versus reward.
- Monitor your progress and adjust as you go.

The crucial factor in this comprehensive strategy is prioritising the second point: developing additional income sources. This is where the strategy gains its momentum, as new income streams can be actively created.

For those in employment, the first action is to create a case to support your request for a raise; charity begins at home. You do not want to leave money on the table. If you have built your skills over the years as expected of a fifty-year-old, your employer should have taken note and may readily consider a pay rise.

Another viable avenue is real estate. Real estate provides various leveraging options, including the following possibilities:

- buying fixer-upper properties, renovating them and selling them for a profit (flipping)
- buying rental properties that offer net positive cash flow immediately (contrary to popular belief, such properties are available for those who search doggedly for them, including at auctions and bank repossessions)
- adding a rental garden flat to your home
- adding a garden flat to your rental property to increase its rental yield.

Chapter 5 deals with leveraging in greater detail.

Freehold properties provide better opportunities to increase rental income, as the owner is permitted to add garden flats if building plans are submitted to the municipality. I used this approach when my children were young. When my daughter was chosen for the primary school swimming team, the family preyed on me and my wife, begging us to swap our home for a bigger one with a swimming pool. I made a compromise and agreed on condition that the new home came with outbuildings that had potential for a garden cottage conversion. I converted the outbuildings into two flats, which had separate entrance access from the service lane behind the house, and installed a wooden fence to provide privacy for my family and tenants. The set-up attracted good tenants and enjoyed an occupancy rate of 100% over the years. The rental from my tenants was enough to cover rates, water and electricity, garden services and maintenance costs, with a small surplus left over. The new home proved comfortable for the family, and my daughter was able to train whenever she wanted to. All this was possible without draining my pocket; in fact, I was better off financially after moving house.

Most of my rental properties are freehold, bought by means of a 100% bond. Once I added garden flats to these rental properties, they generated significantly more positive cash flow.

Other options for generating income fall into the category of side hustles, for example, digital and online businesses, and consulting or part-time work after hours (lecturing, private tutoring and so on). The examples given here demand a better use of personal time (weekends, after hours), which is available in abundance to all. There is not much glamour involved and it can be boring, hard work, but this approach, like building a wall brick by brick, is quite effective.

Just as a serious student does not wait for the last day before the examinations start to pick up a book and begin studying, the build-up to midlife should begin from the time a person finishes high school, college or university and starts working. It is important to take care of your financial affairs, acknowledging that the jacaranda blossoms will fall in due course and accumulating a stash, like the scatter-hoarding squirrel.

Should we retire simply because we have reached the age limit set by our employers? And as for style, should we start dressing more casually or should we maintain a professional appearance? Should we allow all the knowledge and wisdom we have gained over the years to go to waste or should we make it available for the benefit of others at a fee? The lives of Ray Kroc, Dick McDonald and Mac McDonald suggest that long-held stereotypes of age and the default retirement mentality must be challenged.

CHAPTER 7

TIMELESS SUCCESS SECRETS:
Inspired by the wild

'I live in heaven – why would you leave heaven?
I'm literally born again by being up here.'
– David Glasheen in Kelsey-Sugg

1

After more than five years with my seventh employer, I realised I had finally found the right fit. Unlike my previous roles – each lasting around three years by choice, as I sought to build a diverse skill set across various industries – this time it felt different. There was a sense of belonging that I had not experienced before, a sign that I had finally landed where I was meant to be.

Shortly after joining the organisation, I was assigned to lead a team tasked with completing an important project. For many years, the auditors had signed off on the annual financial statements with a qualified opinion. Despite the efforts of those who had preceded me, there had been no significant improvement to shift the opinion of the auditors. However, when I set up the full property, plant and equipment accounting records in compliance with the latest accounting standards, the auditors lifted their sanction and the qualification disappeared for the first time.

With a replacement value of tens of billions, property, plant and equipment was the single largest item on the balance sheet. The audit qualification was a serious matter and had become an albatross around the company's neck. I basked in the glory of the achievement. But my boss retired, and a new one with different ideas and methods took over. Whatever had made me a local hero before was out of the window now. You are only as good as your last game, and the new man had not watched it. I had to earn his trust afresh.

I had dealt with new bosses for many years and had always found a way to adapt. Now, however, I had to work under a person who made everything about him. (Such people are commonly referred to as 'egocentric'.) The dynamic in the whole team changed. In search of much-needed comic relief, my colleagues and I found a name that we used privately for our boss without his knowledge. We nicknamed him 'Mr Burns', after the sadistic hunchbacked cartoon boss character Charles Montgomery Burns in the animated television series *The Simpsons*.

I thought of quitting more than once. Could this be like the notorious wall that marathon runners come up against about thirty-two kilometres into a race, when their energy levels suddenly drop as the finishing line gets close? Sports scientist Tim Noakes attributes the wall to the 'central governor', in reference to the role played by one of the mechanisms deep in the brain (Noakes, 2007). The central governor controls the performance of different parts of the body through the nervous system. Sports trainers drill athletes and encourage them to find a distraction when that feeling starts to kick in. It's in the mind, athletes are told.

I would open my laptop early on Monday morning and watch as the emails downloading on MS Outlook filled the screen. I found myself repeatedly scrolling through the inbox, my eyes trained to seek out the urgent emails that always came from my boss. In our division, the unspoken rule was clear: the boss's emails took priority. This hierarchy was more pronounced here than anywhere else I had worked. My boss had a habit of sending many emails late on a Sunday night. It sometimes felt as if he was trying to set an example of what it meant to be hard-working, but the effect was to make me and my colleagues feel inadequate. We hypothesised jokingly that 'Mr Burns' wrote his emails during the week, deliberately accumulating them in draft mode, only to hit the send button late on a Sunday. The effect was to make every Monday a blue Monday.

I find that happy moments always help me to regain perspective at times such as this. Every morning when my daughter greeted me happily, ready to be dropped off at school, my misgivings about my work situation quickly dissolved. Reminded of my parental responsibilities, I made sure to arrive at work early. It was a conundrum.

I decided to try out the athletes' tactic and find a distraction. At that time, I usually went to gym three times a week, but my interest in gym had somehow waned. I found out about hiking, tried it and got hooked. Every weekend I walked the hiking trails in the nature reserves close to Johannesburg – Kliprivier, Suikerbosrand's Bokmakierie, Muldersdrift's Cradle Moon and many others – and the bush healed me. But Monday would always come again, far too quickly.

By Tuesday, I could not wait for my weekend hike and the peace of the bush. At some point, a defiant attitude came over me. I felt that I wanted to outlast 'Mr Burns'. I worked hard, raising my performance levels higher. I became the first person to meet every deadline and pretended to be fired up every day. If anyone greeted me in the corridors, my response was an enthusiastic, 'Ag man! I'm good, all good!'

I never once missed my weekend hike. However, as time passed, I began adding weights to my rucksack, transforming my weekly activity from hiking to rucking. After two years, packed full of sand, stones and dumbbells, my rucksack weighed twenty-seven kilograms, and the hike became a workout. I thought to myself that something good had happened because of 'Mr Burns'.

2

While relaxing in the late afternoon on Saturdays, I discovered the BBC Earth channel on the DStv satellite service for which I paid a monthly subscription. On the reality TV channel, I watched programmes featuring people who had become fed up with the nine-to-five daily grind and sought a new life. I wanted to understand them better.

Ben Fogle is an Englishman who made his name in the reality TV series *Castaway 2000*. He has climbed Mount Everest, rowed across the Atlantic and engaged in many feats that most people consider extreme and dangerous. Fogle is the United Nations Patron of the Wilderness, a fellow of the Royal Geographic Society, an ambassador for the World Wildlife Fund and an ambassador of the British Red Cross (Pitts, 2020).

Fogle has a genuine interest in languages. In his chosen career, languages are an important way of breaking down communication barriers and establishing quick connections with strangers.

A passionate adventurer, Fogle went on to anchor a documentary series called *Ben Fogle: New Lives in the Wild* on BBC's Channel 5. The show is also aired on BBC Earth, where it goes by the title *Where The Wild Men Are With Ben Fogle*. South African viewers can enjoy it on DStv, MultiChoice's satellite service.

Fogle is a city guy who loves to connect with others. He visits people living alone or with only their immediate family in some of the most remote and desolate off-the-beaten-track places, spending a week with them. His hosts are people who have willingly decided to forsake luxuries and the modern world's lifestyle to live off the grid.

Always displaying a strong interest in and connection with his hosts, Fogle sets out to explore their lives, bringing out the best in them for the benefit of viewers of the television show. During the week that Fogle spends with them, he is followed by TV crews with cameras as he participates in the day-to-day tasks and chores of his hosts, experiencing first-hand the hardships, challenges and fun of their lives.

The idea of leaving a dead-end job, abandoning civilization and retreating into the wilderness is a common fantasy among employees. Most reality TV viewers live in conventional neighbourhoods with little access to remote areas, so the idea is enticing, but the reality of such a lifestyle is usually difficult, monotonous and lonely (Dowling, 2013). In addition, the rewards depend on the vagaries of nature and the individual's own resourcefulness. However, it is this intriguing dream of an off-the-grid existence that attracts people to Fogle's television series.

The two episodes featured here have been selected for the lasting impression that they made on me, although there have been many other touching episodes.

3

The first of these episodes features Dave Glasheen, aged sixty-nine at the time the episode was filmed, which was in 2013. Glasheen, who was Fogle's first subject for the *New Lives in the Wild* TV series, lives on Restoration Island off the remote Cape York peninsula in North Australia. He came to Restoration Island after a friend told him about it, and he has never left (Kelsey-Sugg, 2019).

Glasheen spent most of his early years running a multimillion-dollar mining company. He lived the high life in Sydney, but spectacularly lost the family fortune, £6.7 million, during the 1987 October stock market crash. Soon after, his marriage broke down. He used most of the little that remained after his home was repossessed to acquire a long lease on the hundred-acre volcanic island.

The humiliating experience of losing a fortune would cause many to change their view of modern civilisation. Glasheen concedes that when his marriage broke down, happening as it did soon after he had lost his fortune, he was emotionally battered. Moving to Restoration Island saved him.

At first, Glasheen lived on the island with his girlfriend and their child. However, the loneliness of life with no one else around them must eventually have become unbearable because they left the island, leaving him alone. When Fogle visited Glasheen, he and his dog were the only inhabitants on this section of the island.

Glasheen's state pension cannot provide for all his needs. Certainly, he has nowhere near enough cash to buy the comforts he was used to as a Sydney businessman. To survive, he must fish every day. Oysters and fish dominate his diet. He also has to tend his garden and ensure that he builds up stocks of food for a rainy day. To satisfy his natural human tendency to seek luxuries, Glasheen brews his own beer for refreshment. He has no television or geyser to supply hot water, although he has a solar-powered computer that he uses to do online banking and to access YouTube when he needs DIY help.

Being the master of his own destiny brings Glasheen tremendous satisfaction, and on the surface, his life seems idyllic. However, when his boat leaks and poisonous spiders are a constant menace, with hospitals far away, the daily threats of this type of existence become apparent.

Ten years after Fogle's visit, a journalist from the *Sun* newspaper followed up on Glasheen. Now almost eighty, he admitted that life on his own in this remote spot was now becoming harder. 'I fainted one day and then fell and broke my hip,' he said. 'The phones don't work when you need them half the time, so the best security I could get is more people' (Connor, 2022). But Glasheen can hardly afford to hire hands to help him with the strenuous chores and keep him company. Despite these concerns, though, he has no intention of heading back to the mainland (Kelsey-Sugg, 2019).

4

In 2015, Fogle's subject was a fellow countryman from Wales in southwest Great Britain: Emma Orbach, who has given up her conventional life with family to settle in the Welsh wilderness in Pembrokeshire at the base of the Preseli Mountains.

Now sixty-eight, Orbach had a privileged background. She attended some of the most expensive British boarding schools and studied Chinese at Oxford, graduating with a bachelor's degree. She seemed set to make it in a modern world. Since 2000, however, she has lived in a hut made of mud and straw, cemented by copious quantities of horse manure (O'Grady, 2015).

Fogle spent a week with Orbach in 2015 when she was sixty. As is always the case, Fogle, a likeable fellow, made himself at home with his host, joining her in building a Celtic-style mud hut and kneading horse manure into straw (O'Grady, 2015).

What caused Orbach to turn her back on conventional life? This non-materialistic woman had simply felt a strong urge to say goodbye to the rat race. Away from the convenience of everyday appliances such as microwaves and electric kettles, she lives an extremely off-grid lifestyle. She owns her land (175 acres). She does not have electric lights, ovens or heaters; instead, she has a fireplace. She draws fresh water from a stream, grows her own vegetables, owns seven chickens, keeps three goats for milk and uses two horses for transportation. The hut cost her less than £1 000 to build. There are no computers in her life; she communicates through handwritten letters delivered by the postal system.

Fogle revisited Orbach in 2021, six years later. She has remained happily entrenched in the woodlands of Pembrokeshire, with no intention whatsoever of returning to city life (Williams, 2021, 2023).

5

In both of these episodes of *New Lives in the Wild*, Fogle's subjects, disillusioned, rebelled against the way humans live in the twenty-first century, with unsatisfying jobs, overwhelming debt and the commute to work making life a living hell for many. Glasheen and Orbach decided to opt out of the rat race and sacrifice convenience in order to start a new life in the wild. They are modern-day Robinson Crusoes.

In both instances, several years since Fogle first visited them, they are still convinced that the decision to embark on a new life in the wild was the best choice they have ever made. They have no intention of returning to conventional life in the city. To them, being able to take charge of their own destinies is adequate reward for their choice.

I would not judge the reasons for their actions; lifestyle is a personal choice. For most of us, though, their lives are extraordinary and the stuff of fantasy. I am struck by their tremendous courage in pursuing such a choice.

Their choices were voluntary responses to the strong urge to try another way of life that might deliver a better alternative to the fast-paced, cut-throat urban lifestyle they rejected. However, there are times when such a decision is motivated by the force of circumstances and desperation leaves no other option. The next personal experience shared here falls into the latter category.

6

Patricia took the early morning bus, which joined a long queue of vehicles in a convoy protected by members of the Rhodesian Security Forces, armed to the teeth. She chose a wide two-seater bench and made herself comfortable for what she knew would be a long journey of four hundred kilometres. A studious girl, wearing spectacles that made her look smart and alert, Patricia quickly opened her handbag to pull out a book to keep herself occupied. Too serious to read a Mills & Boon, Patricia preferred something of more substance. She had two books to choose from: the American classic *To Kill a Mockingbird,* by Harper Lee, and the English classic *Great Expectations*, by Charles Dickens.

My literary tastes were similar to Patricia's, since I was also a voracious reader, but the difference was that I could sneak in titles by Agatha Christie or Wilbur Smith in pretty good measure. But we got along very well, as we had much in common, and I was excited that Patricia would be visiting us during the summer school holidays. She and I were first cousins and the same age. Both of us were in boarding schools; during the school term, we communicated by means of letters.

This was the mid-seventies. There was no WhatsApp, Blackberry service, email, internet, Facebook, Instagram or cell phones, and it was considered a privilege to have a telephone at home. Most of us were not that lucky, but the post office was one of the most reliable, efficient organisations, so communication by letter worked just fine. Looking back, however, I cannot believe that we managed to stay in touch through letters; somehow, we did.

Most of my memories of the 1970s are painful, and I have tried my best to push them to the back of my mind. I adored my father, who was ahead of his time; he was a pioneer at one of the first high schools in the country, then called 'Southern Rhodesia'. Dad trained as a teacher and his career was nothing short of phenomenal; he rose to become the manager and inspector of all primary schools in the entire province. At the height of his career, his name was synonymous with success, and he was respected by those with whom he dealt professionally. However, in 1972, having turned fifty a couple of years earlier, Dad lost his job. He later learnt from well-wishers that an ambitious acquaintance, jealous of his success, had reported him to the authorities, falsely claiming that he was aiding the terrorists during the Rhodesian Bush War.

In addition to being fired, Dad was blacklisted; he would never again be permitted to hold a position in any capacity whatsoever in any government department. He had fallen from grace and immediately became an outcast.

Looking after his large family (we were seven children) had been a daunting task even before losing his job. What saved the day was that, during his early working years, Dad built a shop in a settlement in the Lowveld, close to the neighborhood where he had grown up. Without this shop, the situation would have been a great deal more dire. The tenant occupying the shop was immediately served with a notice terminating the lease.

We never quite understood just how Dad managed to negotiate credit lines with wholesalers and other suppliers in the provincial town, then Fort Victoria, and stock the shop at short notice, but I was to learn much later that despite his blacklisting, the reputation he had built over the years stood him in good stead.

According to Warren Buffet (Schwantes, 2021), achieving extraordinary results does not require doing extraordinary things. It also takes many years to build a reputation, but only minutes to ruin it. Keeping that in mind can change how you choose to act.

With a family of seven children, all attending school, my parents' financial circumstances became desperate. Mother was a trained teacher, but her salary was never going to be sufficient. It was time for Dad to be resourceful and find other ways to retain his status as respected head of the family.

The BMW sedan that my father considered a marker of his middle-income status was repossessed after he lost his job, as he could no longer keep up with the hire purchase instalments. What was so special about this BMW Cheetah that my father had found it irresistible even when, in hindsight, the car may have been beyond his means? It was not, in fact, entirely a BMW; it was an 1800/2000 SA series in the BMW model portfolio. Its appearance was strange, as it did not resemble any other vehicle in the German manufacturer's stable, as Adriaan Dorofte observed in his musings in a BMW blog in 2020 (Dorofte, 2020). The Glas 1700 was not a model of choice in BMW's portfolio because of its Italian look. However, it was given a new lease on life in Africa from 1967, when the company began assembling it in South Africa and neighbouring Rhodesia (now Zimbabwe). The BMW 1800 SA, named the BMW Cheetah in Rhodesia, was the grand BMW Cheetah that my father, who loved cars, bought.

As children, we naively believed that the BMW Cheetah had been bought outright. We were proud of the sleek, stunning car, a symbol of success. Aimed at the upper middle class, the BMW Cheetah came with a hefty price tag. What we did not know was that Dad had financed it through a substantial loan. We only discovered this after he lost his job and the bank repossessed the car.

In hindsight, it is no surprise that a man supporting seven children as well as his extended family had to rely on a loan to afford such a luxury. The car's repossession was the first real humiliation we experienced as a family, but looking back, I realise how much harder it must have been for Dad.

This was my first lesson about the folly of debt: some debt is necessary, but most debt should be avoided. A good, basic, functional car would have been much more affordable.

The BMW sedan had been the only vehicle our family ever owned, but with it gone, we were left relying on buses or bicycles to get around. Deliveries for the shop became more complicated. If the wholesalers did not have a scheduled drop-off on our route, we had to hire trucks. On several occasions, my father resorted to donkey- or mule-drawn carts to transport supplies, as these were the only vehicles that could safely traverse mined roads. As the bush war escalated, dirt roads became treacherous, with no way to tell where landmines had been buried. Originally designed to target the Rhodesian Security Forces' military trucks, the landmines posed an indiscriminate threat to any vehicle unlucky enough to cross them – collateral damage in the harshest sense.

I experienced the brutality of the war and witnessed graphic incidents whose telling would demand a separate book. However, some incidents that wormed their way into my brain still occasionally replay themselves in my mind.

Our school bus went up in flames one day when it detonated a landmine. A school worker travelling on the bus died on the spot, while my classmate, Saru, who was sitting next to the driver, lost both her legs, becoming wheelchair-bound for life.

Saru was a beautiful girl, with long legs, built like a model. She was talented and athletic, and being a fine netballer and captain of the school netball team, it was expected that she would be selected to play for the national netball team one day. When she led her team in competitive interschool games, the school community and parents flocked to watch. Saru did her thing from centre position, making the most incredible leaps, passing the ball, screaming and urging her team mates on. She was nimble, her leap majestic – like a deer in full flight. At thirteen, Saru was a happy child with no interest in the violent conflict of the grown men around her. But the country was at war. She and her team were travelling to a netball tournament at a neighbouring school when they met their fate.

An army helicopter flew over to collect Saru from the site of the explosion and transport her to the provincial hospital in nearby Fort Victoria, but although the doctors saved her life, they could not save her legs. We never saw Saru again, as she did not return to school.

Today, events such as this one are described as traumatic. During those days, however, we were forced to take tragic events on the chin and consider them as character-building opportunities. The sounds of mortar bombs and exploding landmines, the rattle of the FN MAG machine gun and the AK-47, the boom of a bazooka, the sight and throbbing *wuppa-wuppa* noise of the rotor blades of army helicopters circling in for the kill, the notorious de Havilland Vampire and Hawker Hunter fighter jets swooping down from the sky – in those days, these were the norm.

Guerrilla tactics are the weapon of choice for those fighting from a weaker position, and in that brutal conflict, they were unrelenting, clashing fiercely with the conventional power of the Rhodesian army.

When you are forced to escape death every day, you eventually grow numb to the ever-present dangers. Now, little stirs fear in me – except the thought of being trapped in the grind of modern life, a slave to the monotony of the working world.

7

The settlement where our shop operated became our new home. It was a far cry from what we had been used to growing up; the new surroundings were welcoming, but to say it was a downgrade is an understatement. How the mighty had fallen!

Human beings adapt; I learnt this fact from our experience, but the scars and trauma of the disruption and disappointment affected each member of the family in different ways. When I once asked my parents to buy me a pair of khaki-coloured trousers and a matching shirt designed like army fatigues, with numerous pockets, made by the latest clothing brand, Sting, Dad just mumbled something like, '*Mwari achida mwanangu tapedza isikweletu kwaFata*' ('God willing, son; we will see once we have paid the fees'), and I knew that I should never have asked. The look on his face told me the whole story.

We lived in a house attached to the back of the shop. Over the years, Dad expanded it room by room, building slowly. He gathered most of the materials from the surrounding area, as it was the only way we could afford to continue the construction. There was not much space in the few rooms, so when we had visitors, we would use the shop as a bedroom at night.

We soon discovered that despite the outwardly calm demeanour of our parents, the fall from grace had taken its toll on their health. Both were diagnosed with severe stomach ulcers attributed to stress. As a result of these ulcers, they could not consume carbonated drinks; a single sip would result in excruciating tummy pain. They could also not consume anything sour or fermented.

Mum appeared to have a solution for everything. If it was present times, you would be sure that she was using Google, YouTube or TikTok to do her research. When I was young, however, I thought that my mother was a miser. She found ways of getting us to buy into a frugal lifestyle; some of these habits have stayed with me. Before our return to boarding school every term, for instance, she would have us take a tablespoon of cod liver oil every day for a week, telling us that the oil would fortify us against infections. We did not have the luxury of cod liver oil capsules; we drank the oil, unflavoured, unsweetened and raw. To complete our fortification, Mother would send us to the nearby bushes on the outskirts of the settlement to gather fresh leaves from a special plant. We would chew the bitter leaves and swallow them whole every day for a week. 'It's a powerful herb, passed down from your grandmother,' she would remind us.

I was taught that the smallest tube of toothpaste (the size that most people pack in a toiletry bag when travelling for a couple of days) would be enough for a three-and-a-half-month term at boarding school. 'It's how hard you brush your teeth that matters, not squirting toothpaste all over your brush until you saturate the bristles and the stuff is wobbling all over! A pea-sized squirt is more than enough,' Mum would say while packing our boarding trunks.

When my youngest sister voiced her dissatisfaction with our meagre provisions compared with those of other children in the dormitory, Mum would remind us how lucky we were because many kids ate only one meal a day, often going to bed hungry. She would glance at her children one by one; if she detected signs of further dissent, she would flash a smile as she laid another guilt trip on us: 'Even worse, many kids are orphans. See how fortunate you are to have parents taking care of you. Think about it.'

I grew a thick skin, no longer envious of the material possessions or pocket money that others brought to school. My primary objective became doing well in class. We all loved our holidays, though; that was when we could return home to spend time with our parents and siblings. The house was small, but our mother made it into a home.

Regardless of having to adjust to our new surroundings, the environment brought fun and adventure into our lives. We could wander into the bush to mind the livestock with children from the village and play games with reckless abandon. It was in the humble circumstances of our new home that I was expected to host my cousin Patricia. The prospect of her visit brought joy to my family.

Our activities varied every day. Sometimes the boys would pair themselves up and then let themselves be provoked into a fight just for fun. Here, even the weakest boy soon toughened up. Inciting boys into a fight proved to be easy. The group hierarchy was based on age. The barefooted leader – the oldest boy in the group – would kick a generous amount of sand loose. Sitting on his haunches, he would cup his calloused hands and build two separate cones of earth. Once he was satisfied with this construction, he would step back and ask the paired youths to step forward. Then he would explain the rules of the game.

Each mound of earth was assigned to one of the two boys. These two heaps of sand became opposing territories under the separate ownership of the two boys. To stress the extent of their responsibility, the leader disclosed that each boy's cone of earth represented his mother's breast. Suddenly this became a high-stakes game. The breast is where the boy had suckled, cementing a strong bond with his mother. This was now about his mother, the one who had generated a narrative of loyalty, entrenched attitudes and personal branding. The two boys would then be asked to challenge each other by kicking the 'breast' of the other boy's mother. Every time, one of the boys would kick the cone of earth and a furious kickboxing fight would follow, stopped only by the intervention of others.

I was an observer during these fights until I was unexpectedly thrown into the ring, paired with the village bully, who came with the reputation of being the best fighter in the neighbourhood. He was a big boy, heavily built for his age. I watched him as he kicked the sand cone that represented my mother's breast, knocking the sand onto the feet of the surrounding spectators. How dare he, I thought, adrenalin pumping through my veins. I knew that I had to fight. But when I looked at the guy's calloused knuckles as he rolled his fists tightly, doubts started to creep in. I was short-tempered as a child, a defense mechanism that worked most of the time. However, by contrast with the adversary in front of me, I was tall and as thin as a beanstalk. I also suffered regular asthmatic attacks. I did not think that I stood a chance, but I resisted the urge to take off and run. What if I did the Muhammad Ali thing I had read about in a feature in the *African Times* newspaper, I wondered: dancing around punching the air and pretending to know what I was doing? I heard a voice shouting in my brain, a memory of my mother's call to action – 'You will fight back, son! *Dzorera!*' ('If they hit you, you hit back. You hit harder, son!') – when I once reported a bullying incident at school. Cornered and driven by pride, I surprised my opponent with a quick-fire volley of chaotic punches and caught him off guard. When he realised that I was not backing down, he took off and ran away. On that day, I won great respect from the other boys.

The quality of life in our settlement depended on how hard families were prepared to work. Hard work was rewarded by good harvests and large herds of livestock if the rains were good. For my family, activities included working in the fields planting and harvesting, buying grain from communal farmers to sell at the state grain company, buying cattle hides and preparing them for sale at the tannery, and tending to the herds of livestock and flocks of sheep. The shop, mill and beer hall opened daily. We had to split the tasks among us and the few workers Dad employed. A roster was prepared for me and my siblings.

I was nine when Dad asked me to mind the shop. The first day went well; customer traffic was slow and steady, but the takings were good. It was beginner's luck.

On the second day, I learnt a tough lesson. An elderly man walked in to buy a packet of cigarettes, but he did not have cash. 'I run a line of credit approved by your father, son,' the man told me. I told him I had been left with no such instruction, but the man persisted. He told me not to be concerned as I surely knew where he lived, and said that he would bring me the cash later in the day when he returned from a family visit. I blinked and wrote down the transaction in the debtor's book. He smiled and walked out with a pack of thirty Peter Stuyvesant cigarettes, the pack that came in a box that opened like a suitcase.

The old man proved to be a scoundrel, a nasty piece of work. He did not come back to pay his debt. When I completed my end-of-day cash-up, I told Dad that I was short because of the old man's promise. Dad, straight-faced, displaying no emotion, looked me in the eye and said, 'Should an ostrich trust its eggs with a raccoon?' I did not reply.

The following day I paid the old man, Mr Hippo, a visit, eager to collect the debt. He lived alone in a small two-roomed house at the edge of the settlement. I had not even begun to explain the purpose of my visit before the old man started telling me a yarn. However, I had already learnt from his actions the previous day that talk is cheap. I grabbed one of the chairs in his tiny, sparsely furnished lounge and took it home. I thought that he would follow later with the cash and collect his chair, but he never did.

The chair was small, like the ones built for children. It had a frame made of pieces of steel tube joined with brackets and screws. The seat and backrest were made of indigenous hardwood with a shine that revealed many years of use. The wood plates were so worn and thin in the middle that it seemed like a carpenter was sanding them every day, but the polished wood grain gave the chair an antique feel. I secretly hoped that Mr. Hippo would not turn up to collect his chair. A chair for a packet of cigarettes seemed like good business. My sisters and brother were careful not to sit in the chair –

which was given the name 'Dani's chair' – in my presence if they wanted to avoid a fight. But six months later, the chair came apart. The wooden plates in the seat cracked and fell off, broken into pieces, and the brackets in the steel frame became so shaky that no one wanted to sit in that chair anymore. The chair crumbled as if it had conspired with its owner. It was a dud. My heart sank. It seemed like the old man had won again.

Whenever I am confronted by similar situations and promises without substance, a picture of Mr Hippo grinning as he walked out of the shop with the Peter Stuyvesant cigarettes flashes in my mind like a red light. Without delay, I walk away.

When rains fell during the summer, it was time to work in the fields. The hubbub of activity that followed pressured everybody in the settlement to do the same. In these parts, laziness attracted ridicule. The day started in the very early morning at around 4 a.m., well before sunrise. We took a lunch break when the heat of the sun became unbearable, and went back to work later in the afternoon, only knocking off after sunset.

The sun was important for timekeeping; it was taboo to wake up after sunrise. Friendly neighbours would dispatch a group of children to embarrass an errant child: beating a drum, they would sing a one-line-and-one-chorus song, creating an early morning racket, '*anomuka rabuda zuva, anomuka rabuda zuva*' ['here is the boy who wakes up after sunrise, here is the boy who wakes up after sunrise, here is the boy who …']. The drum would beat rhythmically, non-stop. The band would position themselves at the edge of the homestead just after sunrise and would sing the chorus in persistent repetition, going on for almost fifteen minutes until the child jumped out of bed and walked into the yard to meet the band of singers in shame.

In the rainy months, it was time to plough, plant and weed. These activities were followed in due course by harvesting. During the winter, it was time to nourish the sandy soil by adding organic matter such as cattle manure. There was always some work to do, and I soon found out that every job – including menial tasks such as shovelling manure – required a specialised technique.

Young and old all joined the work groups that seemed to form spontaneously whenever a neighbour needed help to tackle a difficult project. The younger men called the older men 'Uncle', which was pronounced 'Enkeli'. One Enkeli, respected for owning large herds of livestock, preferred to lean on the handle grip of a shovel while he watched us work, eager to pick on any sign of laziness or weakness. Pointing at his big, strong hands, calloused by years of honest, hard work, he would despair at how none of us, with our soft hands, would be able to survive the piece work in construction contracts. He would step up and explain the right way of doing a task and the correct technique to use.

For shovelling, it was the way you positioned yourself, taking the right distance from the pile of manure and the donkey-pulled cart. A firm grip on the shovel was essential, with one hand holding the handle and the other holding the lower shaft at just the right place, on the neck above the blade. He would demonstrate the lever swing, ending with a subtle and well-timed tip action to decant the contents. The right technique made it possible to load several cartloads without breaking your back. However, if you had not mastered the technique, the task was tardy, awkward, energy-sapping and time-consuming.

The banter, storytelling and singing of the people in the work groups made what initially seemed an insurmountable task quite light work. I soon learnt that what seems daunting can most often be accomplished through good organisation, by breaking down the larger job into small parts and attacking each of them one at a time.

8

Patricia's parents bought her a one-way ticket to our home in the Lowveld. It was quite normal for parents to send their children away to visit relatives with the expectation that the hosting relatives would pay for the child's return fare. Cultural norms of *ubuntu* dictated that it was more important to visit relatives than to worry about the minor matter of paying fares. After all, an uncle was meant to treat his brother's children like his own.

This cultural expectation would not have troubled my parents if their financial situation had not been so dire. But given the circumstances, it became a potential source of embarrassment: where would they find enough money to cover Patricia's return fare?

Something had to be done, so Mother came up with a plan that none of us could have dreamt up. She joined a village club that arranged village 'tea' parties meant to raise cash for its members, which they could use to fund whatever needs they had, such as children's school fees. A roster was in place, ensuring that each member had their turn to host the party, but all members were involved during the preparations for every event, supporting the host in different ways.

Mother negotiated to jump the queue, convincing the club members of the urgency after explaining her family's desperate emergency. The menu for patrons at these stokvel parties consisted of traditional beer, chicken and goat stew served with sadza (pap, the staple thick maize meal porridge) or rice. This meant that she now had to brew traditional beer, which she had never done in her life, having been a reverend's daughter and a devout Christian, but without the beer, the event would not have attracted enough patrons to make it worth the trouble. Mother had no respect for beer, but she was forced to accept the business principles that underpinned the club: the objective was to end up with the much-needed net cash surplus when the event ended. Money has no colour.

Two club members offered to help with the brewing of the vital beverage. Surprisingly, they found Mother a quick learner and the drinkers were impressed when they were invited for a beer tasting. Mother was a trained home economics graduate; cooking was second nature to her and so producing the food for the event was never going to be a problem. She got down to work, with friends and family, including Cousin Patricia, assisting her.

The day of the party arrived. The villagers were curious and keen to attend the party; everyone in the settlement had always treated Mother as some sort of royalty. Despite the family's fall from grace, the villagers accorded my parents an elevated status based on their earlier success. Who would want to miss such an event hosted by 'madam'? This word was normally reserved for the wives of the white reverends; the villagers referred to Mother in this way as a sign of respect.

The event was an overwhelming success. Close to two hundred people from the surrounding villages came to the party. Throughout the day, patrons patiently lined up for food and beer, and by late afternoon, everything had sold out. People spent generously, feasting, dancing and ululating in celebration. The colourful crowd was truly a spectacle to behold. Watching the proceedings while sitting in the shade of a large tree, I quickly estimated what the party takings would be. As a shopkeeper's son, my mind had been trained to focus on the cash.

I was jolted out of my mental calculations by high-pitched voices at the entrance to the tent enclosure. An incident had developed around the master of ceremonies, who was engaged in a heated argument with an angry patron.

The master of ceremonies was a boisterous fellow sporting a short afro, a manicured goatee and sideburns. He looked dapper in a light-blue safari suit and platform shoes. Standing on a disused oil drum, he sought to establish full authority over proceedings. He was loud and full of zeal, constantly using English in place of the vernacular whenever the opportunity arose, eager to prove that he had learnt a few things in the city that set him apart from those in the village. When he spoke English, he did so slowly, emphasising each word as if writing in capital letters. His distinct accent, a legacy passed down by the peoples of southern Africa, bore the unmistakable influence of Swahili, from which their languages originated.

And now he was directing people at the top of his voice: 'We have two stations for food. Those who ordered sadza and stew, please go to the left. The ones who ordered lunch should please present themselves at the station to the right!'

I asked a friend sitting next to me why sadza and stew could not be lunch; why was the master of ceremonies making this distinction? Before my friend had the chance to respond, a man walking past who had overheard my question offered this explanation: 'We eat sadza in the village every day. Lunch, eish, lunch is different ...' I was baffled.

One of the friends sitting in the shade with me explained who the angry patron was, and I came to realise that this was a fellow who was known in the village for wife beating. He appeared incensed by something the master of ceremonies had said to him.

The argument went on, threatening to disrupt the mood of the event. The heated exchange between the two men grew louder and there was enough spectator value to draw my group of friends towards the commotion.

It became clear that the angry patron, Aburama, wanted to enter the enclosure under the giant tent where the club members were serving patrons. Since he had not paid the admission fee and was not a club member, there was no chance that he would be allowed in. Aburama was having none of this; he was livid, with the anger of a man who felt that the world was against him. His eyes blinked wildly as he waved his hands around, pointing his fingers menacingly. But our master of ceremonies held firm.

Aburama realised he was not going to win, but should make a face-saving exit. Having concluded that this battle was lost, he eventually offered his parting shot – '*ubulungu bakho ngeke kukuyise ezulwini!*' ('I hope that the so-called membership of your club will get you admitted to heaven!'). With that, he managed a defiant grin. Humiliated by his exclusion from the ongoing festivities, he walked away, disappeared from our view and was quickly forgotten.

9

Aburama was an enigma. The fact that his parents had named him after Abraham, the rich man in the biblical book of Genesis, became an apparent contradiction as he grew into a young adult. To some in the village, he was a maverick and a hero, but others viewed him differently. When he was in his twenties, he went to the city to seek employment, like most young men, and worked for eighteen months under a very abusive boss.

There was nothing unusual about abusive treatment during those years; the difference lay in how the individual reacted to it. Most people coped as best they could, massaging the boss's ego to get their way and using their small wages to build homesteads in the tribal trust lands they came from.

Those who had survived the trials of working in such demeaning conditions often talked of how they had done it. One oft-repeated story went something like this: 'I would approach the foreman in the morning, making a point to be earlier than everyone else. Now the Boer boss was always early. The Boers are keen timekeepers, you see. They love to speak their language, and you must try to learn some of it and surprise them. So you approach the boss early morning and greet him, saying something like, "*Goeiemôre meneer, hoe gaan dit?* ('Good morning, sir, how are you?') *Baas, laat weet wat anders ek vandag moet doen, maar ek ken die plan vir die week, meneer. En baas, ek sien jou bakkie is vol stof. Jy moes op die plaas gewees het, meneer.* ('Boss, let me know what else you want me to do today, but I know the plan for the week, meneer. And boss I see that your bakkie is covered in dust. You must have been to the farm, meneer.') Let me know, but if you do not mind, I will give the bakkie the hosepipe during my lunch, meneer. A man of your station in life should not drive about in a dirty car, meneer. Very well, meneer, and thank you, meneer. Let me be on my way and immediately get to work, meneer. I've got those targets you set for the week; we must beat them, meneer." '

That always did the trick. Applied persistently and in conjunction with hard work, this kind of behaviour guaranteed that a promotion would follow quite soon.

Tribal trust lands were reserved for the native population groups. For a man to survive in these remote areas, he had to build the necessary capacity – farming equipment and cattle – to work the land, which was allocated to him by the chief. Once he had earned enough money in the city, the man would return to his rural home and enjoy a life where he was the master of his own destiny. It usually took between five and ten years to accumulate enough money to do so, and this implied resilience and discipline.

However, Aburama was a different character. Eighteen months of abuse was too much for him. His work record was erratic; known for reporting late to work, he enjoyed his beer at the local tavern and once he got paid at month-end, he was nowhere to be found for a couple of days. One day he arrived at work as usual, which was thirty minutes late, and the foreman shouted obscenities as he always did; instructions were dispatched with typical factory language. Aburama cracked. He clobbered the foreman into a pulp. Security was called and saved the boss from further punishment. But that was it. As was the practice in those days, no disciplinary hearing was held. Aburama was fired without any terminal benefits.

With no savings to show for his months of work and so nothing to invest back home, Aburama returned to a life of poverty. There were just two huts on his homestead and he was the only family man in the village without a herd of cattle. This meant that he was the last person in the settlement to plough his fields, as he had to wait for everyone else to finish so that they could lend him a couple of cattle to pull the plough. Precise timing in preparing the fields in the rainy season is required to take advantage of the rains. Delays result in stunted crops, leading to poor harvests. Aburama struggled to make ends meet.

The same cycle was repeated every year. The result was grinding poverty. Aburama's tale of beating up his abusive boss won him kudos with a few friends, particularly during the Rhodesian Bush War, but most people were not impressed by the story. The elders argued that anyone interested in building a secure financial future must mind their own business. It is not in anyone's best interests to let their emotions get the better of them when it comes to their livelihood.

Only the previous week, Aburama had been at the village court where villagers had gathered to give a constructive judgment regarding an indecisive young man who had made a girl pregnant. During the court proceedings, Aburama – overzealous in his desire to contribute to the proceedings – made an unsolicited remark.

Courts in the village followed a protocol-driven approach adopted from cultural practices passed down from previous generations. Aburama's punishment was immediate: the court warden, polite as ever, asked him to join the boys and supervise the skinning of a goat. The goat had been brought by the defendant as payment in kind to feed the village elders while the matter was being decided by the court. Feeling humiliated and crushed, Aburama had to leave his peers performing the more intellectual duties of defusing a potential feud between the two families (the family of the errant youth and that of his pregnant girlfriend) and go off to do the work of a boy.

A couple of years before, Aburama's wife and children had run away from his homestead, seeking refuge from the angry man. It was a sad incident, but we found it hilarious at the time.

His eldest child was a young boy who, like most children in the village, had learnt how to trap mice during the winter season following the seasonal harvests. Mice were a delicacy, roasted or fried and served with sadza.

Before Aburama had left home early that morning, he had noticed that his son had been successful and had caught a decent number of mice. When he returned in the evening after a day of drinking the traditional brew with other villagers, his appetite for meat had become a craving. I can imagine his thoughts on the way home as he touched his pocket so that he could feel the hot peri-peri bulbs that he always carried in anticipation of fortuitously coming across a meal wherever he went.

Aburama belonged to the *murambwi* clan; his totem was the *shumba*, also called *Ngonyama* or *ibubesi*, the lion, the fearsome carnivore that feeds on meat. In his drunken stupor, he recalled that during his youth, the elders had ingrained in him the unshakable belief that only members of his *murambwi* clan were entitled to eat meat just as the lion does. The idea of barbecued mice sprinkled with a generous amount of peri-peri and salt was a great prospect to end a day, Aburama mused silently. He could hardly wait for supper. He quickened his stride as he headed homeward.

When he arrived, his wife quickly served him supper, but to Aburama's dismay, there was no meat on his plate, only some amasi (sour milk) and sadza. He was desperate for something salty, something to satisfy his craving.

'Where are the mice that I saw with my own eyes this morning?' Aburama demanded. He did not wait for an answer, kicking the plate so that it flew across the hut.

His wife knew what was coming and together with the children ran for dear life to seek refuge at our house. Finding the incident amusing but saddening, we listened behind closed doors in our bedrooms while Mother asked Aburama's wife about what had happened.

Having witnessed Aburama's reckless lifestyle, which had wrecked his family, and his failure to respect bosses and authority, I decided that I did not want to end up like him.

10

I was excited to be involved in the cashing up at the end of Mother's successful stokvel party and keen to find out whether it had been worth the effort.

The outcome was a handsome profit and a greater amount of net cash than expected. There was more than enough cash for Patricia's bus fare, with the balance available for my parents to deal with other pressing needs. The relief was palpable. Mother had done it. She had succeeded.

This was my first taste of hustling and seeing positive results. What a lesson!

11

When I was in primary school, my teachers would ask, 'What do you want to be when you grow up?' My answer was always quick: 'A doctor!' But instead I became an accountant – a very different career from that of doctor. I knew what jobs my parents did before my father lost his job, but I never asked them what their own dreams had been before everything changed. At the time, it felt insensitive to ask.

I can imagine my parents lying awake at night as they adjusted to their new life, thinking of ways to earn a living. My father probably replayed the events that had led to him being fired, wondering what he could have done differently, while my mother, holding his hand, felt powerless. They must have seen this as the end of their youthful ambitions.

These reflections make me think about what people aim for in life, which led me to explore Aristotle's philosophy, particularly his concept of the 'final cause'.

Aristotle's 'final cause' is the purpose or goal something is meant to achieve. In the context of my family, it relates to how people revise their life goals when circumstances change.

Stephen Hawkins (2007) explains this idea using analogies. Natural beings, such as people or tigers, are made up of physical parts. A tiger hunts and eats to survive, and its body is built for these tasks. One zoologist might see the tiger as clumsy and an ineffectual hunter, while another might see it as perfectly adapted for the hunt. But if the environment changes (for instance, if the tiger's usual prey disappears), it will struggle to survive, no matter how well adapted it is. It will need to find new ways to survive.

Thomas Short (2010) used a different but similar analogy to explain this concept further: imagine putting an obstacle in front of ants as they travel between their nest and a food source. Once they have explored the edges of the obstacle, the ants will find a new path (if one exists) to reach the food. This shows that ants do not just stick to set routes; instead, they adapt and find the best way to get to their goal.

Similarly, people adapt to changes in their lives based on their experiences and the world around them. My parents had to reshape their goals to fit their new circumstances, just as Dave Glasheen and Emma Orbach did in their own lives. My father, like the tiger whose prey had disappeared, faced an uncertain future when he lost his job. It felt like a disaster for him and our family. In his fifties, with fewer options open to him, he had to rethink his definition of success. His goal became ensuring his children received a good education – this was his legacy and his 'final cause'.

He needed money to make this happen, but the shop he ran brought in only a modest income, and my mother's salary was also not enough. Eventually he found a solution that would allow him to increase the family's income: farming.

Having had a peasant upbringing, my parents had worked in the fields in their youth and enjoyed farming. The village chief, who presided over communal land, allocated us additional plots every year, reallocating the plots of non-productive villagers. By nature of his position in the community, the chief was the custodian of cultural rules and practices. No one dared contest his decisions. And so, from around four hectares, the land we had under cultivation grew to over forty hectares, and my parents sold the produce from the plots to the state's Grain Marketing Board.

Dad nurtured his relationship with the chief over the years. After visiting early one morning and being convinced by Mother to join Dad for breakfast, the chief made it his habit to visit Dad twice a week.

Mother understood cultural practices well enough to know that the chief and her husband should be left alone to talk over their breakfast. She had to serve them a simple farmer's breakfast, leave the room and return to the kitchen.

Mother baked scones for these breakfasts in her Welcome Dover cast-iron wood-fired oven. This brand, made in Great Britain, was a household name in the homes of off-the-grid folk in southern Africa. In the early morning, the aroma from the kitchen was irresistible. She served the scones with her homemade wild marula jam and tea with milk and plenty of sugar (the chief had a sweet tooth). Once done, she left the two men deep in conversation. It was wartime and the bush war was raging in what was then Rhodesia. Dad listened to the news on the radio every morning at 7 a.m. The chief would visit on Mondays and Wednesdays, taking his seat by 7 a.m.

The chief was an important man who carried himself well. He was of average height and well built, but no description could adequately capture his presence. He looked like a man used to commanding people. His wealth could only be measured in the livestock he owned: herds of cattle and goats, and flocks of sheep, the numbers of which were only restricted by the district commissioner's grazing quotas. He also owned the only mules (the mule is a cross between a donkey and a horse) in the entire district.

The mules had been gifted to him by the district commissioner, who was desperate to keep the chief on the side of the establishment when the bush war showed signs of getting out of control. They were beautiful beasts with the grace and speed of a horse, but they were as hardy and resilient as a donkey, and so able to survive the arid, hot conditions of the Lowveld.

The chief affectionately named the colt '*ngwindi*' ('the strength of a hippopotamus') and the filly '*mgorogodo*' ('the roaring grace of a horse galloping at full speed'). He had been excited to become the only known owner of mules across the native lands in the Lowveld. He had expected the colt and filly to breed and multiply, but as the years passed, he learnt that mules cannot reproduce. He felt cheated. However, since the mules were more powerful than donkeys and were fast when harnessed to a cart, the chief frequently rented out his beloved mules.

The chief was known to scream at his livestock minders, '*Haibo! Isiphukuphuku semuntu. Wenzani?* ('You fool. What are you doing?') These beasts are not donkeys! Be light with the whip!' Because the yoke chafed the necks of animals used for draught power, the chief did not permit yokes on the mules. He kept a set of leather and rubber harnesses for his mules and personally refurbished the harnesses when necessary.

During the war, the dirt roads were dangerous and impassable for vehicles due to landmines. Delivery truck services refused to send trucks along the treacherous roads. Dad often hired the chief's mules, Ngwindi and Mgorogodo, and used a cart to collect supplies from the shunter off the Fort Victoria–Beitbridge highway forty kilometres away.

The chief wanted to follow the wartime news, and he and Dad always seemed to have something important to discuss. The chief always dropped his voice to a quiet whisper when expressing his opinions about the news. 'The walls and bushes around us have ears; be cautious,' he would warn, and those moments were the only times I saw him look vulnerable. He would glance around nervously, pressing his index finger to his lips in a quiet plea for silence.

The chief did not trust the thinly disguised propaganda that laced the news broadcast in the vernacular, cynically assigning it to the same category as the Ministry of Information's *African Times* newspaper. According to him, the English bulletin was far more reliable, and this is where Dad, who seemed to have taken on the role of his confidant, came in. The chief desperately wanted to get his message across to the district commissioner. He felt that with Dad, who spoke English well, at his side, he could walk into the district commissioner's office complex thirty kilometres away and listen while Dad articulated what the chief wanted to say. He could cut out the unreliable translation of the district commissioner's bureaucrats and get things done for his people.

Dad listened to the English news and translated for the chief, with much interpretation. Dad always called for silence in the house at news time; he did not want to miss anything. He would sit quietly, jaw set in concentration in a posture that resembled a calculating, taciturn man.

The chief would nod and shake his head as the news reader went through the bulletin; he had the habit of muttering under his breath, repeating the words *'Kunogwiwa Mwari chaizvo'* ('Oh God almighty, this forsaken war is dreadful. Ah, ah, no, no, no! The young men are fighting, holding their own, but they are only boys, oh Lord!') until the news ended. At first we had thought that he understood every word of the news, but when he blurted out, '*Kwahi kudini?*' ('What did the newsman say?') as soon as he saw that Dad was ready to talk about the latest goings-on, we realised that this was not the case.

This routine with the chief repeated itself for many years. It was only in my adulthood that I appreciated why Mum tolerated the breakfasts with the chief: it was then that land deals were concluded. Thanks to those breakfasts, the number of hectares of ground that we had under cultivation increased tenfold.

My parents' small enterprise expanded. They bought grain from surrounding small-scale farmers, milled it and sold it back to the villagers during the months before the harvest, when grain reserves in the villages were low. They opened a beer hall. There was also a buzz around our business centre, with customers coming from far and wide. Our family's financial situation improved significantly, although it still took some juggling to ensure that the school fees for all seven of us were paid in time. Indeed, there were instances when some of my siblings almost got sent back home by their school principals due to late payment of fees, but Dad always negotiated for an extension of payment deadlines. He delivered on his promises every time and had the reputation of being a reliable man. Year after year, we focused on our studies and did our best not to disappoint our parents.

Once Dad had recalibrated his goals in life, nothing else mattered more than sending his children to good boarding schools, and he worked tirelessly to achieve this aim.

12

Good schools do not come cheap. In addition, the schools we attended were only good in relative terms; ours were those no-frills spartan schools where the Catholic church prioritised a fine education for members of their parish. The schools had excellent teachers and a good curriculum, but living conditions for boarders were less than basic. Boarders were also assigned cleaning duties, taking turns to clean the dormitories and bathrooms according to a roster.

We all enjoyed the initiation ritual at the school once we became seniors, but for the new kids, it was a reminder that home was far away.

All new kids at my boarding school were assigned to a dormitory named 'Kariba' by inhabitants long gone. (Kariba, built on the Zambezi River in the late 1950s, remains the largest man-made lake in Africa.) At our school, Kariba was a reference to water, plenty of free-flowing water.

Kariba was my maiden dorm too. Like all the other children in the dorm, I was no longer wetting my bed at night by the time my parents sent me off to boarding school. But that changed for many of us when we became Kariba residents; most of us woke up every morning in a pool of wee. I was baffled because I could not recall when I had last wet my bed. I would go to bed each night promising myself that the previous night had been an accident and would not be repeated, but the following morning the bed would be wet again.

Soon I came to accept life in Kariba. The stench in the dorm was horrible, despite daily mopping with lots of detergent, but we got used to it. I had to face the humiliation of taking my bedding and pyjamas to dry on the washing line every morning, but after a while my pattern of wetting the bed stopped abruptly. It took another month before the boarding prefects were satisfied that my bedding was dry every morning before they transferred me to another dormitory.

We had cold showers in winter. Breakfast was a plate of maize meal porridge every morning, and we were given roasted peanuts and a cup of tea during the morning break. Meat was only served on special occasions. We ate pap and vegetables (usually kale, cabbage, sugar beans and butter beans) for lunch and supper, and drank milk. Note that the abundance of vegetables in our diet was thanks to the school's frugality; it is only today, decades later, that a vegetarian diet is not only strongly recommended but fashionable, viewed as a healthy lifestyle choice.

When my two young sisters joined me at boarding school, they complained bitterly about the food and immediately wrote to our parents back home. My parents replied to tell them to hang in there: 'It will get better, children. Remember to pray before bed. Always remember our way. Ask our Father, the Lord, ask him for all the good things you want. He always provides.' That settled the issue and answered the request for more pocket money with a silent rebuff!

Concerned about how my young siblings were adapting to boarding school, I told my little sisters that we should find a way to stretch out our one-dollar-per-term allocation of pocket money so that it lasted for the whole three-and-a-half-month term. I felt that we needed some bonding and to find a way to break the routine after a long week. We agreed to share a snack and a cooldrink from the tuckshop on Sundays when we met to catch up. We would also keep a few pennies in reserve for a rainy day. I told my sisters not to expect any more than that. And then I ended with, 'God willing', following my father's popular line, my voice dropping to a grave tone to inject a measure of big-brother authority as I willed them to control their urges. Boarding school went a lot better after that.

Two of my favourite teachers were German nuns. Sister Radegunda taught Geography, while Sister Angelica taught Physical Science and Biology. The nuns adored me because I was a top student in secondary school, excelling across all subjects, including science, literature and history.

I was an avid reader. The two nuns recommended that I be made a school librarian, which meant opening the library once during the week for two hours and on Saturday mornings. During this time, I issued books, received returns and charged fines. When the library was quiet, I sat and read. I also used this opportunity to reserve the best books for myself.

School life followed a structured routine imposed by the principal. We attended classes in the morning. After lunch, we were assigned chores (manual work) according to a roster. All learners worked in the vegetable gardens and orchards of the school and the nunnery, cleaning the pigsties, feeding the pigs, milking the dairy cows and harvesting corn in the church fields. The produce from the farm subsidised the boarding school budget.

This was followed by homework time, then evening study, after which we went to bed, with the lights being switched off by the head boy.

We attended Catholic mass on Sundays and recited the Benediction Prayer on Tuesdays in church: 'The Lord bless us and keep us. The Lord make his face to shine upon us and be gracious unto us. The Lord lift up his countenance upon us, and give us peace, this day, night and forever more. Amen.'

Because I was brought up in a parish of the Dutch Reformed Church, I found the contrasting Catholic ways both confusing and amusing. The burning of incense and the gestures and rituals performed by the priest during the holy communion were novel. This was different and a lot more fun than the melancholy atmosphere at church back home!

I desperately wanted to eat the bread at mass, but was warned that it was only served to baptised Catholics who had completed catechism: 'God will cast a spell on you!' they warned us. Even at that early age, enrolling for catechism was not an option; Mum told us we were strictly Dutch Reformed Church, so there was nothing to be done about it. But I wanted to taste the communion bread and I was not the only one who felt excluded. Some of my classmates were also not baptised Catholics, and a quiet consensus emerged among us. We did not want to tempt God's wrath, so we watched the spectacle from our pews, kneeling, rising, standing, sitting and invoking the Trinity as we made the sign of the cross along with the rest of the congregation, but not eating the bread.

The strict regimen of Catholic school instilled a lasting discipline in us. Even so, for eleven-year-old children, it felt punitive. Our parents assured us that we were the fortunate ones, reminding us of the prestigious Cambridge examinations we would write that guaranteed university entry both locally and internationally.

When one of my elder sisters graduated from university with a bachelor's degree, we noticed a change in our parents. For many years, these folks had hardly smiled. But when Mum and Dad returned from the graduation ceremony in the big city, we noticed a difference in them: they were smiling and laughing, and had a spring in their step. This was especially true of my father, who suddenly seemed to regain his pre-fall height, looking several inches taller as he walked into the house. The tension at home was defused, replaced by a new optimism. That elusive first milestone had now been achieved.

For many years, our parents had suffered from stress-induced ulcers that erupted from time to time. Suddenly the ulcers went quiet, like Mount Vesuvius.

Over the years, some of the villagers had tried to discourage father in his efforts to send his girl children to high school. One loud farmer blatantly undermined Dad's determination in public when we met him at the market. In our presence, while patting Dad vigorously on the back, he yelled his greetings: '*He Ndaa vhari mini!* My good friend! You work too hard. But you are wasting your hard-earned money on this school thing. Look at you, no rest and haggard with worry. As for me, I am done with my daughters as soon as they learn to read and write … that's it, finish and *klaar!*'

My elder sister's voice trembled with emotion as she recalled the incident. 'I was old enough to understand our financial struggles, but I still wanted so badly to go to university, and now …' She was certain that Dad would give in to the pressure from others, but he stood firm and remained true to his convictions.

13

A second chance in the remote wild may seem inviting, but how easy is life in such environments? When a person makes the decision to turn away from city life and the pressures of the day-to-day grind, they should not assume that a utopia beckons. However, it does come with the opportunity to be the master of your own time. If you embrace the hard work involved, life in the wild can be rewarding.

Those who choose this lifestyle will never retire; they keep working and remain socially engaged. In this new environment, alongside their families and, most importantly, their children, they are taught invaluable life lessons that shape their journey.

When Fogle visited them in the remote wild, Glasheen and Orbach had both settled on large plots of land, one on a very long lease and the other owned outright. Securing the parcels of land gave them peace of mind, which says a lot about real estate.

The value of real estate in my parents' life cannot be understated. If Dad had not built the shop while he was still employed, his family would have fallen into a life of destitution when he was fired. The shop saved us from the storms of poverty.

I learnt that when the chips are down, often all you have left to trade on is your reputation. The credit lines from suppliers were granted based on Dad's good reputation.

After Dad passed on, Mum ran the shop as a side hustle while keeping her teaching job at the local school for another twelve years. She eventually retired and decided to rent out the shop, which she did for almost seven years.

After working for forty-one years, Mum discovered that she did not qualify for a pension as she had not been allowed to join the government pension fund while in service. However, in the hyperinflationary environment in the country at the time she retired, a pension would not have made any difference. With additional support from her children, the rental income from the shop (paid in US dollars) was enough to sustain her during her retirement.

I owe my successful career to the sacrifices my parents made, as their dedication allowed me to receive a quality education. Every aspect of my background has contributed to my achievements as a financial executive, specialising in financial management.

I have also developed a deep and enduring interest in real estate, which I believe was sparked by my early exposure to property. I took great pride in watching my father build a shop on a rocky outcrop in the countryside, and later a house attached to the shop. Over the years, I saw him carefully supervise the construction, adding rooms one by one. That experience left a lasting impression.

Over the years, I have gained extensive experience in investments. My experience managing significant retirement fund investments, along with my direct involvement in real estate, has shaped my strong beliefs and perspectives on investing. I find myself questioning the attitudes of financial advisors and professionals towards direct property investment.

Financial services players often create the impression that real estate is too risky and demands too much effort, and that the costs involved make it an unattractive asset class. I argue that property provides a viable investment opportunity that allows individuals to diversify and control a portion of their capital. A property portfolio serves as an effective hedge against inflationary conditions if a long-term view is considered.

Perhaps a better question to ask is whether investors expect too much from financial advisors.

If we assume that there are standard income outcomes to be achieved, the advisor's role is more defined. The advisor leverages their expertise to safeguard clients from errors and ensure their money earns the expected returns (Graham, 2006). Stock markets, bonds and the like offer a great investment opportunity, but if investors are persistently being advised to balance and diversify their investments, why is it that real estate cannot be added to the basket? But where there is low risk, the returns are known to be much lower. The approach that must be taken is that of wealth creation towards a secure future. Taking real estate out of the equation means that investors depend on asset managers to select stocks, bonds and so forth on their behalf for 100% of their investments.

Real estate investing is not free from risk and running expenses: rates and management fees have to be paid, as well as the cost of repairs and maintenance. But the same applies to all investments. The costs of investing through asset managers should never be underestimated; asset managers are paid a fee, a percentage, based on the assets (capital) held under their management. They measure their performance against certain benchmarks, some of which are inflation plus a normative required rate of return, which should lead to a desired real rate of return that beats inflation relative to the risks involved. However, it should be noted that regardless of whether the investment returns are positive or negative, asset managers and investment consultants still receive their fees.

14

The stories in this chapter capture the profound transformation that comes with leaving behind the nine-to-five grind for life in the remote wilderness. In the vast, untamed wild, the promise of a second chance whispers through the rustling leaves – offering not ease but the raw allure of freedom. Turning away from the city's clamour and the relentless race against the clock allows those who choose this path to embrace a new rhythm, dictated not by schedules, but by the rising and setting of the sun.

The wilderness does not come with a cozy campfire singalong; instead, it presents a landscape of challenges. Here, in nature's untamed embrace, individuals are tested, revealing their truest selves. Time becomes something they control, and the hard work poured into taming the land yields more than crops – it nurtures the soul. Success is redefined, no longer measured by material wealth, but by the richness of a life lived in alignment with their deepest values.

For those who choose this path, retirement is an alien concept. They become stewards of the land, shaping it with their hands as they craft their own destiny. Solitude does not mean isolation; rather, social connections deepen, forged through shared work and mutual triumphs.

When Fogle delved into the lives of Dave Glasheen and Emma Orbach, he encountered people who had carved out their own worlds – one with a lease that spanned lifetimes, the other with a deed as solid as the ground beneath her feet. Their sense of peace was palpable, a testament to the enduring value of land – not just as property, but as a foundation for a life well lived.

My own family's story reflects this truth. The shop and home my father built were more than mere structures: they were a fortress against life's tempests. When the winds of misfortune blew, it was this foundation that shielded us from the cold grasp of poverty.

The experience taught me that when everything else is stripped away, your reputation is your last line of defence. It is the respect you earn and the trust you build that unlocks new doors, revealing opportunities once hidden.

This chapter pays tribute to the resilient spirit within each of us – the spirit that rises after every fall, that sees not an ending but a beginning in every sunset, and that understands that the truest form of success is the one that fulfils the heart.

CHAPTER 8

DEFYING THE ODDS:
Beyond limits and labels

'Can you imagine if I had given in to my fear?'
– Henry Winkler

1

Long before the grandeur that Rome would come to achieve, it was but a humble hamlet, nestled in the Italian landscape. Founded before 600 BC, it began as a small farming community, its ambitions yet unformed. Yet the seeds of greatness were sown early; the Romans, though skilled builders, were not content to rely solely on their own knowledge. They were astute observers, absorbing architectural and engineering marvels from the myriad cultures they encountered – and often conquered – within their burgeoning empire.

The legacy of Roman ingenuity is etched in stone and mortar across the centuries: aqueducts that snaked across the landscape, bringing life-giving water to parched cities; arches that stood as triumphal symbols of victory; domes that soared towards the heavens in a show of might and piety; dams that tamed the wild rivers and bridges that connected a sprawling empire. Each structure is a testament to the adage 'Rome wasn't built in a day'.

However, in the summer of AD 64, disaster struck. The Great Fire of Rome razed more than two-thirds of the city to its foundations, leaving a legacy of ashes. But from those ashes rose the Colosseum. It was built between AD 72 and AD 80, a colossal amphitheatre that dwarfed all before it. Spanning two hectares, with seats for fifty thousand spectators, it rivalled the capacity of modern stadiums such as Newlands in Cape Town or Loftus in Pretoria and surpassed Liverpool's Goodison Park by a fifth.

Today, along with international tourist landmarks such as the Pantheon and the Amphitheatre of Nîmes, the Colosseum attracts travellers from around the globe, eager to check off these wonders from their bucket lists. Rome, now a vibrant metropolis housing more than four million souls (World Population Review, 2024), stands resilient, its glory undiminished by the great fire.

In this chapter, we examine the lives of ordinary individuals whose brilliance and achievements shone through in spite of adversity. Like Rome, reborn from the embers, these individuals rose to prominence, their fame a beacon to all who aspire to greatness. Their stories pose a compelling question: in the face of naysayers, misfortune and setbacks, should we give up or should we forge ahead? Is it hope that sustains us, or the courage to seek unconventional paths?

2

The story of how an insecure upper-middle-class kid from a Manhattan family living beyond its means won the role of 'The Fonz' in the American sitcom *Happy Days* is an unlikely tale.

CNN's Chris Wallace sat down with Henry Winkler, wanting to find out how this man, who had struggled with dyslexia all his life, had beaten the odds by becoming a television star and a celebrated writer.

Winkler opened the conversation on CNN's *Who's Talking to Chris Wallace?* in November 2022 by reflecting on his acting career. He shared that after many years of training to become an actor, he finally had the chance to portray a character, rather than aspiring to be someone else. He expressed how enjoyable the experience was and emphasised the enduring bond he shares with his former colleagues, noting that those who are still alive remain incredibly close and friendly, considering themselves to be family.

Winkler had a challenging childhood in New York City with strict but loving parents. Growing up, his school years, which many consider the most memorable time of their youth, were hard. Despite his enthusiasm for learning, he found school incredibly difficult. His preferred mode of communication, perfected from his school days, was speaking, and he has generously participated in numerous interviews over the years during which he has shared his experiences (Cain, 2023; Drabble, 2014; The Yale Center for Dyslexia & Creativity, 2024).

Winkler's struggles with school were profound. He often felt completely lost and bewildered, no matter how hard he tried. His battle with geometry lasted four long years, repeating the same course over and over until he finally passed through summer school. Despite this achievement, he graduated feeling demoralised, haunted by the notion that he had struggled because he was not intelligent.

Winkler poignantly questions whether the anguish and self-doubt he experienced were necessary, especially since he has never needed to use the term 'hypotenuse' in his professional life. This reflection underscores his belief that education should be tailored to take into account how children learn best, not just what they are expected to learn. He emphasises that children should never be made to feel stupid and that educational support should focus on helping them overcome their challenges.

Life at home mirrored the difficulties he faced at school. Winkler's parents, German Jews who placed a high value on education, misinterpreted his academic struggles as laziness. They frequently criticised him, labelling him as lazy and stupid, and insisted he was not living up to his potential. This constant barrage of negativity made him question his self-worth, despite his inner conviction that he was neither lazy nor stupid. His high school years were marked by prolonged periods of being grounded, as his parents believed that keeping him at his desk would somehow rectify his perceived shortcomings.

Despite these challenges, Winkler developed unique coping mechanisms to navigate his difficulties. He studied meticulously and memorised his material, hoping to retain it during tests, only to feel it slip away when he needed it most. This experience led him to improvise, a skill that would later prove invaluable in his acting career. He could instantly memorise large amounts of information and would creatively fill in the gaps, sometimes with humorous results that helped him stand out in auditions.

When he auditioned for the role of Arthur 'The Fonz' Fonzarelli in *Happy Days*, the producers were initially looking for a taller Italian actor.

However, Winkler's performance impressed them so much that they hired him on the spot, despite his shorter stature.

Remembering the audition, Winkler said, 'And they got you know, this short Jew from New York, but all I did Chris, all I did was change my voice. I introduce myself as Henry, and then as I started to do it, something overtook me … And I changed my voice like this and it unleashed me' (Garvey, 2024).

The role, which Winkler played from 1974 to 1984, marked the beginning of a successful career spanning over fifty years. He went on to produce several television shows, including the popular *MacGyver* in the 1980s, and to direct various movies. His talent and hard work earned him two Golden Globe Awards for Best Actor.

Winkler's literary career is equally remarkable. He has written twenty-six books, including eighteen in the Hank Zipzer series, which chronicles the adventures and misadventures of a resourceful but struggling student, and four in the Ghost Buddy series. Despite initial doubts about his ability to write, Winkler, encouraged by his agent, found joy in creating stories that make readers laugh. His struggles with dyslexia, diagnosed later in life, deeply influenced his writing and advocacy work.

Winkler's experiences shaped his approach to writing, which prioritises ensuring his books are accessible to all readers, including those with reading difficulties. Together with his writing partner, Lin Oliver, he uses a variety of formats, includes plenty of white space and keeps his chapters short in order to make reading less daunting. Their collaboration, in which Winkler dictates and Oliver types, has produced bestselling books that resonate with many young readers.

Over the years, Winkler has become a passionate advocate for those with dyslexia. His books, aimed at children, often draw from his own experiences and encourage resilience and perseverance. He tirelessly promotes the message that learning challenges should not prevent anyone from achieving their dreams. Through personal letters to young readers, he reinforces the idea that overcoming difficulties is possible and that success is within reach.

Attention deficit hyperactivity disorder (ADHD) and reading disabilities are among the most commonly diagnosed disorders in childhood, each affecting nearly 5% of the population. G. Reid Lyon of the National

Institutes of Health, along with Sally E. Shaywitz and Bennett A. Shaywitz of Yale University, have conducted extensive research on dyslexia. They describe it as a learning disorder with a neurobiological origin, indicating a connection between the nervous system and brain function (Lyon et al., 2003; Germanò et al., 2010). Despite significant scientific advances, the task of understanding dyslexia remains a work in progress.

Dyslexia is considered to be a specific learning disorder, distinct from general learning disabilities. It often co-occurs with ADHD, meaning that a diagnosis of one frequently accompanies a diagnosis of the other (in medical terms, this is known as 'comorbidity'). Over 80% of children with ADHD and 60% of those with reading disabilities meet the criteria for another diagnosis, commonly dyslexia.

Dyslexia is characterised by difficulties in accurate word recognition, reading disabilities, and poor spelling and decoding abilities. These challenges are not due to poor eyesight, hearing problems, lack of motivation or inadequate teaching.

To help individuals with dyslexia cope better, experts have implemented various interventions, including behavioural therapy, pharmacological treatments, and music education for children and adolescents (Cogo-Moreira *et al.*, 2012).

Some of the most inspiring interventions come from those who have lived with dyslexia and found ways to overcome its challenges. Winkler is one such advocate. His journey from struggling student to successful actor, producer, director and author is a testament to his resilience and determination. His story inspires others to look beyond their challenges and strive to make their dreams reality. Today, The Yale Centre for Dyslexia & Creativity profiles Winkler as one of its iconic success stories, celebrating his achievements and his ongoing efforts to support and inspire those with dyslexia.

3

The Silence of the Lambs, directed by Jonathan Demme and produced with Edward Saxon, was released in 1991. Featuring the unforgettable Anthony Hopkins as Hannibal Lecter, a terrifying cannibal serial killer, the movie became an instant box office success. It won five major Oscars – Best Picture, Best Director, Best Lead Actor, Best Lead Actress and Best Screenplay – making it one of only three films to win all five top categories. This success catapulted Demme and Saxon into a revered class of film-makers.

For their next project, Demme and Saxon were inspired to create a film about AIDS, a disease caused by HIV. This virus attacks the immune system, leaving the body unable to fight infections. In the 1990s, large numbers of people were being infected by HIV, and without viable treatments, the infection progressed to full-blown AIDS, causing death rates to rise exponentially each year.

The death of Hollywood actor Rock Hudson from AIDS in 1985 brought significant attention to the disease. Further inspiration came from Demme's friend Juan Suárez Botas, a Spanish illustrator who had recently been diagnosed with AIDS, and Saxon's friend Robert Breslo, a writer burdened with the disease (Millea, 2019).

Despite their success, Demme and Saxon faced widespread reluctance in the film industry to address the AIDS pandemic, partly due to the perception that it was predominantly a gay disease. This stigma made it difficult to secure funding for the project. However, the success of *The Silence of the Lambs* gave them the credibility to take a leap of faith and break the perception barrier. They chose Philadelphia as the setting for its historical significance and promotional potential (Millea, 2019). After considering titles such as *At Risk, People Like Us* and *Probable Cause*, they settled on *Philadelphia*. Filming began in 1992 and the movie was released in 1993. It was a box office success, grossing $200 million and winning two Oscars: Best Actor for Tom Hanks and Best Original Song for Bruce Springsteen's 'Streets of Philadelphia'.

The storyline of *Philadelphia* was compelling, and the cast was even more convincing. Tom Hanks lost almost nineteen kilograms in order to portray Andrew Beckett, a successful attorney in a prestigious law firm who is secretly gay and infected with HIV, now progressing to AIDS. Beckett's employers, concerned about the firm's reputation, eventually fire him. Beckett decides to fight his dismissal, but most attorneys refuse his case until he finds Joe Miller, played by Denzel Washington, an initially homophobic ambulance chaser whose prejudices fade as the movie progresses. The courtroom battle is intense, and Beckett's determination to fight for his rights despite his deteriorating health is inspiring.

The film, inspired by the true AIDS discrimination case of Geoffrey Bowers versus the law firm Baker McKenzie, dramatises the real challenges faced by those burdened with AIDS (Associated Press, 1996). Bowers sought to clear his name and explain the impact of losing his job during such a vulnerable time. He passed away shortly after testifying, aged thirty-three, in 1987.

Demme and Saxon's film was groundbreaking, confronting the AIDS epidemic head-on and fighting the stigma associated with the disease. The film's portrayal of the steady progression of AIDS was painful yet necessary, highlighting the ignorance and prejudice of the time. Beckett's defiance and courage were a powerful testament to the human spirit.

During the 1980s and 1990s, AIDS decimated millions of lives. The development and distribution of antiretroviral drugs have since slowed the pandemic. According to the World Health Organization, as of July 2024, HIV remains a major global health issue, having claimed 42.3 million lives (World Health Organization, 2024). Although there is no cure, effective prevention, diagnosis and treatment have transformed HIV into a manageable chronic condition, allowing those infected to lead long, healthy lives.

4

The grim picture painted by the World Health Organization and the statistics of death and infection point to deep turmoil for individuals. What did a typical patient feel in the time before the medical breakthroughs described in the last paragraph of the previous section? The experiences of one of those burdened with the disease are poignantly captured in the memoir of Justice Edwin Cameron, who has lived with the virus since the late 1980s (Cameron, 2005).

Following the news of his HIV diagnosis, Cameron was swept into a whirlwind of emotions and frustration. Reflecting on the life-altering moment, he wrote, 'It meant death ... It has been said that what distinguishes humans from other animals is our conscious apprehension of mortality'

(Cameron, 2005: 50). Cameron writes about the stigma attached to AIDS and HIV, describing it as a social brand that marks disgrace, humiliation and rejection. He notes that many people viewed (and many still view) those with AIDS or HIV as contaminated with a vile, self-induced affliction.

This stigma is one of the most persistent and damaging problems of the epidemic, often feared more than the disfiguring, agonising and prolonged death caused by the disease. Cameron recounts how some of those burdened with the disease were shut out by their spouses, abandoned by their friends, and refused the services, help and support they needed. This external rejection found an ally within the minds of those with HIV or AIDS, fuelling fears, self-loathing and self-blame. The combination of external prejudice and internal self-destruction rendered the effects of the stigma so powerful and destructive.

Given the immense burden of pain, rejection and hopelessness, it seems reasonable to assume that individuals diagnosed with HIV would struggle to imagine a future beyond the looming spectre of death. However, humans are inherently different from each other. Even faced with the same fate and circumstances, some individuals dared to dream differently and fought to live with hope and resilience.

5

Earvin 'Magic' Johnson grew up in the heart of Lansing, Michigan, a Midwestern city where hard work was a way of life. His father, a diligent employee at General Motors, instilled in him the values of dedication and perseverance. Johnson often recalls his father's advice, which left a lasting impact on him: 'Listen, son, if you do this job halfway, everything in life you gonna do halfway. You gonna study halfway. You gonna practice basketball halfway' (Williams et al., 2022). His father's words were a guiding principle, ensuring Johnson never settled for anything less than his best. He learnt to love work, becoming both a perfectionist and a workaholic.

Johnson's childhood was shaped by this relentless work ethic. From a young age, he was encouraged to put in honest, hard work, whether it was shovelling snow or practising basketball. This foundation not only built his character, but also prepared him for the gruelling demands of professional sports. Despite his natural talent, his towering 2.06-metre height and sturdy build, it was his dedication and love for the game that truly set him apart.

Johnson's basketball prowess really began to shine during his time at Michigan State University. He played for two seasons, demonstrating a unique blend of skill, agility and strategic thinking.

Basketball, a game played by two teams of five players each, assigns players to specific positions based on their physique, ball handling, passing and shooting skills. Johnson excelled as a point guard, often considered the team's core. Known as the 'floor general', the point guard is crucial in both offense and defence, requiring high dribbling and passing skills and the ability to minimise turnovers while disrupting the opponent's key players. Johnson redefined this role with his lung-busting drives across the court, uncanny passes to well-positioned teammates and impeccable timing in deciding when to shoot or pass.

Johnson's early career with the Los Angeles Lakers, beginning in 1979, was nothing short of spectacular. Over twelve seasons, he helped the Lakers win five NBA championships, scoring over seventeen thousand points. His charismatic personality and extraordinary talent earned him the nickname 'Magic', and he quickly became a national and international idol. His influence on the game was profound, setting new standards for future generations of basketball players.

However, in 1991, Johnson's life took an unexpected and dramatic turn. Dr Michael Mellman, the Lakers' team physician, delivered a fateful call that changed everything: during a routine pre-season medical test, Johnson had tested positive for HIV. Devastated and in disbelief, Johnson repeatedly asked if there had been a mistake. 'I'm asking him a hundred times, "Are you sure?"' he recalls. 'And they say, "Hey, we ran the tests a couple of times, and yes, you do have HIV." And so, I just lost it right there, you know?' (Stevenson, 1991).

The diagnosis came just months after Johnson had married, and his wife was expecting their first child. The implications were terrifying. How would he break the news to his beloved wife? Gathering the courage, Johnson told her, and to his relief, she received the news with remarkable strength, becoming his best source of support. Miraculously, both his wife and child tested negative for HIV, a rare but welcome outcome.

Determined to face his new reality head-on, Johnson sought to understand the virus that had invaded his body. He met with doctors and specialists, asking countless questions to learn about HIV. His hunger for knowledge was insatiable, but he ensured that his information came from reliable experts.

Accompanied by Dr Mellman, Johnson announced his diagnosis at a news conference, becoming the first high-profile sportsman to publicly reveal such news.

'This was Earvin,' Dr Mellman later recalled. 'I had never known him to back down from or hesitate to go towards whatever he had to do. It's who he is and who he was' (Laughland, 2021).

Despite the prevalent view that an HIV diagnosis was a death sentence, Johnson displayed unwavering positivity. At the news conference in November 1991, he announced his retirement from the Lakers, understanding that the competitive nature of professional basketball could harm his immune system. He stated, 'Life is going to go on for me, and I'm going to be a happy man … When your back is against the wall, you have to come out swinging … I'm going to go on, going to be there, going to have fun' (Stevenson, 1991). His optimism in the face of such a grim prognosis was both surprising and inspiring.

Johnson's promise to advocate for those living with HIV and to raise awareness about the dangers of unprotected sex marked the beginning of his new role as a health advocate. Working closely with renowned experts such as Dr David Ho and Dr Anthony Fauci, Johnson began a regimen of antiretroviral drugs designed to combat the virus and protect his immune system. Dr Fauci, who would later gain fame for his leadership during the Covid-19 pandemic, provided critical guidance, but much of the success of Johnson's treatment was due to his own determination and discipline.

Despite the initial advice he had received recommending that he avoid the physical rigours of basketball, Johnson remained active, maintaining his fitness and health. Just months after his diagnosis, he returned to the court for the 1992 NBA All-Star Game and played for the US Olympic men's basketball team. In the 1995–96 season, he made a brief comeback with the Lakers, fulfilling his desire to end his career on his terms.

After retiring from professional basketball, Johnson transitioned into a new life as a successful businessman and philanthropist. He pursued wealth not just for personal gain but to create generational wealth for his family and community. He expressed his satisfaction with having had a great life and the assurance that his children would be financially secure. He pointed out that historically, black people have not fully grasped the concept of generational wealth and its transfer, explaining that there is now a growing understanding of its importance (Williams et al., 2022).

Throughout his life, Johnson has never displayed signs of self-pity or retreated from a challenge. His relentless pursuit of solutions, even against the odds, and his enduring love for his wife and family have been constants. The effectiveness of his treatment plan and his role as an advocate provided a beacon of hope for many living with HIV.

Commemorating thirty years since his diagnosis, Johnson reflected, 'As we talk today, right now, I'm thinking, "Wow," it's been thirty years and I'm still here, healthy. Everything has gone right. There was one drug then; now we have thirty-something drugs' (Laughland, 2021; Oliviera, 2021).

Johnson's story is a testament to resilience, optimism and the power of a positive outlook. His journey from basketball superstar to health advocate and successful businessman illustrates how determination and hard work can overcome even the most formidable challenges. His advocacy and business acumen have left a lasting legacy, inspiring others to strive for their dreams regardless of the obstacles they face.

6

The privilege of sharing their tale is reserved for those who have been confronted by the grim prospect of death and succeeded – for the moment at least – in skirting its clutches.

Justice Edwin Cameron stood at the precipice, compelled by an urgent need to voice his narrative. His journey was marked by a stark contrast: a childhood marred by poverty gave way to a comfortable existence in South Africa, a transition granted by the colour of his skin. His was not a life of excess or recklessness; he was the epitome of diligence, dedicating himself to the legal profession. Despite this, he was not spared from the ravages of AIDS, a stark reminder of life's unpredictability.

Cameron was not a promiscuous man. In his poignant memoir *Witness to AIDS*, he shares a deeply personal account of how a fleeting lapse in judgment one Easter in 1985 brought him perilously close to succumbing to AIDS.

The grave news came during a phone call on a Friday in December 1986, when Cameron was at the height of his career: his doctor delivered the results of Cameron's recent blood tests, confirming his HIV-positive status.

The weight of the news was palpable, leaving both Cameron and his doctor grappling with the enormity of the situation. The doctor seemed at a loss for words and quickly ended the call.

Because there was no available treatment at the time, for Cameron, this news was equivalent to being told that he must now prepare to die. It was public knowledge that it took ten years on average for the virus to complete its devastation of the body, which in itself gave the feeling of a death-row wait. The need for doctors to counsel patients before delivering such news only became standard practice much later. Patients had to deal with their new reality without professional help, with the stigma associated with the disease making it even more difficult to share the news with friends, family or co-workers.

In 1986, Cameron was thirty-three years old. The young advocate was already successful and upwardly mobile. He had HIV but was not yet sick. He summoned his strength and put all his focus on his life passion: work.

7

Cameron's busy legal career and sense of duty to civil advocacy saw him leading the fight against legislation that permitted employers to conduct HIV tests on workers. This was only one of many successes. Such work motivated him.

Cameron's potential did not go unnoticed. In December 1994, President Nelson Mandela appointed him a judge of South Africa's High Court.

Cameron maintained a regular regime of immune checks and CD4 counts, as prescribed by his doctor. All of these tests confirmed that he was in good health. His only dilemma was whether to reveal the diagnosis to his employers.

For the next few years, officiating as a judge of the High Court in Johannesburg, Cameron climbed the stairs between his chambers and the judges' common room several times a day. He did so as a source of exercise as well as a form of distraction, counting the stairs as he walked up and down them: 'Two flights, four landings, forty stairs' (Cameron, 2005: 9). One day in October 1997, he had counted twenty stairs when all his energy suddenly seemed to disappear and he was forced to stop, leaning his forehead against the wall and breathing heavily.

Over the weeks, Cameron had ignored the growing feeling of reduced energy. His worst fear was that he now had AIDS. He made an appointment to see his doctor that afternoon. The doctor's diagnosis was pneumocystis pneumonia, or PCP.

A few weeks later, the fungal spores on Cameron's tongue became worse. However, he had a strong will to work and despite his physical deterioration, he pushed himself to fulfil his responsibilities as a judge.

Cameron's doctor had looked after him for more than six years, and when his patient's CD4 count deteriorated to below 200, he knew it was time to advise him to consider the latest new therapy of antiretroviral drugs. 1996 had been a great year for the treatment of HIV, with American scientist and physician Dr David Ho announcing a breakthrough. Finally convinced, Cameron took his first dose in November 1997. The costs of the treatment were prohibitive; as a judge of the High Court, he could afford them, although the monthly supply took a big chunk of his salary.

In the coming weeks, Cameron was grateful to have decided to start antiretroviral treatment. He began to feel well and was less tired. A ravenous appetite replaced a dutiful regard for meals. 'Life forces were coursing through my body,' he said (Cameron, 2005: 38).

Being made a judge is a hugely respected and coveted career achievement for a lawyer, but Cameron was not going to stop there. A vacancy on the Constitutional Court became available in 1999 because of the death of respected judge John Didcott, following a long illness. Cameron applied when the position was advertised and he was duly nominated, along with other applicants.

Antiretroviral treatment had revitalised Cameron's health and restored his strength. However, although he was in good health, the secret of his illness continued to bother him, so he sought the advice of the head of the Constitutional Court, Justice Arthur Chaskalson.

The two men met over lunch and Chaskalson considered the matter. He counselled that there was no reason for embarrassment because HIV affected many individuals. It was high time, he believed, for someone with a public profile to start talking openly about it. Chaskalson advised Cameron to consider using his upcoming interview in a fortnight as the platform from which to do this, suggesting that the Judicial Service Commission (JSC) would provide a fitting and respectful setting for such a disclosure.

The interview was the public hearing for the vacant position at the Constitution Court for which Cameron had been nominated. This was not the first time he had applied for a position on the bench of the Constitutional Court. However, his previous attempt had not been rewarded with a nomination. His persistent attempts underlined his ambition to reach the apex of the legal profession.

Cameron found himself being convinced by Chaskalson to do what now appeared to be the right thing to do. Announcing his HIV status to the public was an act of advocacy, after all. He had always wanted to make an impact in life and make a difference for the weak and those burdened by the disease. However, the feeling of apprehension that came with his choice of such a course of action was palpable.

First Cameron had to face his seventy-eight-year-old mother and inform her of the news. He had kept his HIV diagnosis from her since 1986, when his doctor had abruptly broken the news to him.

Chaskalson had agreed that it was not a necessity for Cameron to disclose his HIV diagnosis; it was a matter of personal choice to do so. Cameron took the JSC – which included judges, lawyers and politicians – by surprise when he revealed his HIV-positive status and the fact that he had been managing the condition since 1986. His declaration was driven by a powerful message: he emphasised that he was not succumbing to AIDS; rather, he was living with HIV, continuing his life and work despite the diagnosis.

The members of the JSC, who were impressed by Cameron during the interview, recommended and shortlisted him for the position, but this latest attempt was again not successful.

Cameron was not deterred by this second unsuccessful attempt and tried again in 2008. This time he was successful: he was appointed Justice of the Constitutional Court from the beginning of 2009. He served a ten-year term, retiring in 2019. Since then, Cameron, who was a recipient of a Rhodes Scholarship in his early years and studied law at Oxford University, has served in various other public capacities.

Since its inception in 1902 thanks to Cecil John Rhodes's generous endowment, the Rhodes Trust has been recognising and rewarding exceptional students with scholarships. The selection criteria have stood the test of time, with academic prowess being a cornerstone (Rhodes Trust, 2024). Yet the Trust looks beyond scholarly achievements, seeking candidates who exhibit a zest for fully harnessing their talents, as evidenced by their proficiency in collaborative endeavours such as sports, music, debate, dance, theatre and the arts. The trustees value integrity, bravery, commitment, empathy, kindness, generosity and community spirit, alongside a strong moral compass and a propensity for leadership and compassion.

Cameron epitomises these qualities. He has distinguished himself with a remarkable career that extends well beyond the legal world. At the height of the AIDS epidemic in the 1980s, he was one of the tireless activists relentlessly pressuring governments and decision-makers to find solutions and ensure treatments were accessible to all.

When I reached out for Cameron's approval on how I had presented excerpts from his memoir, he reflected on the fierce struggle of those living with the virus for dignity. He quickly corrected me: 'If you don't mind, could you say "surviving" rather than "suffering" where it first appears, and "burdened" for its third occurrence?' This request stemmed from a deliberate resistance by AIDS activists in the 1980s to the prevalent term 'AIDS sufferers'.

Faced with the challenges posed by HIV, Cameron did not waver in his ambitions. Instead, this adversity only intensified his drive, propelling him to imprint an indelible mark on the world.

8

Health is a private, personal matter. The courageous and selfless announcement of their HIV diagnoses by Earvin 'Magic' Johnson and Justice Edwin Cameron in those early years of the disease helped shatter the ignorance about and the stigma associated with the AIDS epidemic.

The two men – one an American and the other a South African – live on different continents, but they share an unflinching desire to overcome the odds that cannot be underestimated.

Johnson and Cameron should have died. That was the fate of millions who were infected with HIV in the 1980s and 1990s, the period during which both men were infected at almost the same age (approximately thirty-two). But both were determined to live and to achieve their desires. By dogged determination, one became a wealthy businessman; the other became a respected and successful Justice of the Constitutional Court.

Success is often romanticised. Successful people are at times viewed as having been destined to do better than the rest, or simply as having been lucky. This may well be true in certain cases: we see their current lifestyle, luxury house, expensive cars and all the other trappings of wealth that represent the fruits of their hard work along the way. But the trail walked by individuals is relegated to history and in most cases is never told. Johnson and Cameron's stories reveal the experiences of remarkable humans who fought like wounded dogs backed into a corner when death came calling. They succeeded despite the odds being stacked against them.

9

Movies are crafted for maximum entertainment, and producers often rely on shock and awe to deliver high-energy thrillers. Facts are frequently exaggerated for dramatic effect, with films such as *Mission Impossible* and *Die Hard* serving as prime examples.

The 2015 movie *San Andreas* follows this formula, using the backdrop of the infamous San Andreas Fault to create a catastrophic storyline. The film, which dramatises the potential for a massive earthquake stretching from Los Angeles to San Francisco, is based on real warnings from seismologists.

The plot is filled with classic movie elements: villains, weasels, heroes and romantic sub-plots – all centred around the calm, unflappable super-saviour, played by Dwayne 'The Rock' Johnson. The movie's scenes of destruction are spectacular, with skyscrapers being reduced to rubble as earthquakes measuring between 9.1 and 9.6 on the Richter scale rock the earth. A 9.6-magnitude quake would, in reality, be the largest ever recorded, but the film takes it a step further, unleashing a massive tsunami that causes a container ship to crash into the Golden Gate Bridge. The iconic bridge is hit at its centre span, causing unimaginable destruction and loss of life.

This jaw-dropping spectacle justified the film's $110-million budget, and Warner Bros was rewarded with box office earnings of $474 million (Wikipedia, 2024).

Interestingly, *San Andreas* is not the first film to feature the Golden Gate Bridge. It has been destroyed or threatened in numerous movies, including *James Bond: A View to a Kill* (1985), *Pacific Rim* (2013) and *Godzilla* (2014). The bridge remains a popular symbol in American cinema, often meeting a dramatic fate on screen. Its cultural significance is undeniable, as major travel sources such as CNN Travel and Tripadvisor regularly list the Golden Gate Bridge as one of the top tourist attractions in the United States (Tripadvisor, 2024).

San Fransisco was founded by the Spanish in 1775. According to Richard Thomas Loomis, 'San Fransisco … is located on a narrow, hilly tip of a peninsula bounded on the west by the Pacific Ocean, on the north by the Golden Gate, on the east by the San Fransisco Bay … The entrance to the Bay, the Golden Gate, is a picturesque strait one mile wide at its narrowest point and some three miles long' (Loomis, 1958: 3–4). Across the Golden Gate to the north of San Fransisco is Marin County.

Gifted with natural beauty, the San Fransisco Bay boasts one of the most well-known natural harbours in the world. Surrounded by the Pacific Ocean waters, its climate is mild throughout the year.

The discovery of gold in 1848 spurred a gold rush and exponential growth in economic activity and population in the area. Transportation of goods and people across the Golden Gate Strait in the nineteenth and early twentieth centuries was by ferry. When demand increased, more ferries were added. However, the emergence of automobile transportation in the first twenty years of the 1900s created logistical problems for the ferry system. Ferries were designed to transport passengers and could cope with carrying a small number of horse-drawn carriages. When motor vehicle numbers skyrocketed, the time had come for ferries to be replaced by a bridge spanning the Golden Gate Strait, connecting San Fransisco to Marin County and other northern settlements.

The Brooklyn bridge in New York City (built in 1883), which links Manhattan Island with the mainland, served as inspiration and encouragement that this feat was possible.

The Golden Gate Bridge was built during the Great Depression. The first proposal for its construction was made in 1872 by railroad infrastructure engineer Charles Crocker, but it was dismissed as too visionary and lacking in implementation practicality. The final decision by the authorities to proceed with construction was only made in 1930 and the bridge was opened for public use in 1937.

For twenty-seven years, the Golden Gate Bridge held the envied title of the longest suspension bridge ever built. Developing technology has made it possible for longer-span bridges to be built and ten bridges have since overtaken the Golden Gate Bridge in terms of length.

Suspension bridges generally feature two parallel cables, spaced about the same width as the roadway deck they support. These cables stretch from anchors at both ends, passing over the tops of intermediate towers. The deck is then suspended by strong ropes that connect from the deck level to the main cables (Golden Gate Bridge Highway & Transportation District, 2024).

The length of the Golden Gate Bridge is 2 337 metres, while the two towers on either side reach a height of 227 metres. There are two parallel cables anchoring from one side of the bridge over the towers to the other side. Each cable is made up of 27 572 galvanised steel cables grouped into

61 cable groups bunched together into a diameter of just under one metre (Game *et al.*, 2016).

The Golden Gate Bridge is renowned as one of the most spectacular and famous bridges globally. The American Society of Civil Engineers has even declared it one of the wonders of the modern world (Arsla, 2020). Today the bridge carries symbolic, historic and cultural meaning, and is 'always associated with San Fransisco' (Chang & Choo, 2009). That the bridge has become integral to the branding of San Fransisco as a tourist destination is explained by tourist destination experts. This is attributed to landmarks in the city: typically, a sightseer's first interaction with a destination is through its representation rather than the actual place. The term 'marker' refers to information about a specific site. Sightseers do not empirically see San Francisco; instead, they experience Fisherman's Wharf, a cable car, the Golden Gate Bridge, Union Square, Coit Tower, the Presidio, City Lights Bookstore, Chinatown and perhaps the Haight-Ashbury district or a nude go-go dancer in a North Beach-Barbary Coast club. Each of these items is a symbolic marker representing the city. Individually, each site also requires its own marker. Thus, two frameworks give meaning to these attractions: one where the sightseer visits the Golden Gate Bridge as a crucial piece of information to complete their experience of San Francisco, and another where they see the bridge as an impressive suspension structure worth admiring on its own (Berger, 2019).

The man who was responsible for this amazing feat of engineering was Joseph Strauss. A few years after graduating from the University of Cincinnati, he formed his own hugely successful business, which operated in the Chicago area.

JB Strauss Company designed bascule bridges across the country and had patents registered. (Bascule bridges are bridges with moveable spans that can be lifted to allow big ships to pass through.) When Strauss learnt about the plan to build a bridge across the Golden Gate, he immediately became interested. After years of building bascule bridges, he wanted to join the Super League by constructing such a long-span bridge.

The general belief of the engineering firms approached by the city engineer was that construction of such a bridge was not possible: 'Everybody says it can't be done and that it would cost over $100 million if it could be done' (Griggs Jr, 2010: 71). However, Strauss learnt from the city engineer that the preliminary budget for the bridge was set at $25 million – reflecting what the city could realistically afford. This presented a stark contrast in terms of expectations and affordability.

Strauss's direct inquiry to the city engineer proved to be a shrewd move. He promised to prepare a design that would come within the indicated budget, and various iterations of the designs were prepared and considered between the early 1920s and 1929, when the final suspension bridge design was concluded.

During these years, Strauss repeatedly faced opposition from the engineering profession. In March 1926, for instance, the Joint Council of Engineering Societies of San Fransisco issued a statement questioning his credibility and stating that although no skilled engineer had claimed that constructing a bridge over the Golden Gate was impossible, there was, in their considered view, a significant difference between what could be achieved regardless of cost and what was financially practical. They concluded that without supporting data, it was unfortunate for the engineering profession that no proposal had yet met any or all of the financial feasibility requirements.

More naysayers emerged in late 1927, when taxpayers hired a local board of engineers to prove that it was not possible to build the bridge for less than $112 million. But if those who opposed Strauss believed that he would give up, they must have been surprised at how he found his way through the roadblocks, manoeuvring around the obstacles thrown at him.

Strauss had earned the nickname 'the drawbridge king' for his expertise in constructing bascule bridges. However, he had no experience with suspension bridge construction, leading some to believe he was overreaching by taking on such a project. His design skills were limited, and at first glance, it might have seemed like a step too far. Yet in hindsight we could argue that his technical limitations fuelled the bold, almost naive enthusiasm necessary to see the project through – especially at a time when more seasoned suspension bridge engineers had already lost their nerve.

In the 2004 documentary *Golden Gate Bridge*, Strauss is profiled as a visionary and a showman (Bittel, 2004) who defied his critics and successfully persuaded the city's residents to support him, explaining that the bridge was crucial for the city's people as well as its growth. He also appealed to their interests, offering the promise of real estate profits and new opportunities that the great bridge would unlock for the future.

The darker side of Strauss lay in his tendency to embellish his credentials and overstate his expertise (Griggs Jr, 2010). Yet his unwavering determination and leadership at every stage of the project were undeniably crucial to its success. If it was an almost impossible but necessary task to pacify taxpayers and engineers in the Bay Area, Strauss knew that it was much more critical to prove to the city authorities team appointed to manage the bridge project that JB Strauss Company had the required capacity.

Strauss was well aware of the level of design skills needed for such a mammoth project. He found the person with the desired skills in Charles A. Ellis, whom he hired in 1921. Strauss made use of Ellis's credentials – Ellis had a strong civil engineering background in private firms and had been a professor at the University of Illinois for nine years – in his dealings with the city authorities.

The rest of the team was assembled on the same basis of credentials and competence: Strauss employed individuals and consulting firms who were experts in their fields, including architects, geologists and engineers versed in all aspects of bridge design (for instance, traffic engineers and structural engineers).

Named in 1929 as chief engineer for the construction project, Strauss was credited with the strict safety procedures implemented on site. Between 1931 and 1937, only one worker died on the construction site. The workers always wore hard hats, which was a first in the country. In addition, safety nets were installed along the bridge channel. However, three months before completion of the bridge in 1937, a scaffold collapsed, breaking the safety net, and ten workers plunged to their death. In total, eleven workers died during construction, a considerably better safety record than projects of similar magnitude. By way of comparison, twenty-four people died during construction of the San Fransisco Bay Bridge, which was built at the same time; safety nets were not used for that bridge.

10

The Golden Gate Bridge is painted International Orange, a colour typically used in the aerospace industry. The current hue of the bridge harmonises seamlessly with the seasonal shades of its surroundings, complementing both the San Francisco cityscape and the Marin Hills (Golden Gate Bridge Highway & Transportation District, 2024).

The bridge was constructed for the functional purpose of transporting goods and people by connecting San Fransisco and the northern cities, but it quickly became a landmark of immense significance. It has since become a favourite setting for Hollywood producers, gracing the backdrop of numerous blockbuster films. As a tourist attraction, it draws visitors year round.

The grandeur that we see when we look at the Golden Gate Bridge today masks the tremendous effort, toil and activity that went into its creation. Indeed, the fact that the bridge was constructed at all during the Great Depression era can be attributed to Strauss's unwavering resolve and dedication, which were pivotal factors in its completion. He was the underdog and outsider who set out to disrupt the strongly held belief that what he proposed to do could not be done.

When the city engineer received the first bridge site survey report in May 1920 and Strauss offered to do the design, he was fifty years old. The city authorities only accepted the final designs and decided to start construction ten years later, and by the time the bridge was completed in 1937, Strauss was sixty-seven years old. Finding himself backed into a virtual corner, he had fought like a wounded dog, succeeding where those who were known to have better skills and experience could not rise to the challenge. He dealt with that perceived weakness by assembling an A team of skilled professionals with a solid reputation in bridge construction, and leading with legendary vision and relentlessness.

The final estimated and consensus cost of construction of the Golden Gate Bridge was $35 million, a remarkable achievement compared with the wild estimates of $100 million proposed by other engineers.

Large-scale projects such as the construction of the Golden Gate Bridge are rarely completed without internal conflicts, power struggles and ethical dilemmas, issues that are often underplayed in business school case studies. Joseph Strauss, the chief engineer and the visionary who brought the idea of the bridge to life, was determined to retain his position as the key figure behind its creation, no matter the cost. In his efforts to keep control and ensure that his name remained synonymous with the prestigious project, he insisted that all reports submitted to the city prominently featured his name and signature, often at the expense of other key contributors.

This created friction, particularly with Charles Ellis, the engineer widely credited with developing the actual design of the Golden Gate Bridge. In a move intended to solidify his own legacy, Strauss fired Ellis in late 1931 and systematically erased Ellis's contributions from the official narrative (Griggs Jr, 2010). By the time Strauss issued his final report on the bridge in 1937, Ellis's name had been completely removed. This act of sidelining key contributors for personal gain highlights the ethical tensions that often arise in major projects – tensions that, while significant, are frequently downplayed in discussions about leadership and management.

Strauss passed away just one year after the Golden Gate Bridge opened, but he had already left behind a legacy.

11

This chapter provides a vivid portrayal of the resilience required to confront adversity and the indomitable spirit needed to fight against the odds. It tells us several things about the psychology of facing challenges:

- Resilience in the face of uncertainty: The inability to predict life's challenges, such as illness or overwhelming projects, requires a psychological resilience that allows individuals to persist despite not knowing what difficulties lie ahead.
- Faith and skill as tools for overcoming adversity: As we saw in Chapter 1, the biblical story of Joseph illustrates how faith coupled with unique skills (such as dream interpretation) can turn dire situations into opportunities for significant breakthroughs.
- Relentless pursuit of goals: The figures mentioned in this chapter (Winkler, Johnson, Cameron and Strauss) exemplify the tenacious mindset, akin to that of a wounded dog backed into a corner, which is often necessary to achieve success against all odds.

- The power of unconventional strategies in overcoming obstacles.
- The role of determination in achieving purpose: Individuals who face adversity head-on with determination are more likely to fulfil their life's purpose and succeed.
- The importance of action: The chapter suggests that taking action, even when a person is faced with serious obstacles, is crucial. Those who actively confront their challenges rather than succumbing to them increase their chances of creating wealth and finding success.

In summary, the psychology of confronting adversity and fighting against the odds involves a complex interplay of resilience, faith, skill and determination as well as the willingness to employ unconventional methods when necessary. It is about harnessing the power within to transform challenges into stepping stones towards success.

The ability to overcome adversity is intertwined with success and the creation of wealth. There is no way of forecasting what curveballs will befall us and in what form. The curveball could be a dread disease, a severe genetic condition or the perception that a project is simply too big for anybody to do. These are the forces that afflicted the individuals showcased in this chapter. Joseph encountered comparable challenges, initially when he was sold into slavery by his brothers and later during his imprisonment in a dungeon. His steadfast faith and his unique ability to interpret dreams were both instrumental in bringing about his pivotal encounter with Pharaoh.

Winkler, Johnson, Cameron and Strauss remained relentless in their pursuit of success, never allowing themselves to falter. In some ways they were like a dung beetle, which hangs in what seems like a precarious inverted posture while it shapes cow dung into a large ball weighing up to fifty times its own weight (Sabi Sabi, 2014). Once it has completed this task, the beetle rolls the massive dung ball along the ground up the embankment towards its burrow.

For anyone watching the beetle do its thing, it seems like an impossible and futile task. Who does that? Who walks backwards while hanging upside down? But the dung beetle survives on faeces; it needs them for food and breeding, and to play its role in the ecosystem. In its inverted posture, the dung beetle directs enormous force into its hind legs to move the cow dung, and so achieves its life purpose. Its technique is unorthodox but effective.

Those who come out swinging when confronted with serious obstacles give themselves a fighting chance, keeping their objective of creating wealth and finding success alive.

SOURCES

Chapter 1

Alexander, W. (2009). Mathematics vs pattern recognition in water resource studies. *Civil Engineering*, 44–46.

Aling, C. (2003). Joseph in Egypt. *Bible and Spade*, 10–13.

Bengen, W. (1992). Asset allocation for a lifetime. *Journal of Financial Planning*, 58–67.

Bengen, W. (1994). Determining Withdrawal Rates Using Historical Data. *Journal of Financial Planning*, 7(4), 171–180.

Berners-Lee, T. (2000). *Weaving The Web: The Original Design and Ultimate Destiny of the World Wide Web*. New York: HarperCollins.

Brown, D. & Brown, D. (2000). *Mesopotamian planetary astronomy-astrology*. Groningen: Styx.

CE Noticias Financieras. (2020). *Stories of bad people: Vlad the impaler that inspired the legend of Dracula*. Miami: Content Engine LLC.

CE Noticias Financieras. (2021). *He executed more than 100 000 people with the cruelest methods: the story of Vlad the Impaler, the real Dracula*. Miami: Content Engine LLC.

Corey, J. (2014). Dreaming of Droughts: Genesis 37:1–11 in Dialogue with Contemporary Science. *Journal for the Study of the Old Testament*, 38(4), 425–438.

Graves, T., Gramacy, R. & Watkins, N. (2017). A Brief History of Long Memory: Hurst, Mandelbrot and the Road to ARFIMA, 1951–1980. *Entropy*, 19, 1–21.

Haleem, A. M. A. S. (2007). The story of Joseph in the Qur'an and the old testament. *Islam and Christian Relations*, 1(2), 171–191.

Hern, A. (2019). *Tim Berners-Lee on 30 years of the world wide web: 'We can get the web we want'*. The Guardian. [Online] Available at: https://www.theguardian.com/technology/2019/mar/12/tim-berners-lee-on-30-years-of-the-web-if-we-dream-a-little-we-can-get-the-web-we-want

Hodell, D. A., Brenner, M., Curtis, J. H. & Guilderson, T. (2001). Solar Forcing of Drought Frequency in the Maya Lowlands. *Science*, 292(5520), 1367–1370.

Holland, J. H. (1995). Hidden order. *Business Week – Domestic Edition*, 21.

Holy Bible: New King James Bible. (2004). Nashville: Thomas Nelson (Original work published 1982).

Indah, K. (2023). *How Many People Use Yahoo Mail in 2023? (User Stats)*. [Online] Available at: https://earthweb.com/yahoo-mail-users/

Jonathan, G. (2014). It Was 20 Years Ago Today. *Journal of Financial Planning*, 27(10), 24–28.

Meinert, R. G. (1973). Futures forecasting. *Oxford Journals (Oxford University Press) – Social Work*, 48–51.

Press, G. (2016). *Why Yahoo Lost And Google Won*. Forbes. [Online] Available at: https://www.forbes.com/sites/gilpress/2016/07/26/why-yahoo-lost-and-google-won/?sh=11afc295e155

Rota, G.-C. (1985). The Barrier of Meaning. *Letters in Mathematical Physics*, *10*(2–3), 97–99.

Tamplin, T. (2023). *Joseph Effect*. Finance Strategists. [Online] Available at: https://www.financestrategists.com/wealth-management/fundamental-vs-technical-analysis/joseph-effect/

Von Rad, G. (1973). *Genesis: A commentary*. s.l.: Westminister John Knox Press.

World Wide Web Foundation. (2019). *30 years on, what's next #ForTheWeb?* [Online] Available at: https://webfoundation.org/2019/03/web-birthday-30/

Chapter 2

Arthur, C. V. (1994). The Impact of the Second World War on Los Angeles. *University of California Press: Pacific Historical Review*, 289–314.

Britannica. (2024). *Israel-Hamas War*. [Online] Available at: https://www.britannica.com/event/Israel-Hamas-War#ref1320682

Bullock, A. (1971). *Hitler and the Origins of the Second World War*. London: Oxford University Press (Proceedings of the British Academy, v. 53), pp. 189–190.

Ciotti, M., Anglett, S., Minieri, M., Giovanetti, M., Benvenuto, D., Pascarella, S. … Ciccozzi, M. (2020). Covid-19 Outbreak: An Overview. *Chemotherapy*, *64*(5–6), 215–223.

Finkel, I. (2014). *The Ark Before Noah: Decoding the Story of the Flood*. New York: Random House LLC.

Fourie, B. (2023). *House prices in these CT suburbs have nearly doubled in 10 years*. IOL. [Online] Available at: https://www.iol.co.za/property/house-prices-in-these-ct-suburbs-have-nearly-doubled-in-10-years-8e95d22a-5b87-4c77-9b6f-5e2a62a54 57f#:~:text=House%20prices%20in%20these%20CT%20suburbs%20have%20 nearly%20doubled%20in%2010%20years,-Some%20Cape%20Town&text=Te

Graves, T., Gramacy, R. & Watkins, N. (2017). A Brief History of Long Memory: Hurst, Mandelbrot and the Road to ARFIMA, 1951–1980. *Entropy*, *19*(9), 1–21.

Hald, K. S. & Coslugeanu, P. (2020). The preliminary supply chain lessons of the Covid-19 disruption – What is the role of digital techlogies? *Operations Management Research*, *15*(1–2), 282–297.

Holland, T. (2014). *Review: Non Fiction: So much older than the Bible: The Ark was originally conceived as round and made of plant fibre*. [Online] Available at: https://www.proquest.com/newspapers/review-non-fiction-so-much-older-than--bible-ark/docview/1498233010/se-2?accountid=15083

Holy Bible: New King James Bible. (2004). Nashville: Thomas Nelson (Original work published 1982).

Lockheed Martin. (2020). *Lockheed During World War II: Operation Camouflage*. [Online] Available at: https://www.lockheedmartin.com/en-us/news/features/history/camouflage.

html#:~:text=At%20the%20Lockheed%20plant%2C%20Ohmer,in%20with%20
the%20surrounding%20grass

Macrotrends. (2023). *Lockheed Martin – 47 Year Stock Price History | LMT.* [Online]
Available at: https://www.macrotrends.net/stocks/charts/LMT/lockheed-martin/stock-
price-history

Moneyweb. (2023). *Distressed house sales soar 80% since last year.* [Online]
Available at: https://www.moneyweb.co.za/news/south-africa/distressed-house-sales-
soar-80-since-last-year/#:~:text=%2D%20JSE%3ASBK&text=The%20number%20
of%20homeowners%20being,increase%20of%20more%20than%2080%25

National Park Service. (2024). *World War II Shipbuilding in the San Francisco Bay Area.*
National Park Service. [Online] Available at: https://www.nps.gov/articles/000/world-
war-ii-shipbuilding-in-the-san-francisco-bay-area.htm#:~:text=San%20Francisco%20
Bay%20Area%20shipbuilders,ship%20a%20day%2C%20on%20average

NBC News. (2012). *10 companies profiting most from war.* [Online] Available at:
https://www.nbcnews.com/businessmain/10-companies-profiting-most-war-330249

Pam Golding Properties. (2023). *Residential Property Market Report by Pam Golding
Properties.* [Online] Available at: https://blog.pamgolding.co.za/residential-property-
market-report-by-pam-golding-properties/

Richter, W. (2019). *"Where the American Dream Goes to Die": Changes in House Prices,
Rents, and Incomes since 1960 by Region & Metro.* Wolf Street. [Online] Available at:
https://wolfstreet.com/2019/07/12/changes-in-house-prices-rents-and-household-
incomes-since-1960-in-the-us-by-region-and-major-metro/

Ryan, W. & Pitman, W. (1998). *Noah's Flood.* New York: Simon & Schuster.

Soskice, J. (2014). *Review – Books: Make Yourself an Ark.* [Online] Available at:
https://www.proquest.com/newspapers/review-books-make-yourself-ark/docview/
1525188349/se-2?account=15083

Statistics South Africa. (2023). *Stats SA's new property price index: Cape Town has become
more expensive.* [Online] Available at: https://www.statssa.gov.za/?p=16242#:~:text=Stats
%20SA%27s%20new%20residential%20property,metropolitan%20municipalities%20
(Figure%201)

The Economist. (2022). *The new winners and losers in business.* [Online] Available at:
https://www.economist.com/business/2022/11/27/the-new-winners-and-losers-in-
business

Walter, C. (2014). Benoit Mandelbrot in finance. In M. Frame & N. Cohen (Eds.), *Benoit
Mandelbrot: A Life in Many Dimensions*, p. 457. Singapore: World Scientific.

Weinberger, M. (2016). *This is why San Francisco's insane housing market has hit the crisis
point.* Business Insider India. [Online] Available at: https://www.businessinsider.in/
this-is-why-san-franciscos-insane-housing-market-has-hit-the-crisis-point/articleshow/
52771354.cms

Wikipedia. (2024). *George Smith (Assyriologist).* [Online] Available at: https://en.wikipedia.
org/wiki/George_Smith_(Assyriologist)

Williams, J. (2017). *Cape Town: African city of opportunity.* [Online] Available at:
https://www.pwc.co.za/en/publications/city-of-opportunity.html#:~:text=Unlike%20

many%20African%20cities%2C%20Cape,as%20city%20improvement%20districts%3B%20and

World Health Organization. (2023). *COVID-19 epidemiological update – 22 December 2023*. [Online] Available at: https://www.who.int/publications/m/item/covid-19-epidemiological-update---22-december-2023

Xiling, W., Caihua, Z. & Wei, D. (2021). An Analysis on the Crisis of "Chips shortage" in Automobile Industry – Based on the Double Influence of Covid-19 and Trade Friction. *Journal of Physiscs: Conference Series*. 1971. 012100. 10.1088/1742-6596/1971/1/012100.

Yi-Chi, W., Ching-Sung, C. & Yu-Jiun, C. (2020). The Outbreak of Covid-19: An Overview. *Journal of Chinese Medical Association, 83*(3), 217–220.

Chapter 3

Andreou, C. & White, M. D. (2010). The Thief of Time: Philosophical Essays on Procrastination. In: *Coping With Procrastination*. New York: Oxford University Press, pp. 206–215.

Augustine, of Hippo, Saint, 354–430. (19401949). *The Confessions of Saint Augustine*. Mount Vernon: Peter Pauper Press.

Australian National Maritime Museum. (2023). *HM colonial cruisers HMS KATOOMBA, MILDURA and WALLAROO*. [Online] Available at: https://www.google.co.za/url?sa=t&rct=j&q=&esrc=s&source=web&cd=&ved=2ahUKEwiMzoqctMm DAxVGTUEAHfkZAYkQFnoECAoQAQ&url=https%3A%2F%2Fcollections.sea.museum%2Fen%2Fobjects% 2F42758%2Fhm-colonial-cruisers-hms-katoomba-mildura-and-wallaroo%3 Bjsessionid%3D0334F2

CarMag. (2006). *Opel Corsa Lite Sport*. [Online] Available at: https://www.carmag.co.za/road-tests-blog/opel-corsa-lite-sport/

Clason, G. S. (1988). *The Richest Man in Babylon*. New York City: Signet.

CNBC News releases. (2023). *Full Transcript from CNBC's "Charlie Munger: A Life of Wit and Wisdom"*. [Online] Available at: https://www.cnbc.com/2023/11/30/full-transcript-from-cnbcs-charlie-munger-a-life-of-wit-and-wisdom-.html

Crane, A. B. (2006). The Hidden Costs of Mutual Funds. *Better Investing, 7*, 22–23.

Duignan, B. (2023). *Financial crisis of 2007–08*. Brittanica Money. [Online] Available at: https://www.britannica.com/money/topic/financial-crisis-of-2007-2008/Key-events-of-the-crisis

Ellis, C. D. (2012). Investment Management Fees Are (Much) Higher Than You Think. *Financial Analysts Journal, 68*(3), 4–6.

Fox, M. (2023). *Charlie Munger riffed on bitcoin, the woes of stock picking, and the simple habit behind his billionaire status in a recent interview. Here are the 8 best quotes*. Business Insider Africa. [Online] Available at: https://africa.businessinsider.com/markets/charlie-munger-riffed-on-bitcoin-the-woes-of-stock-picking-and-the-simple-habit/tjq3w17#:~:text=markets-,Charlie%20Munger%20riffed%20on%20bitcoin%2C%20the%20woes%20of%20stock%20picking,are%20the%208%20best%20quot

Haslem, J. A. (2004). Are Mutual Fund Expenses Too High. *Journal of Investing: London, 13*(2), 8–12.

Hogg, A. & Wessels, V. (2020). *End of an era for 91-year-old Edgars as it owes local and foreign creditors billions.* BizNews. [Online] Available at: https://www.biznews.com/briefs/2020/06/12/end-era-edgars-edcon-creditors#:~:text=%F0%9F%94%92BN%20portfolios-,End%20of%20an%20era%20for%2091%2Dyear%2Dold%20Edgars%20as,local%20and%20foreign%20creditors%20billions&text=(Bloomberg)%20%E2%80%93%20Goldman%20S

Holy Bible: New King James Bible. (2004). Nashville: Thomas Nelson (Original work published 1982).

Mahlangu, I. (2020). *22,000 Edcon employees get retrenchment notices.* TimesLIVE. [Online] Available at: https://www.timeslive.co.za/news/south-africa/2020-06-17-22000-edcon-employees-get-retrenchment-notices/

MarketWatch. (2008–). *MarketWatch.* [Online] Available at: https://www.marketwatch.com/investing/index/alsh/download-data?startDate=3/6/2008&endDate=12/31/2008&countryCode=za

Nadkarni, A. (2020). *How I made my first million: 'You can't save yourself to riches'.* Stuff. [Online] Available at: https://www.stuff.co.nz/business/118845209/how-i-made-my-first-million-you-cant-save-yourself-to-riches

National Treasury, South Africa. (2014). *Statement on the Impact of the Proposed Retirement Reforms| Press Release.* [Online] Available at: https://www.treasury.gov.za/comm_media/press/2014/2014070901%20-%20Statement%20on%20the%20Impact%20of%20the%20Proposed%20Retirement%20Reforms.pdf

Poliquin, R. (2018). *Redeeming Augustine, Redeeming the Body: Critiquing Popular Readings of Augustine's Theology of the Body and their Historical Consequences.* [Online] Available at: https://scholars.carroll.edu/handle/20.500.12647/7344

Primedia Broadcasting. (2024). *Money Show host Bruce Whitfield to leave Primedia.* Bizcommunity. [Online] Available at: https://www.bizcommunity.com/article/money-show-host-bruce-whitfield-to-leave-primedia-236117a

Sharpe, W. F. (2013). The Arithmetic of Investment Expenses. *Financial Analysts Journal, 69*(2), 34–41.

Smith, C. (2020). *Edcon, like SAA, 'on life support for a long time' – analyst.* News24. [Online] Available at: https://www.news24.com/fin24/edcon-like-saa-on-life-support-for-a-long-time-analyst-20200328-2

Whitfield, B. (2018). *This woman is on track to grow a slice of her salary into more than R60 million – by doing one free thing.* News24. [Online] Available at: https://www.news24.com/news24/bi-archive/bruce-whitfield-why-you-need-to-start-saving-now-2018-7

Whitfield, B. (2021). *BRUCE WHITFIELD: How to make R2.7m with just 40 hours of work.* Financial Mail. [Online] Available at: https://www.businesslive.co.za/fm/opinion/2021-08-03-bruce-whitfield-how-to-make-r27m-with-just-40-hours-of-work/

Wierzycka, M. (2015). *RA 101: The Compounding Impact of Costs, Compared.* Sygnia for all. [Online] Available at: https://www.sygnia.co.za/press/ra-101-the-compounding-impact-of-costs-compared

Chapter 4

Asch, S. E. (1956). Studies of Independence and Conformity: I. A Minority of One Against a Unanimous Majority. *Psychological Monographs: General and Applied, 70*(9),1–70.

BBC Radio. (2023). *'The Wolf of Crypto'. Podcast.* [Sound Recording] (BBC Radio).

Borrel, L. (2023). *How a quaint British village went from rags to crypto riches … and then lost it all.* Metro. [Online] Available at: https://metro.co.uk/2023/08/02/crypto-bbc-radio-winchmore-hill-koda-19222796/

Bouri, E., Gupta, R. & Roubaud, D. (2019). Herding behavior in cryptocurrencies. *Finance Research Letters, 29*, 216–221.

Carswell, J. (1960). *The South Sea Bubble.* (1st ed.). London: The Cresset Press.

Ciaran, R. (2021). *Will the FSCA's R50m fine on Viceroy have a chilling effect on research?* Moneyweb. [Online] Available at: https://www.moneyweb.co.za/news/companies-and-deals/will-the-fscas-r50m-fine-on-viceroy-have-a-chilling-effect-on-research/

Graham, B. (2006). *The Intelligent Investor. The Definitive Book on Value Investing.* (Revised ed.). New York: HarperCollins.

Hamrick, J. T., Rouhi, F., Mukherjee, A., Feder, A., Gandal, N., Moore, T. & Vasek, M. (2021). An examination of the cryptocurrency pump-and-dump ecosystem. *Information Processing and Management, 58*(4), Article ID 102506.

Hermanus Whale Watchers. (2024). *Whale Watching with Hermanus Whale Watchers.* [Online] Available at: https://hermanuswhalewatchers.co.za

Holmes, S. & Jermyn, D. (2004). *Understanding Reality Television.* (1st ed.). s.l.: Psychology Press.

Holy Bible: New King James Bible. (2004). Nashville: Thomas Nelson (Original work published 1982).

Isaac Newton Institute. (2024). *Isaac Newton's Life.* [Online] Available at: https://www.newton.ac.uk/about/isaac-newton/isaac-newtons-life/

Kindleberger, C. P. (2000). *Manias, Panics, and Crashes. A History of Financial Crises.* (4th ed.). s.l.: John Wiley & Sons, Inc.

King, A. J., Wilson, A. M., Wilshin, S. D., Lowe, J., Haddadi, H., Hailes, S. & Morton, A. J. (2012). Selfish-herd behavior of sheep under threat. *Current Biology, 22*(14), R561–R562.

Koornhof, P. (2022). *Capitec: The way to build a bank.* Allan Gray. [Online] Available at: https://www.allangray.co.za/latest-insights/companies/capitec-the-way-to-build-a-bank/

Landsberg, G. & Deneburg, S. (2014). *Social Behavior of Sheep.* [Online] Available at: https://www.msdvetmanual.com/behavior/normal-social-behavior-and-behavioral-problems-of-domestic-animals/social-behavior-of-sheep

Livni, E. (2023). *Bitcoin Jumps as Court Ruling Paves Way for Cryptocurrency E.T.F.* [Online] Available at: https://www.nytimes.com/2023/08/29/business/cryptocurrency-grayscale-bitcoin-etf.html

Maas, J. B. & Toivanen, K. M. (1978). Candid Camera and the behavioral sciences. *Teaching of Psychology, 5*(4), 226–228.

Mattke, J., Maier, C., Reis, L. & Weitzel, T. (2020). Herd behavior in social media: The role of Facebook likes, strength of ties, and expertise. *Information & Management, 57*(8), Article ID 103370.

Ninety One Value Fund. (2023). *Ninety One Value Fund.* [Online] Available at: https://ninetyone.com/en/south-africa/funds-strategies/funds/value-a-inc-zar-zae000024154

Nowak, R., Porter, R. H., Blache, D. & Dwyer, C. M. (2008). Behavior and the Welfare of Sheep. *Animal Welfare, 6,* 81–134.

Planting, S. (2020). *Biccard: A contrarian who finds opportunity where others fear to tread.* Daily Maverick. [Online] Available at: https://www.dailymaverick.co.za/article/2020-02-11-biccard-a-contrarian-who-finds-opportunity-where-others-fear-to-tread/

Pröllochs, N. & Feuerriegel, S. (2023). Mechanisms of true and false rumor sharing in social media: Collective intelligence or herd behavior? *Proceedings of the ACM on Human-Computer Interaction, 7,* 1–38.

Rakoff, D. (2000). *The Lives They Lived: Questions for James B. Maas; Candid Classroom.* The New York Times Magazine. [Online] Available at: https://www.nytimes.com/interactive/2022/12/14/magazine/gun-violence-america-child-deaths.html

Robbins, J., Dalla Rossa, L., Allen, J. M., Mattila, D. K., Secchi, E. R., Friedlaender, A. S. … Steel, D. (2011). Return movement of a humpback whale between the Antarctic Peninsula and American Samoa: a seasonal migration record. *Endangered Species Research, 13,* 117–121.

Selyukh, A. (2013). *Hackers send fake market-moving AP tweet on White House explosions.* Reuters. [Online] Available at: https://www.reuters.com/article/technology/hackers-send-fake-market-moving-ap-tweet-on-white-house-explosions-idUSBRE93M12Y/

The Newton Project. (2024). *Isaac Newton's Personal Life.* [Online] Available at: https://www.newtonproject.ox.ac.uk/his-personal-life

Van Niekerk, R. (2022). *True value investing allows a trusted share its ups and downs.* Moneyweb. [Online] Available at: https://www.moneyweb.co.za/moneyweb-podcasts/be-a-better-investor/true-value-investing-allows-a-trusted-share-its-ups-and-downs/

Viceroy Research. (2018). *Capitec – A wolf in sheep's clothing.* [Online] Available at: https://viceroyresearch.org/2018/01/30/capitec-a-wolf-in-sheeps-clothing/

Westfall, R. (1994). *The Life of Isaac Newton.* (Canto ed.). Cambridge: Cambridge University Press.

Yaffe-Bellany, D. (2024). *Regulators Approve New Type of Bitcoin Fund, in Boon for Crypto Industry.* The New York Times. [Online] Available at: https://www.nytimes.com/2024/01/10/technology/sec-bitcoin-approval-exchange-traded-funds.html?campaign_id=190&emc=edit_ufn_20240110&instance_id=112195&nl=from-the-times&regi_id=2232 96897&segment_id=154813&te=1&user_id=2a13e19fae68e4d0cecca0f173583481

Chapter 5

Anon. (2024). *James Coddington: Building a future Auckland.* Auckland Tāmaki Makaurau. [Online] Available at: https://industry.aucklandnz.com/business/resources/Voices-of-Auckland/James-Coddington

Bone Fide Wealth. (2024). [Online] Available at: https://bonefidewealth.com

Brown, S. (2023). *Using credit to build wealth*. [Online] Available at: https://www.
moneyweb.co.za/moneyweb-podcasts/moneyweb-now/using-credit-to-build-wealth/

Elkins, K. (2020). *The budget breakdown of a 27-year-old millionaire who brings in $615,000 and owns 6 properties*. CNBC Make It. [Online] Available at:
https://www.cnbc.com/2020/02/28/budget-of-millennial-millionaire-who-saves-80percent-of-his-income.html

Graham, B. (2006). *The Intelligent Investor. The Definitive Book on Value Investing*.
(Revised ed.). New York: HarperCollins.

Hecht, A. (2019). *How to stop obsessing over your debt, according to experts*. CNBC Make It.
[Online] Available at: https://www.cnbc.com/2019/12/19/how-to-stop-obsessing-over-your-debt-according-to-experts.html

Holy Bible: New King James Bible. (2004). Nashville: Thomas Nelson (Original work published 1982).

International Accounting Standards Board (IASB). (2018). *Conceptual Framework for Financial Reporting*. [Online] Available at: https://www.ifrs.org/login/?resource=/
content/dam/ifrs/publications/pdf-standards/english/2024/issued/part-a/conceptual-framework-for-financial-reporting.pdf&bypass=on

Jackson, A. (2023a). *Barbara Corcoran: A $320 coat was the 'best investment I ever made' at age 23 – 'it changed my life'*. CNBC Make It. [Online] Available at: https://www.cnbc.
com/2023/08/21/barbara-corcoran-expensive-coat-was-best-investment-i-ever-made.
html

Jackson, A. (2023b). *When Barbara Corcoran sold her company for $66 million, she didn't know how much it was worth – here's how she negotiated anyway*. CNBC Make It.
[Online] Available at: https://www.cnbc.com/2023/05/02/barbara-corcoran-negotiated-company-sale-not-knowing-its-value.html#:~:text=The%20large%20dollar%20
figure%20wasn,%2C%20I%20had%20no%20idea.%E2%80%9D

Jensen, M. C. & Meckling, W. H. (1976). Theory of the Firm: Managerial Behaviour,
Agency Costs and Ownership Structure. *Journal of Financial Economics, 3*(4), 305–360.

McNair, K. (2023a). *31-year-old self-made millionaire: How to get started in real estate investing*. CNBC Make It. [Online] Available at: https://www.cnbc.com/2023/05/21/
todd-baldwin-how-to-get-started-in-real-estate-investing.html#:~:text=Save%20
and%20Invest-,31%2Dyear%2Dold%20self%2Dmade%20millionaire%3A%20
How%20to,started%20in%20real%20estate%20investing&text=Whether%20you%20
buy%20a%20ho

McNair, K. (2023b). *Self-made millionaires say 'saving won't bring you wealth' – here's what will*. CNBC Make It. [Online] Available at: https://www.cnbc.com/2023/06/16/self-made-millionaires-saving-wont-bring-you-wealth.html

Peng, I. (2024). *Why Cocoa Prices Spiked and What It Means for Chocolate Lovers*.
Bloomberg. [Online] Available at: https://www.bloomberg.com/news/
articles/2024-03-31/why-cocoa-prices-spiked-and-what-it-means-for-chocolate-lovers?embedded-checkout=true

Sanchez, C. (2024). *Cocoa price surge in global market lures Colombian farmers away from coca cultivation*. El País. [Online] Available at: https://english.elpais.com/economy-and-business/2024-04-04/cocoa-price-surge-in-global-market-lures-colombian-farmers-away-from-coca-cultivation.html

Schroth, G., Läderach, P., Martinez-Valle, A. I., Bunn, C. & Jassonge, L. (2016). Vulnerability to climate change of cocoa in West Africa: Patterns. *Science of the Total Environment*, *556*, 231–241.

Vasquez, L. A. (2020). If you don't owe, you don't own: debt, discipline and growth in rural Colombia. *Journal of Rural Studies*, *78*(1), 271–281.

Chapter 6

CaringKind. (2022). *NYC Marathon's oldest runner was adventurous mogul Alan Patricof, 88*. [Online] Available at: https://caringkindnyc.org/nyc-marathons-oldest-runner-was-adventurous-mogul-alan-patricof-88/

Cartner-Morley, J. (2022). *Get louder every decade: the new rules for dressing your age after 50*. The Guardian. [Online] Available at: https://www.theguardian.com/lifeandstyle/2022/jun/01/the-new-rules-for-dressing-your-age-after-50

Delgado, M. M. & Jacobs, L. F. (2017). Caching for where and what: evidence for a mnemonic strategy in a scatter-hoarder. *Royal Society Open Science*, *4*(9).

Graham, B. (2006). *The Intelligent Investor. The Definitive Book on Value Investing*. (Revised ed.). New York: HarperCollins.

Hazera, A. (2017). John Lee Hancock, The Founder (2016) – Review. *Markets, Globalization & Development Review*, *2*(4).

Henderson, L. (1990). *Jacaranda*. [Weeds no. A_30/1990.] Pretoria: Department of Agricultural Development.

Hyken, S. (2022). *Forty-three Percent Say 40-Plus is Old: Discrimination In the Workplace*. LinkedIn. [Online] Available at: https://www.linkedin.com/posts/shephyken_forty-three-percent-say-40-plus-is-old-discrimination-activity-6994727969860571136-jZt1

Love, J. F. (1986). *McDonald's Behind The Arches*. (1995 ed.). New York: Bantam Books.

Museums of History New South Wales (NSW). (2015). *The dream tree: Jacaranda, Sydney icon*. [Online] Available at: https://mhnsw.au/stories/general/dream-tree-jacaranda-sydney-icon/

National Geographic. (2017). *Squirrels Gone Wild: Their Quirky Behaviors Explained*. [Online] Available at: https://www.nationalgeographic.co.uk/video/tv/squirrels-gone-wild-their-quirky-behaviors-explained

Srivastava, L. M. (2002). Shedding. *Plant growth and development. Hormones and the environment*. Oxford: Academic Press.

Stewart, D. (1946). 'The jacaranda'. *The dosser in springtime*. Sydney: Angus and Robertson.

Stewart, T. (n.d.). *Ray Kroc Biography, "The Founding father" of McDonald's*. s.l.: s.n.

The Economist. (2024). *Our Big Mac index shows how burger prices are changing*. [Online] Available at: https://www.economist.com/big-mac-index

SOURCES

The Founder. (2016). [Film] Directed by John Lee Hancock. USA: FilmNation
Entertainment; The Combine; Faliro House Productions S.A.

Whiteley, P. J. (2017). *Ageing With Attitude: Daring To Be Different After 50.* [Online]
Available at: https://sixtyandme.com/aging-with-attitude-daring-to-be-different-after-50/

Chapter 7

Connor, F. (2022). *ISLAND LIFE I'm a real life castaway – I gave up being millionaire
stockbroker to live on deserted island with two female mannequins.* The Sun. [Online]
Available at: https://www.thesun.co.uk/news/18942360/real-life-castaway-deserted-
island/

Dorofte, A. (2020). *The BMW 1800/2000 SA series: A look at an intriguing Bimmer.*
BMWBLOG. [Online] Available at: https://www.bmwblog.com/2020/04/05/the-
bmw-1800-2000-sa-series-a-look-at-an-intriguing-bimmer/#:~:text=The%20main%20
distinction%20between%20the,by%20the%20nickname%20%E2%80%9CCheet-
ah%E2%80%9D

Dowling, T. (2013). *Ben Fogle: New Lives in the Wild – TV review.* The Guardian. [Online]
Available at: https://www.theguardian.com/tv-and-radio/2013/apr/23/ben-fogle-new-
lives-in-the-wild

Graham, B. (2006). *The Intelligent Investor. The Definitive Book on Value Investing.*
(Revised ed.). New York: HarperCollins.

Hawkins, S. B. (2007). Desire and Natural Classification: Aristotle and Peirce on Final
Cause. *Transactions of the Charles S. Peirce Society, 43*(3), 521–541.

Kelsey-Sugg, A. (2019). *When David Glasheen lost everything, moving to a remote island
saved him.* Australian Broadcasting Corporation (ABC). [Online] Available at:
https://www.abc.net.au/news/2019-07-23/ex-millionaire-david-glasheen-revived-by-
remote-island-living/11310184

Noakes, T. D. (2007). The Central Governor Model of Exercise Regulation Applied to the
Marathon. *Sports Medicine, 37,* 374–377.

O'Grady, S. (2015). *Ben Fogle: New Lives in the Wild UK, TV review – 'Oh, to run away
from it all and live in a mud hut with goats'.* Independent. [Online] Available at:
https://www.independent.co.uk/arts-entertainment/tv/reviews/ben-fogle-new-lives-
in-the-wild-uk-tv-review-oh-to-run-away-from-it-all-and-live-in-a-mud-hut-with-
goats-a6741291.html

Pitts, L. (2020). *Ben Fogle on the power of immersion.* Cambridge. [Online]
Available at: https://www.cambridge.org/elt/blog/2020/02/20/ben-fogle-power-
immersion/#:~:text=%E2%80%9CTravel%20is%20nothing%20without%20
communication,a%20new%20form%20of%20communication

Schwantes, M. (2021). *Warren Buffett Says You Can Ruin Your Life in 5 Minutes by Making
1 Critical Mistake.* Inc. [Online] Available at: https://www.inc.com/marcel-schwantes/
warren-buffett-says-you-can-ruin-your-life-in-5-minutes-by-making-1-critical-mistake.
html

213

Short, T. (2010). Did Peirce have a cosmology?. Transactions of the Charles S. Peirce Society. *A Quarterly Journal in American Philosophy*, *46*(4), 521–543.

Williams, K. (2021, 2023). *The Oxford graduate who grew up in a castle and now lives off-grid in Welsh woodland*. WalesOnline. [Online] Available at: https://www.walesonline.co.uk/lifestyle/tv/oxford-graduate-who-grew-up-19897194

Chapter 8

Arsla, A. (2020). Bridges as City Landmarks: A Critical Review on Iconic Structures. *Design Studio*, *2*(2), 85–99.

Associated Press. (1996). *Filmmakers admit 'Philadelphia' was based on real life*. Deseret News. [Online] Available at: https://www.deseret.com/1996/3/20/19231740/filmmakers-admit-philadelphia-was-based-on-real-life/

Berger, A. A. (2019). San Francisco as a Brand. *Brands and Cultural Analysis*, 99–105.

Bittel, C. (2004). Golden Gate Bridge (Commentary on Ben Loeterman documentary film). *The Journal of American History*, *91*(3), 1132–1133.

Cain, B. (2023). *The Fonz is coming to Raleigh. But first, Henry Winkler talks to us about his new memoir*. The News & Observer. [Online] Available at: https://www.newsobserver.com/entertainment/tv-movies/warm-tv-blog/article280963213.html

Cameron, E. (2005). *Witness to AIDS*. New York: I.B. Taurus & Co Ltd.

Chang, S.-P. & Choo, J. F. (2009). Values of Bridge in the Formation of Cities. *IABSE Symposium Report, International Association for Bridge and Structural Engineering*, *95*(1), 25–46.

Cogo-Moreira, H., Andriolo, R., Yazigi, L., Ploubidis, G., De Ávila, C. & Mari, J. (2012). Music education for improving reading skills in children and adolescents with dyslexia. *Cochrane Database of Systematic Reviews*, *8*.

Drabble, E. (2014). *Henry Winkler: I didn't read a book myself until I was 31 years old*. The Guardian. [Online] Available at: https://www.theguardian.com/childrens-books-site/2014/may/26/henry-winkler-the-fonz-interview-hank-zipzer-dyslexia

Game, T., Vos, C., Morshedi, R., Grafton, R., Alonso-Marroquin, F. & Tahmasebinia, F. (2016). Full Dynamic Model of Golden Gate Bridge. *AIP Conference Proceedings*, *1762*(1).

Garvey, M. (2024). *Henry Winkler explains the trick that allowed him to transform into The Fonz*. CNN. [Online] Available at: https://edition.cnn.com/2022/11/13/entertainment/henry-winkler-the-fonz/index.html

Germanò, E., Gagliano, A. & Curatolo, P. (2010). Comorbidity of ADHD and dyslexia. *Developmental Neuropsychology*, *35*(5), 475–493.

Golden Gate Bridge Highway & Transportation District. (2024). *Bridge features*. Goldengate.org. [Online] Available at: https://www.goldengate.org/bridge/history-research/bridge-features/color-art-deco-styling/

Griggs Jr, F. E. (2010). Joseph B Strauss, Charles A Ellis, and the Golden Gate Bridge: Justice at Last. *Journal of Professional Issues in Engineering Education and Practice*, *136*(2), 71–83.

Laughland, O. (2021). *Magic Johnson: The NBA superstar who smashed HIV stigma – then built a huge fortune*. The Guardian. [Online] Available at: https://www.theguardian.com/society/2021/jun/24/magic-johnson-the-nba-superstar-who-smashed-hiv-stigma-then-built-a-huge-fortune

Loomis, R. T. (1958). *The History of the Building of the Golden Gate Bridge*. Stanford University.

Lyon, R. G., Shaywitz, S. E. & Shaywitz, B. A. (2003). Defining Dyslexia, Comorbidity, Teachers' Knowledge of Language and Reading. *Annals of Dyslexia*, *53*, 1–14.

Millea, H. (2019). *Looking Back at 'Philadelphia,' 25 Years Later*. Smithsonian Magazine. [Online] Available at: https://www.smithsonianmag.com/arts-culture/looking-back-philadelphia-25-years-later-180971011/#:~:text=What%20would%20the%20breakthrough%20movie,if%20it%20were%20made%20today%3F&text=These%20were%20the%20early%20fighters,at%20Action%20Wellness%20in%20Phi

Oliviera, N. (2021). *Magic Johnson opens up about his health, career 30 years after HIV diagnosis: "You just sit there and say, what does this mean? Am I gonna die?"*. CBS News. [Online] Available at: https://www.cbsnews.com/news/magic-johnson-30-years-hiv-diagnosis/

Rhodes Trust. (2024). *Rhodes Scholarships Selection Criteria*. [Online] Available at: https://www.rhodeshouse.ox.ac.uk/scholarships/the-selection-criteria/

Sabi Sabi. (2014). *Sabi Sabi Wild Facts: Dung Beetles Part 1*. [Online] Available at: https://www.sabisabi.com/discover/wild-facts/dung-beetles

Stevenson, R. W. (1991). *BASKETBALL; Magic Johnson Ends His Career, Saying He Has AIDS Infection*. The New York Times. [Online] Available at: https://www.nytimes.com/1991/11/08/sports/basketball-magic-johnson-ends-his-career-saying-he-has-aids-infection.html

The Yale Center for Dyslexia & Creativity. (2024). *Success Stories; Henry Winkler, Director & Actor*. The Yale Center for Dyslexia & Creativity. [Online] Available at: https://dyslexia.yale.edu/success-stories/

Tripadvisor. (2024). *Travelers' Choice - Best of the Best Destinations*. [Online] Available at: https://www.tripadvisor.com/TravelersChoice-Destinations-cTop-g191

Wikipedia. (2024). *San Andreas (film)*. [Online] Available at: https://en.wikipedia.org/wiki/San_Andreas_(film)

Williams, J., Sanzgiri, L. & Schwartz, D. (2022). *Magic Johnson on basketball, business, and being the face of HIV*. NPR. [Online] Available at: https://www.npr.org/2022/10/04/1126788790/magic-johnson-on-basketball-business-and-being-the-face-of-hiv

World Health Organization. (2024). *HIV and AIDS*. [Online] Available at: https://www.who.int/news-room/fact-sheets/detail/hiv-aids?gad_source=1&gclid=Cj0KCQjw-5y1BhC-ARIsAAM_oKmfn8Kf65Jl9SQbx8KHFKd0Q6 ButgO1x1jWYfqCQVD6GR8oIu8hCqkaAspXEALw_wcB

World Population Review. (2024). *Rome, Italy Population 2024*. [Online] Available at: https://worldpopulationreview.com/cities/italy/rome

ACKNOWLEDGEMENTS

The idea of Joseph and Noah grew over a period.

When I was first appointed as an employer representative on the board of trustees of the retirement fund of a major South African university, Wits, my expectations were modest. However, I quickly encountered the full breadth of responsibilities entrusted to each board member. From the excitement of investing member funds to the critical yet often understated work of addressing member welfare and distributing death benefits, I have experienced it all.

I have the privilege of serving alongside a diverse group of individuals – pension law attorneys, professors in investment finance, chartered accountants and psychologists – each of whom brings their unique expertise to the table. Together, as a board, we engage in thoughtful, often intense discussions and tackle the challenges we face as best we can. However, from the many talented colleagues with whom I've had the pleasure of working, I must single out Bob (now retired from the board), who, with an honours degree in English and Drama from Rhodes University, had previously spent several years of his career as a director in an arts theatre. Bob often began his questions to investment consultants with the following words: 'Forgive my ignorance, but please explain to me …' Yet the depth of his questions revealed a profound understanding of the subject and a keen focus on matters of importance – especially money. When the board reviewed the minutes of previous meetings, Bob would meticulously correct the tenses, grammar and punctuation, reminding everyone that a misplaced hyphen, comma or bracket could alter the intent of a board resolution.

One of the most significant changes I witnessed was the restructuring of the fund's operations. We moved from a one-stop administrator model, where a single entity managed all services, including investments, to a more modern structure that segregates different activities to mitigate conflicts of interest.

Various financial crises, especially the 2008 global financial crisis and the Covid-19 pandemic, forced us to confront the harsh realities members faced, particularly those approaching retirement. Timing, as it turned out, could be devastating, with market crashes erasing years of savings. Over the two decades that followed, I attended every annual general meeting, listening to the concerns that mattered most to our members. These experiences planted the seeds for this book.

I owe much of my inspiration to Malcolm Gladwell, whose books *Outliers* and *David and Goliath* demonstrated the power of thoroughly researched stories. My thinking is shaped not only by my experiences but also by my academic qualifications. The rigour of my master's thesis in commerce has been foundational to my understanding of finance.

To Justice Edwin Cameron, who graciously allowed me to quote excerpts from his memoir, *Witness to AIDS*, and who took time out from his busy schedule to review a significant section of a chapter, providing invaluable insights and feedback, I am deeply humbled and sincerely grateful. Thanks also go to Veronica Klipp, publisher at Wits University Press, who was the first person to review selected chapters of my manuscript. Her belief in the work and her feedback were invaluable. Although her critique initially scared the hell out of me, it ultimately helped shape the rest of the manuscript. I am profoundly grateful to my editor, Louise Rapley, whose persistence and attention to detail were unwavering. Without her, this book may have been finished sooner, but it would have been far less complete. I also thank my publisher at Quickfox, Vanessa Wilson, for guiding me through the process, and Adele Wilson, also at Quickfox, for her strict project management of the publishing process. The responsibility for the content of this book is entirely mine, and any remaining errors are mine.

Finally, I am eternally grateful to my parents, Thamary and Henson Magiga, who raised our family of seven children on a shoestring budget, making enormous sacrifices during a civil war and teaching us many things along the way. To my siblings, who shaped my world view. And to my beloved wife, Elly, and our children, Kai and Ngaa, who continuously encouraged me, patiently giving me the space I needed to write.

About the author

Daniel Gozo is a seasoned finance executive with over thirty-five years of experience across diverse industries, including mining, insurance, engineering, FMCG, sugar, tobacco and higher education. He holds a master's degree in commerce from Wits University and an honours degree in Business Sciences. He is a Chartered Management Accountant (CIMA) and a Chartered Global Management Accountant (CGMA). Daniel has served in various senior roles, including that of financial director. He is currently Director of Finance at Wits University.

His passion for investments was honed during twenty years as a board trustee of a large retirement fund, where he played a pivotal role in overseeing asset managers, investment consultants and other service providers, steering the fund through two global crises: the global financial crisis of 2008 and the Covid-19 crisis. He directed key operations such as strategic asset allocation, annual review of the fund's investment policy statement, compliance monitoring, governance and annual financial statement reviews.

Daniel's writing on success, investment and wealth management is enriched by his deep knowledge of financial operations and his personal enthusiasm for real estate. Outside of his professional endeavours, Daniel enjoys hiking, rucking and various other sports, including athletics, rugby, tennis and soccer. He resides in both Johannesburg and Cape Town with his wife and two children.